Béla Bartók

A Celebration

Benjamin Suchoff

The Scarecrow Press, Inc.
Lanham, Maryland, and Oxford
2004

SCARECROW PRESS, INC.

Published in the United States of America
by Scarecrow Press, Inc.
A wholly owned subsidary of
The Rowman & Littlefield Publishing Group, Inc.
4501 Forbes Boulevard, Suite 200, Lanham, Maryland 20706
www.scarecrowpress.com

PO Box 317
Oxford
OX2 9RU, UK

British Library Cataloguing in Publication Information Available

Library of Congress Cataloging-in-Publication Data

Suchoff, Benjamin.
  Bâela Bartâok : a celebration / Benjamin Suchoff.
    p. cm.
  Includes bibliographical references (p.   ) and index.
  ISBN 0-8108-4958-5 (alk. paper)
  1. Bartôk, Bâela, 1881–1945—Criticism and interpretation. I. Title.
ML410.B26 S835 2003
780'.92—dc22

                                                                    2003016345

♾™ The paper used in this publication meets the minimum requirements of
American National Standard for Information Sciences—Permanence of
Paper for Printed Library Materials, ANSI/NISO Z39.48-1992.
Manufactured in the United States of America.

For Eleanor

Contents

PART TWO

Musical Folklore

PART THREE

General Studies

Preface

Béla Bartók: A Celebration—a selection of my writings on Bartók as man, composer, and folklorist—commemorates a half century of my career in Bartók studies. The actual immersion in Bartókiana occurred in 1950, during the preparation of my dissertation on Bartók's *Mikrokosmos*. It was indeed fortuitous that in 1953 the investigation led to a meeting with Victor Bator, then cotrustee of the Bartók estate, and thereafter to employment as his assistant, appointment as curator of the New York Bartók Archive, and, following his death in 1967, designation as successor-trustee. When the Bartók trust terminated in 1982, I continued the investigation of Bartók's lifework in composition and systematic ethnomusicology—now with emphasis on a theoretic-analytical approach.

The concomitant purpose of this book is to provide music students, specialists, and performers with those published essays, unpublished lectures, and other papers that served as essential sources for my recent publications, *Béla Bartok: Life and Work* (2001) and *Bartók's* Mikrokosmos: *Genesis, Pedagogy, and Style* (2002).

Part I is devoted to Bartók as composer, beginning with program notes on selected masterpieces that are intended for music lovers as well as students. Other essays examine folk-music sources in the composer's works, point to stylistic aspects in his early piano pieces, determine the sources of his unique musical language, and investigate his principles of composition.

Part II includes those prefatory writings that were the outcome of my editorial preparation for publication of Bartók's collections of musical folklore: Hungarian, Romanian, Slovak, Turkish, and Yugoslav. These essays provide the background to Bartók's research and findings in comparative musicology, and they underscore why he is considered one of the forefathers in the field of ethnomusicology.

Part III consists of general studies, including the development and holdings of the former New York Bartók Archive, the composer as litterateur, and Béla Bartók's trials during his last years as an émigré in America.

This book marks the completion of my "Bartók trilogy," a project that began in 1996 and achieved fruition through the efforts and advice of Bruce Philips, music editor of Scarecrow Press. I am also greatly indebted to his editorial assistants, Rebecca Massa and Melissa Ray and to production editor Niki Averill and copy editor Jen Sorenson. Special thanks go to my good friend and distinguished colleague, Elliott Antokoletz, for his continuing support that began so many years ago at the New York Bartók Archive. And the dedication page to my wife reflects my heartfelt appreciation for her help and encouragement during the preparation of this book.

Acknowledgments

To Boosey & Hawkes Music Publishers Ltd., London, acknowledgment is due for musical examples from the following of Béla Bartók's works: *Mikrokosmos*, Sixth String Quartet, Second Violin Concerto, Concerto for Orchestra. Acknowledgment is made to Boosey & Hawkes Inc., New York, for musical examples from the following works: Second String Quartet, Second Violin Sonata, Music for Strings, Percussion, and Celesta, Dance Suite, First Piano Concerto.

To Universal Edition A. G., Vienna, for musical examples from the following works: Second String Quartet, Second Violin Sonata, Music for Strings, Percussion, and Celesta, Dance Suite, First Piano Concerto.

Acknowledgment is due to the following publishers for extracts from my editorial prefaces: Princeton University Press (Béla Bartók: *Turkish Folk Music from Asian Minor*) and State University of New York Press (Béla Bartók: *Yugoslav Folk Music* I).

Abbreviations

BBA	Budapest Bartók Archívum
BBCO	Benjamin Suchoff: *Béla Bartók: Concerto for Orchestra: Understanding Bartók's World.* New York: Schirmer, 1995
BBE	Béla Bartók: *Béla Bartók Essays*, selected and edited by Benjamin Suchoff. Reprint. Lincoln and London: University of Nebraska Press, 1992
BBGM	Benjamin Suchoff: *Béla Bartók and a Guide to the* Mikrokosmos. Ann Arbor, Mich.: UMI, 1957
BBGR	Elliott Antokoletz: *Béla Bartók: A Guide to Research.* 2d ed., rev. and enl. New York: Garland, 1997
BBL	*Béla Bartók Letters*, ed. János Demény. Trans. Péter Balabán and István Farkas, rev. trans. Elisabeth West and Colin Mason. New York: St. Martin's Press, 1971
BBLW	Benjamin Suchoff: *Béla Bartók: Life and Work.* Lanham, Md.: Scarecrow Press, 2001
BBSE	Béla Bartók: *Béla Bartók Studies in Ethnomusicology*, selected and ed. Benjamin Suchoff. Lincoln and London: University of Nebraska Press, 1997
BC	*The Bartók Companion*, ed. Malcolm Gillies. Portland, Ore.: Amadeus Press, 1994
BM	Benjamin Suchoff: *Bartók's Mikrokosmos: Genesis, Pedagogy, and Style.* Lanham, Md. and Oxford: Scarecrow Press, 2002.
BP	*Bartók Perspectives*, ed. Elliott Antokoletz, Victoria Fischer, and Benjamin Suchoff. New York: Oxford University Press, 2000
HFS	Béla Bartók: *The Hungarian Folk Song*, ed. Benjamin Suchoff. Trans. M. D. Calvocoressi, with annotations by Zoltán Kodály. Albany: State University of New York Press, 1981
LMBB	Halsey Stevens: *The Life and Music of Béla Bartók.* 3d ed. Preparation by Malcolm Gillies. Oxford: Clarendon Press, 1993
MBB	Elliott Antokoletz: *The Music of Béla Bartók: A Study of Tonality and Progression in Twentieth-Century Music.* Berkeley and Los Angeles: University of California Press, 1984

xiii

NYBA	New York Bartók Archive (now in *PBA*)
PBA	Peter Bartók Archive, Homosassa, Florida
RFM.i–v	Béla Bartók: *Rumanian Folk Music*, ed. Benjamin Suchoff, trans. E. C. Teodorescu. The Hague: Martinus Nijhoff, 1967, 1975
*SV.*i–iii	Béla Bartók: *Slowakische Volkslieder*, ed. Alica Elscheková, Oskár Elschek, and Jozef Kresánek. Bratislava: Academia Scientiarum Slovaca, 1959, 1970 (vol. iii is unpublished)
TFM	Béla Bartók: *Turkish Folk Music from Asia Minor*, ed. Benjamin Suchoff. With an afterword by Kurt Reinhard. Princeton: Princeton University Press, 1976
YFM.i–iv	Béla Bartók: *Yugoslav Folk Music*, ed. Benjamin Suchoff. Albany: State University of New York Press, 1978

1

Béla Bartók: A Celebration[1]

INTRODUCTION[2]

When the centenary of Béla Bartók's birth arrived, in March of 1981, the music world rushed to pay homage. It was not that Bartók had been unknown in his own day; no major composer ever is. The concept of a great musical mind starving in a garret is a romantic invention. But in the decades following his death in 1945 the true picture of Béla Bartók began to emerge.

Most experts would agree that Bartók was one of the three major composers of the twentieth century, the other two being Igor Stravinsky and Arnold Schoenberg. And there is no disagreement about the value of his music. It is conceded that his string quartets are the most important works in that medium since the last Beethoven quartets. Perhaps no twentieth-century work for symphony orchestra is as much played as Bartók's Concerto for Orchestra, which has edged out even Stravinsky's *Le Sacre du printemps* in popularity. Where pianists are, the Bartók concertos are not far behind. Violinists find the Bartók sonatas and concertos a perpetual challenge. His opera, *Duke Bluebeard's Castle*, has entered the international repertory.

It is all the more tribute to Bartók that his music is not "easy." Béla Bartók, a small, frail man with burning eyes, wrote music of unprecedented power and dissonance. Even today, when music of total dissonance and lack of obvious melody is the norm, Bartók's music can cause problems. Listening to it for the first time can be an unsettling experience. Those savage thrusts! Those complicated rhythms! That uncompromising intent to avoid anything that can be described as "pretty"!

And, above all, that web of Hungarian peasant music underlying almost everything the man composed. Bartók was a nationalist composer who went back to the roots of his country for his music. He started collecting peasant music in 1905, going around the country with an Edison cylinder machine, and he kept at it all his life. But his was not the sophisticated virtuoso music of Liszt and his Hungarian Rhapsodies. (Liszt, incidentally, was a composer Bartók admired.) In *his* music Bartók went back to something stark and fundamental, trying to achieve the Hungarian *melos*—the basic, underlying spirit of his people's music —in a powerful, contemporary texture. Charles Ives, in his way, was doing

1

much the same thing in America.

No composer springs from nowhere, and Bartók was no exception. Like all important musicians, he started early, playing the piano at five and composing at nine. He came under the influence of Richard Strauss and Claude Debussy, and his early music reflects something of those composers as well as of Liszt. But after he saturated himself in Magyar and Romanian folk music a completely new element began to appear in his compositions. He used peasant scales and melodies, which were based on the old church or Greek modes and on the pentatonic scale. He developed a new chordal system, often using fourths instead of the traditional thirds. It was a music that puzzled most listeners of the 1920s and 1930s.

Yet Bartók was internationally famous after World War I. Like it or dislike it, audiences knew they were in the presence of something larger than life. Bartók was kept busy, teaching at the Budapest Academy, concertizing all over the world (his American debut took place in 1927), writing music for commissions, continually researching folk music—and getting into trouble with the authorities.

For Bartók was a fierce anti-Nazi who hated everything that Hitler and fascism stood for. He remained in Hungary at the beginning of the war to take care of his mother. But when she died, he managed to get out, and he came to the United States in 1940.

There were stories about Bartók's struggles with poverty during his American years. Not true. He did experience financial difficulties, but he never starved. Columbia University hired him to work on his own and the Parry collection of Yugoslav folk music. Serge Koussevitzky commissioned a work that turned out to be the Concerto for Orchestra. Yehudi Menuhin commissioned a sonata for solo violin. William Primrose commissioned a viola concerto. Bartók settled in. As he wrote to his sons, he was beginning to be Americanized. He found central heating too hot. He liked the bus ride, which took him to the middle of town from Forest Hills for a nickel. He ate "American" breakfasts: grapefruit, puffed wheat, eggs, and bacon. He had trouble coping with American gadgets, such as the electric can opener.

But he became ill soon after he arrived in the United States, and the prognosis was grave: Bartók had leukemia. Did his last works reflect a calm fatalism? Certainly they had little of the savage power of his European works. He wrote his Third Piano Concerto for his wife—Ditta Pásztory Bartók—as an annuity for her, and she did play it in concert. It proved to be the most popular of his three piano concertos, far removed from the austerities of No. 1, which still hits the listener like a rock slide. The Concerto for Orchestra, with its spacious melodies, wit, and haunting "Intermezzo interrotto" movement, is much more relaxed than, say, the early *Miraculous Mandarin* score. Would he have continued in this vein? On his deathbed he lamented, "I have to go with so much still to say."

If those late works are relatively easy to understand, the middle-period pieces still demand some effort for the listener. Pieces like the Piano Concerto No. 1 or the Music for Stringed Instruments, Percussion, and Celesta are not going to unravel themselves on a single hearing any more than a late Beethoven quartet or *Tristan und Isolde* will. But, as with Beethoven and Wagner, the music more than repays the effort put into it. After several hearings—and that is what records are for—the form of the music suddenly becomes clear. The harmonies become expressive instead of merely dissonant. And where at first the melodies tend to sound angular, acquaintance with them reveals their Hungarian coloration, their drive and joie de vivre, their rakish rhythms and irresistible individuality. Composers who strive for an easy success are generally forgotten ten years after their death. Composers of genius who have a bigger vision and go their uncompromising way live eternally. And nobody in the twentieth century has had as big a vision as Béla Bartók.

Notes on the Music[3]

Béla Bartók's compositions can be divided into three stages of stylistic development, each one growing out of a two-year period of creative "stagnation." The first stage, which Bartók modestly referred to as his student years, was the recapitulation of romantic (nineteenth-century) Hungarian popular music dialect. The second was the discovery and methodical articulation of the true folk music of Hungary and of the national minority peoples and the resultant applications in Bartók's composed works. The third and highest stage was purposefully integrative: the combination of the newly mastered language of east European musical folklore with specific techniques derived from west European composers.

Summary of Hungarian Musical Dialect (to 1905)

In 1903, his last year as a student of piano and composition at the Budapest Academy of Music, Bartók composed a symphonic poem based on the life of the Hungarian patriot Louis Kossuth and his ill-fated revolution against the Austrian rule of the Magyar nation. The young composer, a dedicated nationalist who was carried along in the wave of resurgent national longing for independence, wrote that:

> Everyone, on reaching maturity, has to set himself a goal and must direct all his work and actions toward this. For my own part, all my life, in every sphere, always and in every way, I shall have one objective: the good of Hungary and the Hungarian nation. I think I have already given some proof of this intention in the minor ways which have so far been possible to me.

The *Kossuth* symphonic poem combines the dissonant harmonic novelties of

Richard Strauss with the Hungarianisms of Franz Liszt to such an artful degree that Hungarian press reviews hailed the twenty-two-year-old genius as the "Hungarian Tchaikovsky." Other similarly styled works quickly followed: Rhapsody for Piano and Orchestra (op. 1), Scherzo for Piano and Orchestra (op. 2) in 1904, and Suite No. 1 for Orchestra (op. 3) in the spring of 1905. All these works are based on Hungarian popular art song as source material, for Bartók and his predecessors—indeed, the rest of the musical world—erroneously assumed that such music, which was mainly composed by amateurs from the educated classes and disseminated with typical distortions by city Gypsy bands, was the true Hungarian folk music.

FUSION OF NATIONAL MUSIC STYLES (1906–1925)

But during the summer of 1904, while Bartók was working on the Rhapsody, he overheard a girl singing a melody that had very unusual qualities. She was of Székely origin, born and raised in a Hungarian-speaking community in the southeast corner of Transylvania. He annotated and analyzed her song repertory, convinced that he had chanced upon an ancient melody type unknown until then and totally different from the so-called Hungarian folk songs that pervaded Budapest's musical life. He decided to investigate further. In his autobiography, he recalled that:

> I set out in 1905 to collect and study Hungarian peasant music unknown till then. It was my great good luck to find a helpmate for this work in Zoltán Kodály [1882-1967], who, owing to his deep insight and sound judgment in all spheres of music, could give me many a hint and much advice that proved of immense value. I started these investigations on entirely musical grounds and pursued them in areas which linguistically were purely Hungarian. Later I became fascinated by the scientific implications of my musical material and extended my work over territories which were linguistically Slovakian and Romanian.

He continues with a description of those elements from the "collected treasure" that were of "decisive influence upon my work." Among them were the ancient pentatonic scale that the Magyars brought with them from central Asia into the Danube Basin in the ninth century, and an incredible variety of old ecclesiastical or old Greek modes that "freed me from the tyrannical rule of the major and minor keys [and that] eventually led to a new conception of the chromatic scale, every tone of which came to be considered of equal value and could be used freely and independently."

It was Bartók's great talent that enabled him to homogenize polyglot musical folklore, beginning in 1907, and develop five levels of complexity for using his newly found materials.

(1) Genuine folk tunes are featured in a composition, and the invented material is of secondary importance. In other words, the folk tune is the "jewel" and

the added parts function as its "mounting."
(2) In this level of construction, the folk tune and the invented material are treated equally.
(3) The folk tune is presented as a kind of musical "motto," and the invented material is of greater significance.
(4) The melody is composed in imitation of a genuine folk tune.
(5) The highest level is that in which neither folk tune nor its imitation is used, but the work is pervaded by the atmosphere of folk music. Thus, for example, the music might have Hungarian pentatonic turns, Romanian bagpipe motif structure, Slovak modal features, and so on.
The first three levels are readily apparent in the Rhapsody No. 1 for Violin and Piano (1928), and all levels can be located in the Concerto for Orchestra (1943).

Synthesis of East and West (1926–1945)

In 1939, Bartók, talking about Debussy with an interviewer, raised certain questions that had been preoccupying him for a decade. "Debussy's great service to music," he said, "was to reawaken among all musicians an awareness of harmony and its possibilities. In that, he was just as important as Beethoven, who revealed to us the meaning of progressive form, and as Bach, who showed us the transcendent significance of counterpoint. Now, what I am always asking myself is this: is it possible to make a synthesis of these three great masters, a living synthesis that will be valid for our time?"

It is interesting that Bartók broached this seemingly fantastic concept in the form of a question, for he had achieved the synthesis stage years before, with the composition of his *Cantata profana* in 1930. But this third and highest stage of development did not emerge full-blown like Venus in Botticelli's masterpiece. He felt a need to incorporate a distinctive polyphonic dimension in his work, to be added to his innovative permutations of classical sonata and rondo forms and of French musical "Impressionism" (for example, Bartók's use of the whole-tone scale in Sonata No. 2 for Violin and Piano, 1922).

But Bartók, looking for direction in 1924 and 1925, turned to the style of Bach's Italian predecessors and contemporaries—for example, Frescobaldi and della Ciaia. He found the Italian musical temperament more closely identifiable with his Hungarian predilection for the variation principle and for flexibility in fugal writing. (See the related comments in my program note to Concerto No. 1 for Piano and Orchestra.)

Briefly summarized, then, Bartók's last stage of development was the synthesis of Eastern folk-music materials and Western art-music techniques of composition, whose outcome is illustrated in such masterpieces as Music for Stringed Instruments, Percussion, and Celesta (1936); Concerto No. 2 for Violin and Orchestra (1938); and the previously mentioned Concerto for Orchestra. And it is these compositions among his other works, particularly his six string quartets, that have led to his acclamation—during his lifetime—as the fourth in the procession of Bs in music: Bach, Beethoven, Brahms, and Bartók. There is mounting evidence that by the year 2003 Béla Bartók will have been designated composer par excellence of the twentieth century.

CONCERTO FOR ORCHESTRA[4]

It was in 1941, the year after Bartók emigrated to the United States, that the first link can be traced in the chain of events that ultimately led to the composition of his Concerto for Orchestra.

Bartók, working at Columbia University on the transcription of Yugoslav folk music, was particularly struck by a unique recording of Dalmatian two-part chromatic folk melodies. As he later remarked, during his 1943 lectures at Harvard University, he was impressed by the "unity, higher development and unusual effect on listeners" of the pieces. The replication of this Dalmatian folk-music style in the second movement of the Concerto is a direct outcome of his scholarly research.

A second important event was a letter from his London publisher, Ralph Hawkes, in April of 1942:

> I believe that you would be interested in composing a series of concertos for solo instrument or instruments and string orchestra. By this I mean piano and string orchestra, solo violin and string orchestra, flute and string orchestra, etc., or combinations of solo instruments and string orchestra. I have in mind the *Brandenburg* Concertos by Bach, and I believe you are well fitted to do something on these lines.

At that time, however, Bartók was involved with the Yugoslav materials, including a highly technical introductory study, for publication by the Columbia University Press. In addition, he was preparing the fair copy of his monumental collection of Romanian folk music and committed to a second transcontinental concert tour. Moreover, as he replied to the publisher on 3 August :

> I am ill since the beginning of April. And the doctors cannot find the cause, in spite of very thorough examinations. Fortunately, I can continue my work at Columbia Univ. I only wonder how long this can go on in this way. And whether it is perhaps a general breakdown? Heaven knows. Just before my illness I began some composition work, and just the kind you suggested in your letter. But then, of course, I had to discontinue it because of lack of energy, tranquillity and mood— I don't know if I ever will be in the position to do some new works.

The overall structural concept and title of the Concerto, and particularly the plan of the second movement, indicate the extent to which Bartók was motivated by his publisher's ideas.

The third event occurred during the broadcast of the NBC Symphony on 19 July 1942, as Arturo Toscanini conducted the Shostakovich *Leningrad* Symphony No. 7. According to Bartók's younger son, Peter:

> During the part of the work which I believe was supposed to signify the advance of the German army [the first movement], my father became aware of numerous repetitions of a theme which sounded like a Viennese cabaret song. . . . My father was surprised to hear such a theme used for such a purpose in such great abundance.

Bartók uses a variant of the same tune as the *interrotto* theme in the fourth movement of the Concerto. According to the conductor Antal Dorati, Bartók showed him the movement soon after its completion and stated that:

> The big, overblown *Leningrad* Symphony of Shostakovich is no good. While I was doing my piece, suddenly I thought of the *Leningrad*. It made me very angry. I put that anger into the Concerto and then laughed at the Russian work.

Concurrent with his preparation of the Yugoslav material for publication, Bartók worked on his monumental collection of Romanian folk music in the hope that the New York Public Library would serve as the publisher. In the first volume of instrumental melodies, which includes a chapter on folk dance and its choreography, he concludes that bagpipe dance tunes, seemingly of indeterminate structure, are actually composed of shorter or longer motifs strung together in a way recognizable by the dancers. These bagpipe motifs and their imitations on violin and peasant flute were extracted, classified, and tabulated by Bartók as an appendix to his study. An outcome of this work was his idealization of bagpipe motifs as the thematic basis of the Concerto's Finale.

After he completed the second volume of Romanian folk music in December 1942 Bartók began to prepare a series of lectures to be given at Harvard. In March, however, following the third lecture, he had a sudden breakdown ("There is no hope of recovery," he said), which was aggravated by the Library's rejection of his Romanian material because of the high cost. He was deeply troubled by the apparent failure of his doctors to diagnose his illness, and he was unaware that he had incurable leukemia. Nevertheless, and with indomitable will—"I always work, even when I am sick!"—he found the strength to complete his 1936 collection of Turkish folk music, for he had the impression that the Library might accept a smaller, less-complicated publication project.

In May, while Bartók was still hospitalized, he was visited by Serge Koussevitzky, conductor of the Boston Symphony Orchestra, who offered Bartók a grant of $1,000 to write an orchestral composition. His wife, Ditta, wrote that "plans, musical ambitions, compositions are stirring in Béla's mind—a new hope, discovered in this way quite by chance, as if it were incidentally. One thing is sure: Béla's 'under no circumstances will I ever write any new work' attitude is gone. It has been more than *three* years now." And so the last and most important link in the chain of events was forged. A special grant from the American Society of Composers, Authors, and Publishers (ASCAP) enabled Bartók to convalesce during that summer in a small cottage at Saranac Lake, New York. He brought his Turkish field sketchbook for reference purposes in the preparation of the fair-copy draft of his book on the subject. On 20 July, Ralph Hawkes wrote to Bartók, asking whether any new compositions were under way. The 31 July response included a long description of the illness and the various medical diagnoses: "I feel better [when I have periods of lower fever]. But, on the whole there is no perceptible change! Now about the doctors . . . they are groping about in the darkness."

On 15 August, Bartók began composing the Concerto, using the field sketchbook for the purpose, and beginning with the third movement (Elegia) and its opening quotation of the "darkness" theme from his opera *Duke Bluebeard's Castle*. The work was completed on 15 October 1943.

In 1944 Bartók wrote the following program note, "Explanation to Concerto for Orchestra," for the Boston premiere at Symphony Hall on 1 December:

> The title of this symphony-like orchestral work is explained by its tendency to treat the single instruments or instrument groups in a *concertant* or soloistic manner. The "virtuoso" treatment appears, for instance, in the *fugato* sections of the development of the first movement (brass instruments) or in the *perpetuum mobile*-like passages of the principal theme in the last movement (strings), and, especially, in the second movement, in which pairs of instruments appear consecutively with brilliant passages.
>
> As for the structure of the work, the first and fifth movements are written in a more or less regular sonata form. The development of the first movement contains *fugato* sections for brass; the exposition in the finale is somewhat extended, and its development consists of a fugue built on the last theme of the exposition.
>
> Less traditional forms are found in the second and third movements. The main part of the second movement consists of a chain of independent short sections, by wind instruments consecutively introduced in five pairs (bassoons, oboes, clarinets, flutes and muted trumpets). Thematically, the five sections have nothing in common and could be symbolized by the letters "*a, b, c, d, e.*" A kind of "trio" — a short chorale for brass instruments and side-drum—follows, after which the five sections are recapitulated in a more elaborate instrumentation.
>
> The structure of the third movement likewise is chain-like; three themes appear successively. These constitute the core of the movement, which is enframed by a misty texture of rudimentary motives. Most of the thematic material of this movement derives from the "Introduction" [Introduzione] to the first movement. The form of the fourth movement—*Intermezzo interrotto*—could be rendered by the letter symbols "A B A—interruption—B A."
>
> The general mood of the work represents—apart from the jesting second movement—a gradual transition from the sternness of the first movement and the lugubrious death song of the third, to the life-assertion of the last one.

Introduzione and First Movement. The two contrasting themes that form the Introduzione have a four-section melodic structure characteristic of Hungarian folk song. Theme 1 is pentatonic and in the parlando (free) rhythm typical of the "old" style (Ex. 1.1).

Ex. 1.1. Bartók, Concerto for Orchestra, Introduzione, bars 1–6.

It has properties in common with the melody in the second piece in Bartók's Four Dirges for Piano (Ex. 1.2)

Ex. 1.2. Bartók, Four Dirges for Piano (op. 8b, 1908), No. 2, bars 1–7.

and it is in closer relationship to the Prologue theme from *Duke Bluebeard's Castle* (Ex. 1.3).

Ex. 1.3. Bartók, *Duke Bluebeard's Castle* (op. 11, 1911), Prologue, bars 1–17.

This theme also closes the opera as Bluebeard sings, "Henceforth all shall be darkness." Since thematic transformations of this "darkness music" appear cyclically in the Concerto, the first and perhaps most important of the composer's extra-musical intentions is thus made apparent.

A flourish of trumpets announces theme 2, which has other features of "old"-style Hungarian folk song. The four melody sections have twin-bar motifs that descend sequentially (Ex. 1.4).

The motifs, inverted and rhythmically altered, are taken up by the strings

Ex. 1.4. Bartók, Concerto for Orchestra, Introduzione, theme 2, bars 39–43.

and high woodwinds. Suddenly there is an ominous pounding by the timpani, followed by a transition passage in which the orchestra iterates the first bar of the exposition main theme, *poco a poco accelerando e crescendo.* The main theme combines *tempo giusto* (strict) rhythm with the interval of the tritone (augmented fourth)—characteristic features of Slovak folk music (Ex. 1.5).

Ex. 1.5. Ibid., exposition main theme, R.N. 76.

The lyrical secondary theme, played in turn by the oboe, clarinets, and then flutes with strings, provides a pastoral mood until it is overwhelmed by an arching of the main theme motif, tossed *forte* between strings and woodwinds (Ex. 1.6).

Ex. 1.6. Ibid., exposition secondary theme, one bar before R.N. 155.

The development contains three sections, all contrapuntally textured. The first section is a main-theme *fugato* for strings and double reeds; the second section features the clarinet in a broadened, lyrical transformation of the same material, in approximation of the pastoral mood previously met in the secondary theme. The third section, also a *fugato*, is assigned to the brass. The full-orchestra crescendo culminates in a great unison which is quickly punctuated with a crashing chord to end the development.

The recapitulation begins with the secondary theme as a clarinet solo. The return of the main theme is again preceded by the same kind of motivic treatment in the transition between the Introduzione and the exposition.

An eight-bar codetta—the main theme motif in augmented note values—ends on a cadence in the Phrygian mode, thus emphasizing the atmosphere of folk music that pervades the movement.

Second Movement. Several holographs of the second movement show "Presentando le coppie" (presenting of the couples) and not "Giuoco delle coppie" (game of the couples) as the caption for the second movement. The lightsome tunes and unusually interesting orchestral effects are in sharp contrast to the tense, foreboding music of the preceding movement.

The bassoons, in parallel at the interval of a major sixth, begin with a melody in imitation of Yugoslav *kolo* (round dance) style (Ex. 1.7).

Ex. 1.7. Ibid., second movement, theme 1, bars 8–12.

The oboes brighten the dance with a perky tune of irregular phrase structure, in minor thirds—the inverted form of the bassoon intervals (Ex. 1.8).

Ex. 1.8. Ibid., second movement, theme 2, R.N. 25.

The clarinets, substituting for the traditional *sopel* (a kind of folk oboe) prelude, in a peculiar type of Dalmatian folk song, play their duet at the unusual but characteristic interval of a minor seventh (Ex. 1.9).

Ex. 1.9. Ibid., second movement, theme 3, R.N. 45.

The flute duet, whose rhythm, mode, and parallel fifths betray "foreign" (that is, western European) influence, maintains the chromaticism common to the preceding dance tunes (Ex. 1.10).

Ex. 1.10. Ibid., second movement, theme 4, R.N. 60.

The muted trumpets are given the role of Dalmatian folk singers—that is, a duet in major seconds (the inverted form of minor sevenths) to follow an instrumental prelude (here, the clarinet duet). Unlike folk-music performance, however, the trumpet tune differs in rhythm and especially in tonality (Ex. 1.11).

Ex. 1.11. Ibid., second movement, theme 5, R.N. 90.

The "Sunday order of dances"—a feature of village life that Bartók observed during his field trips—is interrupted by a chorale tune in the brass. The antique harmonic flavor is achieved bimodally: the intervallic fifths of the second trombone and the tuba are in the pentatonic scale, while above them the trumpets and first trombone are given simple triads in the major-minor tonal system. The chorale ends with a "Yugoslav cadence"—that is, on the dominant chord—and the horns with the tuba repeat the last half of the melody in a new key.

The closing section is a reprise of the dances in the same order of tone color and intervallic distance but with added instrumentation and string contrapuntal passages. The movement ends with a repetition of the side-drum solo that served as its introduction.

Third Movement. The Elegia is a funereal lament interspersed with sounds of Bartók's cherished "night music," as if in tearful remembrance of happier times that he had among the Romanian villagers of northern Transylvania. A mourning song text that he collected there in 1913 seems appropriately related to the musical content of this movement:

> O you black and woeful earth!
> Whosoever gets inside you

Nevermore comes back again.
Many people have you swallowed,
Yet you haven't had your fill.

The two Introduzione themes open the movement, each briefly developed and followed by interludes which represent the nocturnal sounds of nature. Then the violas play this chromatically compressed imitation of a folk lament (Ex. 1.12).

Ex. 1.12. Ibid., third movement, R.N. 62.

Introduzione theme 2 returns in inverted form in the violins, followed by flute and clarinet arpeggios and by the reprise of theme 1 in the low strings. The subsequent whispering string tremolos below the continuous swirling of woodwind arpeggios are similar to the texture in *Duke Bluebeard's Castle*, when the sixth door is opened to reveal the Lake of Tears—formed out of the weeping of Bluebeard's murdered wives. Theme 1, the "darkness" motif, is again heard but the healing "night music" prevails as piccolo, horn, and timpani quietly bring the movement to a close.

Fourth Movement. In the first draft of his "Explanation to Concerto for Orchestra," Bartók struck out the words "the only programmatic" in his discussion of the structural features of the "Intermezzo interrotto." He obviously intended to give the listener some kind of extra-musical description, but changed his mind. Therefore I propose the following narrative based on a musical interpretation of the themes:

> Once in Greater Hungary, prior to its dismemberment in 1920, there were three kinds of popular music. The genuine, unaccompanied folk songs were preserved in the rural areas, and they were of such high quality that Beethoven used them in his *Pastoral* Symphony. A composer who has made a scientific study of such village music can produce high-quality imitations, as in this melody in Slovak style (Ex. 1.13).
>
> In the cities and towns amateur and professional musicians composed melodies in folk-song style. Some of these melodies were adapted by the villagers and became part of rural repertory; others were propagated by city Gypsy bands in such a distorted way that a delighted, worldwide audience thought of this kind of

Ex. 1.13. Ibid., fourth movement, theme 1, R.N. 5.

Gypsy music as the genuine Hungarian folk music. And so thought Liszt and Brahms.

It is in the adaptable and unadulterated case, however, that pseudo folk songs can be used by a composer in higher art forms. For example, the melody of Zsigmond Vincze's patriotic song, "You are lovely, you are beautiful, Hungary," is fitted with interesting chord progressions to replace its commonplace harmonies (Ex. 1.14).

Ex. 1.14. Ibid., fourth movement, theme 2, R.N. 43.

Viennese song hits, like the vulgar "Chez Maxim" from Léhar's operetta, *The Merry Widow,* are unfit for village use or to depict the German assault on Leningrad in 1941. They serve best as parody music, provided the setting incorporates Bulgarian or syncopated rhythms to avoid monotony (Ex. 1.15).

Ex. 1.15. Ibid., fourth movement, theme 3, bars 76–80.

A reprise of theme 2, followed by several of theme 1, enframes the movement in a rondolike form.

Fifth Movement. The entire finale is a fantasy of transformed bagpipe motifs that Bartók collected from Transylvanian-Romanian villagers between 1907 and 1917. These twin-bar or four-bar motifs were usually accompanied by a kind of two-string guitar to provide the missing tonic-dominant drone pipes when a violin replaced the bagpipe—as in this *Jocul fecioresc* (bachelor's round dance) Bartók transcribed in 1913 (Ex. 1.16).

1.16. *RFM*.v, melody No. 161c, bars 12–15, 20–21.

The movement begins with an introductory statement of the secondary theme by the horns; the violas and cellos follow with their impersonation of a guitar accompaniment, whereupon the second violins strike up the dance with a four-bar motif, Presto, that forms the nucleus of the exposition main theme (Ex. 1.17).

1.17. Bartók, Concerto for Orchestra, fifth movement, theme 1, bars 8–11.

The texture thickens as the *divisi* violins enter at four-bar intervals and in parallel thirds and fifths. A long crescendo leads to a new motif, marked by the addition of woodwinds. A sudden drop in intensity finds the flutes, oboe, clarinets and piccolo in a musical argument as one of the harps and the strings shift to syncopated chordal-accompaniment patterns. A short transition section follows the reprise of the main theme by the strings, and the second bassoon leads a brief stretto canon of the secondary theme (Ex. 1.18).

1.18. Ibid., fifth movement, theme 2, R.N. 148.

A choralelike episode, reminiscent of the "trio" in the second movement, precedes the closing theme, which is partly derived from the clarinet "Dalmatian prelude" duet of that same movement (Ex. 1.19).

Repetition of the closing theme, in inverted form, is followed by a canonic reprise of the theme and its inversion, crashing orchestra chords, and timpani.

The development is introduced by harps 1 and 2 and the *divisi* violins. This

1.19. Ibid., fifth movement, theme 3, R.N. 201.

short but striking introduction—perhaps a final homage to Debussy?—is an imitation of a Balinese gamelan (tuned percussion) orchestra.[5] The development proper is a fugue whose subject, announced by violin 2, is the closing theme from the exposition. The unmistakable musical atmosphere of the development is the art of the fugue merged with the spirit of the dance.

The recapitulation is ignited by a three-bar burst of chords in strings and brass. The main-theme motifs are hardly touched when the chorale theme returns, Tranquillo. And then—Più presto!—arching scalar passages in triplet rhythm sweep across the strings as the bassoon plays the secondary theme in augmented note values. A crescendo leads to the coda in which the fugue subject is proclaimed with mighty chords to bring the concerto to a stunning end.

SONATA NO. 2 FOR VIOLIN AND PIANO[6]

At the end of the First World War, defeated Hungary was governed by a short-lived communist dictatorship and, following a counterrevolution, by a reactionary regency on 1 March 1920. Bartók recalled the war years in his autobiography:

> Then came the outbreak of the war, which—apart from general human considerations—hit me very hard, because it put an end to my work. Only a small part of Hungary remained open to my studies, and I worked there under hampered conditions till 1918.
>
> The year 1917 brought a change in the attitude of the Budapest public toward my compositions. . . . After these promising beginnings there followed, alas! the complete political and economic breakdown of 1918.
>
> The sad and troubled times that followed for about a year and a half were not conducive to serious work.
>
> And even today conditions are not such as would allow us to think of continuing our studies in musical folklore. They are a "luxury" we cannot afford on our own resources. Political conditions are another great impediment. The great hatred that has been worked up makes it almost impossible to carry out research in parts of countries that once belonged to Hungary. Journeys to faraway countries are out of the question.

The Treaty of Trianon (1920) dismembered Greater Hungary, Slovakia, Transylvania, and Croatia. Other southern territories were now lost and their borders closed to Hungarian nationals. The disillusioned Bartók, further depressed by debilitating illness, withdrew to his study to prepare scholarly works that would summarize his research and findings in Hungarian, Romanian, Slovak, and North African Arab musical folklore.

> I have no time for composing, [he wrote in May of 1921], even if I were in the right mood for it. But my mood is far from right—and no wonder. . . . And I am hopelessly cut off from the one thing which is as necessary to me as fresh air is to other people—the possibility of going on with my studies of folk music in the countryside.
> Yet at this moment my compositions are arousing interest abroad. In November I was the subject of a 12-page (approx.) article in a London music periodical in which the writer placed me in the ranks of the world's greatest composers, not merely the greatest living composers but of all time . . . anyhow, even if they [international music periodicals] were to make me the High Pope of Music, it would be no help to me so long as I remain cut off from peasant music.

The now-famous forty-year-old composer, roused from scholarly retreat by a request to give a recital of his piano pieces in London (thanks to the efforts of the d'Arányi sisters, both violinists, who had moved there from Budapest), decided to write a piece for violin and piano as part of the program. Thus his First Violin and Piano Sonata came into being on 12 December 1921, composed for Jelly d'Arányi, his onetime pupil and now a close friend.

The first London performance, by Jelly and Bartók, on 24 March 1922, was a great success—so much so that Bartók was apparently inspired to write his Second Sonata, also for Jelly, which he completed at the end of November 1922. The first performance was given in Berlin by Bartók and the Hungarian violinist, Imre Waldbauer.

The completion of the Second Sonata in 1922 is the high point of the second stage in Bartók's stylistic development, which had begun in 1906 with simple settings of Hungarian folk songs. Until then his quest to make "a living synthesis" of Debussy's harmonic innovations, Beethoven's progressive form, and Bach's counterpoint had been concerned with the mastery of the first two aspects of composition and with their application to his collected musical folklore as source materials.

Perhaps it is Bartók's emphasis on harmonic and formal development that has prompted performers and analysts of the Second Sonata to write such comments as "most complex and severe of Bartók's chamber works," "formal principles which are the subject of speculation among musicologists," "one of Bartók's most difficult and dissonant scores," and "one of his most adventurous and problematic works."

Not so! The listener's difficulties fade when the work is approached as program music based on a specific genre of Transylvanian Romanian instrumental music style: the *cântec lung* or *hora lungă* ("long-drawn" song). This unique melody type, which Bartók was the first to discover during his collecting trips in Transylvania in 1913, is entirely improvisatory but with irregularly recurring sections that feature sustained tones and richly ornamented passages.

Bartók also noted that the *cântec lung* was played by shepherds on the peasant flute and that it was sometimes called "When the Shepherd Lost his Sheep" to express sorrow over one of the most tragic events in shepherd life. Village musicians took over this slow-tempo improvisatory piece and followed it with a faster one consisting of dance melodies and designated "When the Shepherd Found his Lost Sheep." Bartók's Sonata No. 2 for Violin and Piano is such a Transylvanian double piece, whose composite structure was also to be found in Hungarian villages (designated there as *lassan* or *lassú* [slow piece] and *friska* or *friss* [fast piece]), in city Gypsy-band repertory, and even in some of Liszt's Hungarian Rhapsodies.

An important clue to the understanding of Bartók's tonal language in the sonata can be found in the melodic structure of the *cântec lung*, which is unaccompanied music for solo performance. The scale consists of five and sometimes six tones, in which the third and fourth degrees are variable in pitch—including quarter tones! The resulting alternations and fluctuations in pitch yield major or minor thirds and perfect or augmented (tritone) fourths. And there is emphatic use of minor and major seconds throughout the melody.

First Movement. The sustained tones of the opening bars, in typical *cântec lung* style, serve as a prelude to theme 1 ("when the shepherd lost his sheep"), played by the violin as personator of the peasant flute (Ex. 1.20).

Ex. 1.20. Bartók, Second Sonata for Violin and Piano, first movement, theme 1, bars 4–7.

The independent piano part, in which intervallic doublings of seconds, fourths and sevenths replace traditional triadic sonorities, seems to function as a musical spectator uttering some kind of bitter commentary (perhaps the composer himself, despondent over being cut off from his folk-music sources—"the all-important work that makes my life worth living").

Theme 2, played by the piano, is harmonized throughout by dissonant sonorities that mask the "old"-style Hungarian provenance of the melodic skeleton: pentatonic flavor and the so-called dotted (syncopated) rhythm schema.

The return to theme 1, in the piano and in augmentation of note values, reveals the basic rondo structure of the movement.

Theme 3 follows in the violin; it is a narrow-range chromatic melody whose complex rhythmic organization is matched by an equally complex chordal structuring of the piano part. The violin reprise of theme 1 is accompanied by pianisms in the form of arpeggios and scale passages.

Theme 4, in the violin, introduced by sustained harmonics, features dissonant double-stops as the piano plays octave passages in contrary motion.

The last, full return of theme 1 is followed by a short coda in which the theme is rhythmically transformed. At the same time the piano plays a series of descending fourths, ending with the Lydian tritone (F-B), which temporarily displaces the principal tone E in the violin. The latter, however, continues with a whole-tone pentachordal figure—actually the retrograde form of the first theme's opening motif—thus guiding the ear downward in place of the now-silent piano, toward the final concordance: a simple E-major triad.

Second Movement. This movement is for the most part a series of dance tunes in rondo-variation form. It is perhaps symbolic of the "happy shepherd who has found his lost sheep," since the opening motif of theme 1 is the retrograde form, in augmented note values, of the same motif from the first theme of the preceding movement (Ex. 1.21).

Ex. 1.21. Bartók, Second Sonata for Violin and Piano, second movement, theme 1, bars 5–9.

Another similarity between the two movements is represented by theme 2. Here, too, it is assigned to the piano and features pentatonicism and "dotted" rhythm characteristic of old Hungarian folk-music style (Ex. 1.22).

Ex. 1.22. Ibid., second movement, theme 2, R.N. 3.

Theme 2, in the dominant key, thus exhibits another Hungarianism: fifth transposition structure. Uncharacteristic, of course, is the dissonance resulting from the bimodal treatment of the melody, which is performed simultaneously with its inverted (mirror image) form.

Theme 1 returns in diminution of note values, also in the dominant key. It is repeated a fifth higher, then a transition section leads back to the piano repetition of theme 2 in the tonic key of C. A second repetition of theme 2, transposed down a fifth to F as principal tone, is accompanied by violin figurations.

Theme 3, constructed of typically Romanian rhythm patterns, ♫♩, ♫♫, and ♫♫♩, marks the unique middle section of the movement.

The piano "accompaniment" is nothing else but the exploitation of the whole-tone scale as chord clusters, scalar patterns, and even bitonal passagework, all as if in commemoration of Debussy's earlier innovations along such tonal lines.

The development of theme 3 is interrupted in both parts by the insertion of six bars of theme 4 from the first movement. Then the violin plays a chromatically compressed version of theme 3 while the piano is heard in a descending sequence of related motifs. Another cyclic return of theme 4 from the first movement is followed by a repetition of the chromatically compressed theme 3 and the piano-motif sequences, both instruments transposed downward by a tritone.

The return of theme 1 in the violin is in irregular quintuple meter. The piano accompaniment features major-second doublings in each hand, in the tonic key of C. Two repetitions of the theme are in successive fifth transpositions. Theme 2, yet again given to the piano, is in a variant form that is even more strongly Hungarian in character. The variant, in the dominant key, is repeated in fifth transposition in the tonic.

Theme 1 is heard for the last time, repeated in a sectional arrangement that concludes with accompanying piano configurations that are more or less similar to the thematic ones in the violin.

The coda provides an architectonic or rounded shape to the sonata, for it is a cyclic memento of the "shepherd bewailing his lost sheep." And like the procedure in the first movement, the closing bars lead to a cadence on the tonic major triad—this time fully sounded by violin and piano.

VIOLIN CONCERTO NO. 2[7]

Bartók's Second Violin Concerto was commissioned by and dedicated to "my dear friend Zoltán Székely." Székely, a distinguished Hungarian violinist and composer, had commissioned Bartók's Second Rhapsody for Violin and Piano in 1928. Eight years later he approached Bartók for a larger work. Bartók, overburdened with another commission (the Music for String Instruments, Percussion, and Celesta), with scholarly folk-music research at the Hungarian Academy of Sciences (Budapest), and with concert tours as pianist, offered to compose an extended one-movement work in variation form. Székely, however, insisted on the traditional concerto form.

The composer agreed, but with some reservations, since he had mastered classical sonata and rondo form and was eager to explore the problems of variation form that had been a structural feature in the music of Mozart, Beethoven, and Brahms. Preliminary thematic sketches made in 1936 were put aside, however, to prepare for a previously postponed visit to Turkey, where Bartók had been invited to give lectures, play concerts, and—more important—to record the music of nomadic tribes in southern Turkey. On his return and up to the summer of 1937 he devoted most of his time and energy to transcription and scientific analysis of the folk music that he had collected in Turkey, for he had made an astonishing discovery there: that certain specimens were in close variant relationship with the "old" style of folk song that the Magyars had brought with them when they migrated to present-day Hungary from central Asia during the ninth century A.D.

Other, perhaps more interesting or challenging commissions were offered to Bartók—the Sonata for Two Pianos and Percussion, featuring the composer and his wife, Ditta, as soloists, and *Contrasts* for clarinet, violin, and piano, for Benny Goodman. In August, at long last, he began work on the Violin Concerto but, as he wrote in a January 1938 letter, "It is not yet finished—not having finished it is a very oppressing burden on me."

A further delay resulted from the European political situation. Preparations for war, the Nazi annexation of Austria, and the subsequent German-Hungarian alignment were the contributing factors in Bartók's decision to try to emigrate from Hungary as soon as possible. The one outstanding musical commitment was the Székely commission. He therefore completed the work on 31 December 1938.

The fact that Bartók's masterpiece has become a part of the standard repertory—acclaimed repeatedly as "the best violin concerto since Brahms's"—is an indication of how successful he was in achieving his ultimate goal as a composer: the perfect fusion of Eastern folk-music elements with Western art-music techniques.

As the original tempo designation in one of the manuscripts shows (Tempo di Verbunkos), Bartók's inspiration for the first movement was the *verbunkos*, a specifically Hungarian musical genre that, like the Romanian *Ardeleana*, probably stems from the Ukrainian *kolomyjka* (round dance) melody type.

The *verbunkos* began as recruiting music at the end of the seventeenth century. Hussar officers, accompanied by the bagpipe or a Gypsy band, performed an alternation of slow and fast dances in Hungarian villages—a theatrical kind of performance. The *Verbunkos* style became the national Hungarian musical idiom of the nineteenth century, and it was used by composers in dance suites and other forms. In the Bartók Concerto the *verbunkos* style is represented by the alternation of Risoluto and Vivace with Calmo and Tranquillo, as well as by the bravura of the solo violin.

The older stratum of Hungarian folk music is represented by the main theme, which has pentatonic and modal characteristics, and above all by the syncopated rhythm schema which Bartók found to be a peculiarly Hungarian "dotted"-rhythm attribute in his scholarly studies of Hungarian musical folklore.

There is also a well-hidden programmatic aspect in the first movement, remarkably similar in purpose to the fourth movement of the Concerto for Orchestra. The "secondary" theme is a transmutation of the main theme but in the guise of the twelve-tone technique formulated by Arnold Schoenberg and propagated by his disciples, Anton von Webern and Alban Berg.

Indeed, the first four notes of the secondary theme are a direct quotation of those employed by Berg in his *Lyric Suite*: A, Bb, B♮, F. These four notes, which Berg had previously located as the first and last two of Wagner's *Tristan und Isolde* motif, are an acronym in German music notation of Alban Berg's initials and those of his paramour, Hanna Fuchs.[8] Bartók was not only present at the 16 July 1927 performance of the *Lyric Suite* in Baden-Baden, but he was aware of the motivic borrowing in Berg's twelve-tone theme.

The secondary theme therefore suggests that both the theme and its treatment are a Bartókian commentary, similar to the waggery directed at Shostakovich in the *interrotto* section of the Concerto for Orchestra. Bartók's higher purpose, apparently, is to thus aurally communicate his belief that twelve-tone formulaic composition cannot be reconciled with folk-music applications—"because folk melodies are always tonal," as he explained in 1931. "Folk music of atonality is completely inconceivable. Consequently, music on twelve tones cannot be based on folk music. . . . Far be it from me to maintain that to base his music on folk music is the only way to salvation for a composer in our days. But I wish that our opponents had an equally liberal opinion of the significance of folk music."

First Movement. The movement, in sonata form, begins with an introductory motif, accompanied by strumming harp (Ex. 1.23).

Allegro non troppo

Ex. 1.23. Bartók, Second Violin Concerto, first movement, introductory motif, bars 3–7.

The violin solo enters with the exposition main theme that is built of seconds and fourths in the previously mentioned "old"- style of Hungarian folk music (Ex 1.24). The harp accompaniment in major triads with the main theme in the Phrygian-colored G-Lydian mode—a Bartókian polymodal innovation—is a stylistic hallmark intended to yield a "neutral" tonality.

(Allegro non troppo)

Ex. 1.24. Ibid., theme 1, bars 8–11.

A transition theme in quicker tempo features a dialogue between soloist and first clarinet, which emphasizes another of the composer's musical logos—the tritone (augmented fourth interval).

The secondary theme, a permutation of the main theme, has the twelve tones of the chromatic scale organized in imitation of serial composition technique.

The ensuing dialogue between the solo and the orchestral choirs is a parody of the twelve-tone technique of composition. Instead of treating the theme in accordance with rigid procedural rules based on order of tones—the original theme, its inversion, retrograde form of the original theme, and the retrograde inversion—Bartók simply varies his material so that all twelve tones are present but within a tonal context (Ex. 1.25).

Ex. 1.25. Ibid., variations of the secondary theme, beginning at R.N. 73.

When the orchestra breaks into three loud guffaws (at R.N. 92), the solo tries to camouflage its "atonality" with Romanian *Ardeleana* (round dance) rhythm patterns, ♪♪♪♪ ♪♪♪. But the string section insists on a traditional accompaniment in tonally based triads until the trombones end this sorry state of chromatic affairs with a snort of derision.

The development opens with the solo playing the introductory motif—now expanded into an extended lyrical structure.

The sudden change to Vivace tempo signals the start of the fast *Verbunkos*, as the solo, now in Gypsy costume, plays dazzling *figuras* (whirling scalar patterns) and the orchestra adds chordal motifs in Hungarian "dotted" rhythm. This is followed by the English horn with an augmentation and then a varied diminution of the main theme. The woodwinds and horns continue with the syncopation patterns, which lead to a solo reprise of the main theme—now in inverted form as a transitional passage.

The recapitulation of the main theme, Tranquillo, is followed by more repetitions of the "dotted"-rhythm motif in the brass and woodwinds, and the solo's Romanian rhythm patterns serve as a surprising introduction to an attenuated reprise of the "atonal" secondary theme. When this enfeebled attempt is later echoed by the first clarinet, the orchestra again breaks into laughter. Sheepishly the solo takes up the Romanian rhythm schemata, and the orchestra applauds with a burst of pentachords from the traditional chromatic scale and turns the stage over to the solo for the traditional cadenza. Before the solo begins the display of instrumental pyrotechnics, Bartók slips in a last musical comment on another possibility for this "Age of Chromaticism"—a six-bar introductory passage featuring quarter tones!

The coda is a reprise of main-theme motif permutations as the solo continues on in quasi-cadenza style. The movement ends on a crescendo in unison, on B, the same tonality with which it began.

Second Movement. The main theme has the same Phrygian-colored, G-Lydian tonality as the main theme in the preceding movement (Ex. 1.26).

Andante tranquillo

Ex. 1.26. Bartók, Second Violin Concerto, second movement, main theme, bars 1–3.

There are six variations of the theme:

1. Un poco più andante. The solo, at first accompanied only by contrabass and timpani and then by the string section, plays an ornamented variation of the melody.

2. Un poco più tranquillo. The French horn introduces the new tonality, and the solo's performance of the variation is in a rhythmically free (parlando) style.

3. Più mosso. Sustained intervals in the horns and flutes parallel the double-

stops in the solo as the tempo quickens.

4. Lento. The florid passages (*figuras*) in the solo are contrasted by the theme in augmented note values in the low strings. The second violins and violas enter in canonic imitation of the theme.

5. Allegro scherzando. A bright dance variation in strict rhythm (Tempo giusto). The rhythm patterns recall bagpipe motifs in Romanian dance melodies (Ex. 1.27).

Allegro scherzando

Ex. 1.27. Ibid., bars 83–84.

6. Commodo. The last variation is a dancelike canon for the string section, with percussion punctuations.

A coda provides the reprise of the main theme. Muted violins, *divisi*, bring the movement to a hushed close.

Third Movement. The entire movement is a thematic and structural variation of the first movement, thereby realizing the composer's original intention to focus on variation form as the basis for the Székely commission in 1936 (Ex. 1.28a).

Allegro molto

Ex. 1.28a. Bartók, Second Violin Concerto, third movement, main theme, bars 5–10.

The rondo form calls for a different architecture. Bartók thus separates the various themes with connective musical tissue that is related to material in the development of the first movement. When the secondary twelve-tone theme makes its appearance in the solo—introduced by percussion and harp—it is greeted by *divisi*, muted string tremolos in chromatic hexachords (Ex. 128b).

Ex. 1.28b. Ibid., secondary theme, bars 138–145.

But the chromaticism is organized in the form of modal segments, and the work ends emphatically in B major. So much for "atonality"!

Rhapsody No. 1 for Violin and Piano[9]

Bartók's first American concert tour began in New York on 22 December 1927 at Carnegie Hall. Willem Mengelberg conducted the New York Philharmonic Orchestra, with the composer as soloist, in Bartók's Rhapsody for Piano and Orchestra, op. 1. This early (1904) work, representative of Bartók's first stage of creative development, was substituted for his First Piano Concerto— inadequate rehearsal time forced the cancellation of the Concerto. One review criticized the Rhapsody for Piano and Orchestra as being so free in style that it lacked cohesion, and suggested that it had enough good musical ideas to make two works instead of one.

On 5–6 February 1928, also in New York, Bartók and Szigeti played concerts which included the Sonata No. 2 for Violin and Piano (1922), Romanian Folk Dances from Hungary (1915), and Szigeti's transcription of pieces from Bartók's *For Children* for piano (1908; the transcription was made in 1927 and titled Hungarian Folktunes).

The success of his tour with Szigeti and the apparent resolve to give his partner new material were the basic motives that prompted Bartók to compose his First Rhapsody for Violin and Piano during the early fall of that same year. "I've written a minor (12-minute) composition for you (based on folk dances)," he wrote Szigeti on completion of the first draft, "and I want to talk to you about one or two points."

Soon thereafter Bartók made transcriptions for cello and piano and for violin and orchestra. As he wrote to a Hungarian journalist in 1931:

> Both the First and Second Rhapsody were originally written for violin and piano (or orchestra), later I transcribed the First for the cello, too; or to be more exact, I had always imagined, from the very outset, both for violin and piano and for cello and piano; but it wasn't until sometime later that the cello and piano version was written out. This is shown, incidentally, by the fact that the First Rhaps. is dedicated to a violinist [Szigeti]!

The first performance, by Szigeti and the composer, took place in Budapest on 22 November 1929. The original recording, like that of the Second Sonata, was made during their recital at the 1940 Coolidge Festival (Library of Congress) in Washington, D.C.

The First Rhapsody is in very close relationship to the Second Sonata with regard to form: two movements in contrasting tempos. A *lassú* (slow piece) is followed by a *friss* (fast piece), with a short reprise of the *lassú* to provide an architectonic or rounded (ABA) form. The score has an alternate ending in the second movement that Bartók originally composed so that this movement could be played as an independent piece.

The Sonata and the Rhapsody are also connected umbilically to Romanian instrumental folk music, indeed, by single references to Hungarian folk music as well. The Sonata, however, represents the two highest levels of Bartókian transmutation of folk music into composed music: the invention of melodies in imitation of real folk tunes and the creation of a musical atmosphere that is pervaded by certain characteristics of Romanian, Hungarian, and other ethnic musical folklore. The Rhapsody, on the other hand, is based on a less complex level of composition, in which actual folk melodies are used in simple settings or as a kind of "motto" material for the construction and development of the work.

A quite obvious difference between the two works is tonality. The Sonata was written at a time when Bartók thought he was approaching a species of twelve-tone music—that is, along the lines of Arnold Schoenberg's approach to composition. Bartók always emphasized, however, that even then "the absolute tonal foundation is unmistakable." The Rhapsody is, of course, pronouncedly tonal in type.

The folk tunes that Bartók assembled for the construction of the Rhapsody seem to suggest an underlying program which I have conjectured in the following narrative for the amusement of the listener:

> *Lassú* (slow). In a Romanian village the Gypsy musicians strike up the tune.
> *De ciuit* (calling to the dance), The villagers shout with joy as they gather to begin the dance festival. "Jaj de szépen muzsikálnak—Oh, how beautifully they are playing music" (for the Hungarian gentleman, Bartók, who has come to the village with his recording machine to collect melodies) is sung in praise of the honored guest. The *de ciuit* is struck up again as the villagers, with loud huzzas, make ready for the first dance.
> *Friss* (fast). *Judecata* (judgment) is the appropriate first dance whose melody is also sung to the following text: "I shall pass out judgment to you, / A Romanian [peasant] judgment, / May the Lord let it endure."
> Next the bachelors dance the *crucea*, stepping nimbly between crossed sticks; couples alternate steps and leaps to the *pre loc*; then the bachelors return to dance the *cuiesdeanca*. The Hungarian gentleman wants to hear the *pre loc* melody again: he is fascinated by the "strange" modern sound of the second violin's chordal accompaniment.
> The *judecata* is danced again as the gentleman tries to decide which dance was the best. He likes them all, he tells the villagers, and he decides to arrange their melodies in a concert piece.

First Movement. Theme 1, in the Lydian mode (a major scale with an augmented fourth degree or tritone), is introduced by pedaled fifths in the piano part, in imitation of tonic-dominant pipes of a peasant bagpipe (Ex. 1.29).

The thematic source is a *de ciuit* (calling to the dance) melody, played as a kind of prelude to Sunday dancing or dance festivals. The music does not be-

Ex. 1.29. Bartók, First Rhapsody for Violin and Piano (1928), first movement, theme 1, bars 2–6.

long to the dance genre nor does it serve as such. The villagers usually accompany the tune with "dance words" or huzzas (Ex. 1.30).

Ex. 1.30. Bartók, *RFM*.i, melody No. 232, bars 1–4.

Theme 2 is in the parallel Phrygian mode: a G-minor scale with a lowered second degree (Ex. 1.31).

Ex. 1.31. Bartók, First Rhapsody for Violin and Piano (1928), first movement, theme 2, R.N. 5. The Phrygian folk mode is G-A♭-B♭-C-D-E♭.

This theme, transcribed by Bartók from a recording of a Hungarian Gypsy violinist (Ex. 1.32), stems from a Hungarian folk song whose text is:

> Oh, how beautifully they are playing music
> For the outlaw in the green forest;
> In the tent of the weeping willow
> Sándor Rózsa is dancing.[10]

Ex. 1.32. Hungarian folk song melody, played by János Balog, a Gypsy, and recorded by Béla Vikár.

The piano repetition of the theme in fifth transposition—a characteristic tonal shift in Hungarian folk music—is imitated canonically by the violin. The return to theme 1 provides a temporary feeling of rounded (ABA) form, but the last six bars echo theme 2.

Although the movement consists of seemingly disparate ethnic musics, the second half of the Romanian and Hungarian tunes are in very close variant relationship.

Second Movement. The first theme of this movement is in the major mode, whose principal tone, E, is heard as a drone in the piano part (Ex. 1.33).

Ex. 1.33. Bartók, First Rhapsody for Violin and Piano, second movement, theme 1, R.N. 1.

The theme is hardly recognizable as such in the treble of the piano part, for it appears there in retrograde and in augmented note values. The tune itself is a *judecata* (judgment), a dance piece collected by Bartók in 1912 (Ex. 1.34).

Ex. 1.34. *RFM*.i, melody No. 404, bars 1–4.

It is fascinating to speculate about the provenance of the *judecata* in the light of a variant melody brought by the Shakers (an English Quaker sect) to New York in about 1774, called "The Gift to Be Simple" and transcribed by Aaron Copland as the fifth theme in his ballet, *Appalachian Spring* (Ex. 1.35).

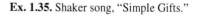

"Tis the   gift to be sim-ple, 'tis the   gift to be free, 'Tis the   gift to come down

Ex. 1.35. Shaker song, "Simple Gifts."

The second dance (theme 2), also in E major but in 2/4 time, is introduced by two 4/4 bars in slower tempo (Ex. 1.36). These bars, however, are a rhythmic expansion of the first bar of the *crucea* source melody (Ex. 1.37).

Ex. 1.36. First Rhapsody for Violin and Piano, second movement, theme 2, R.N. 6.

Ex. 1.37. *RFM*.i, melody No. 298b, *Crucea* (Crossed sticks: young man's solo dance), bars 1–4.

In the second dance, too, canonic imitation is established between the instruments when the piano plays the melody with inverted motifs.

The third dance (theme 3) is in faster tempo and is based on D♯ as principal tone (Ex. 1.38).

Ex. 1.38. Bartók, First Rhapsody for Violin and Piano, second movement, theme 3, two bars before R.N. 11.

The ostinato (repeated figure) accompaniment by the piano is derived from the second violin part of the *pre loc* source melody (Ex. 1.39).

Ex. 1.39. *RFM*.i, melody No. 215, *Pre loc* (Couples' dance), bars 1–5.

The fourth dance (theme 4) is in even quicker tempo and in canonic form (Ex. 1.40). The source melody is a *cuiesdeanca*, which Bartók collected in 1914 (Ex. 1.41).

Theme 4 is followed by a reprise of theme 3 (the *pre loc*) in the piano part as the violin plays accompanying figurations. When the Rhapsody is performed as

Ex. 1.40. Bartók, First Rhapsody for Violin and Piano, second movement, theme 4.

Ex. 1.41. *RFM*.i, melody No. 226, *Cuiesdeanca*, (Bachelors' dance), bars 1–4.

a complete two-movement work, a short development section follows in which the Bartókian innovation of so-called chromatic compression of motivic matter is evident. Then comes a return of theme 1 of the first movement (*de ciuit*), the same architectural procedure to be found in the earlier Second Sonata. A violin passage, *Rubato, quasi-cadenza*, ends the work.

The score of the second movement includes an alternate ending, which Bartók originally intended to be performed when only this movement of the Rhapsody is presented in concert. Thus, instead of the "chromatically compressed" development section following the reprise of theme 3 (*pre loc*), the *judecata* melody—theme 1 of this movement—is brought back, briefly developed, and the Rhapsody closes with a glissando leading to an E-major triad.

MUSIC FOR STRINGS, PERCUSSION, AND CELESTA[11]

The conception of this orchestral masterpiece was the outcome of the newly established relationship between Bartók and Paul Sacher, founder and director of the Basel (Switzerland) Chamber Orchestra.

It was on 23 June 1936 that Sacher asked Bartók for a new work in celebration of the tenth anniversary of the founding of the orchestra. Because of financial and technical difficulties, Sacher asked for elimination of wind players and their substitution by "a piano or cembalo (as a continuo, so to speak) or some kind of percussion instrument."

Bartók responded immediately. His letter of acceptance, dated 27 June, specified the instrumentation of the planned work and addressed the question of difficulty:

> It is a more delicate problem to satisfy your request that the work not be too difficult. Technical difficulty I will certainly be able to avoid. But it is more difficult to avoid rhythmic difficulty. If one writes something new, the very fact of its unusualness already causes difficulties in performance. At any rate, I will en-

deavor to write something that is easily playable. In conclusion, I never write something with the conscious intention of combining everything that is hard to perform."

Sacher's reply of 30 June raised questions about the number of percussion players that would be needed, with obvious emphasis on the xylophone part and within the context of a situation where "we do not have only virtuosos in our service but also players of modest ability." On the last day of August, Bartók wrote to a staff member of the orchestra that "the [xylophone] part is not at all difficult and there is also little to be played. An amateur—I believe—could play this part, too, if he works with the instrument for a little while."

On 7 September the composition was completed, and on September 25— Bartók was quite obviously much concerned about the possibility that the work might be performed without the xylophone—he wrote: "I assure you that the xylophone part is very easy to play, and thus that it can be handled by a person who has never in his life seen a xylophone. I myself have hardly looked at an instrument like this (except for the arrangement of the keys) and had not the slightest difficulty when I tried to play the part on it."

Dedicated to the Basel Chamber Orchestra and its director, Paul Sacher, the first performance was given in Basel on 21 January 1937. In March 1937, Bartók wrote program notes on the work for his publisher, Universal Edition, Vienna. These were misplaced, however, so that Bartók had to redraft them for publication in the study-score edition:

> **Movement I.** *in A*—On certain principles fairly strictly executed form of a fugue, that is, the 2nd entry appears a fifth higher; the 4th again a fifth higher than the 2nd; the 6th, 8th and so on, again a fifth higher than the preceding one. The 3rd, 5th, 7th and so on, on the other hand, each enter a fifth lower. After the remotest key—E-flat—has been reached (the climax of the Movement) the following entries render the theme in contrary motion until the fundamental key—A—is again reached, after which a short Coda follows. N.B.—(1) Several secondary entries appear in *stretto*. (2) Some entries show the theme incompletely, that is, in fragments.

> **Movement II.** *in C*—Sonata form (secondary theme in G). In the execution the theme of Movement I also appears, however, in altered form, and so does an allusion to the main theme of Movement IV. The Recapitulation changes the 2/4 rhythm of the Exposition into a 3/8 rhythm.

> **Movement III.** *in F-sharp*—"*Brueckenform*" (Rondo): A, B, C, B, A. Between each section a part of the theme of Movement I appears.

> **Movement IV.** *in A*—Formula: A + B + A, C + D + E + D + F, G, A. The G part (measures 203–234) shows the main theme of Movement I. which is extended, however, by diatonic expansion of the original chromatic form.

In Bartók's corrected copy of the printed full score is a holographic draft which lists the instrumentation—including the specification of two string players per part—and the approximate disposition of the orchestra in the following diagrammatic form (Ex. 1.42).

Vc. 1 Cb. 1	Timp.		Cb. 2 Vc. 2
Viola 1	Gr. cassa, Piatti		Viola 2
	Tamb. picc.	Xyl.	
Viol. 2	Celesta, Arpa		Viol. 4
Viol. 1	Pianoforte		Viol. 3

Ex. 1.42. Bartók's diagram of the "Approximate disposition of the orchestra."

First Movement. The fugue subject or theme comprises four motifs and is announced by violas 1 and 2, on A as principal tone (Ex. 1.43).

Vle. 1.2. (*8va bassa*)

Ex. 1.43. Bartók, Music for Stringed Instruments, Percussion, and Celesta (1936), first movement, fugue subject, bars 1–4.

The exposition continues with successive entries by violins 3 and 4, cellos 1 and 2, violin 2, and contrabasses 1 and 2. The entry of violin 1 signals episodic development at the tritone (augmented fourth interval), which features the contrapuntal device of stretto. Now the percussion makes its appearance beginning with the timpani.

A crescendo leads to the climactic part of the movement, which is marked by a stroke of the bass drum and a unison on E♭ (the twelfth tone in the series of chromatic entries at alternately higher and lower fifths).

The return to the fundamental tonality features the contrapuntal devices of inversion (melodic reflection) and retrograde (backward melodic direction). There is emphasis on tritone relationships. The celesta ostinato configurations, the repetitions of motif 1 on the principal tone, and the unison ending underscore Bartók's unwavering allegiance to the concept of tonality as the basis for twentieth-century composition.

Second Movement. This movement could be designated "Dance of the Brotherhood of Nations," since motif 1 of the main theme is "old"-style Hungarian pentatonic (C-Eb-F-G-A) and motif 2 has characteristic rhythmic and modal (Lydian: C-D-E-F♯-G) features of Romanian and Slovak folk music (Ex. 1.44).

Ex. 1.44. Ibid., second movement, main theme, bars 1–5.

The antiphonal effect is maintained throughout by division of the orchestra into two string "quintets," the percussion instruments involved with the full-string ensemble or, less frequently, with the first orchestra.

The exposition begins with the main theme (Ex. 1.44) which is transformed and tossed between the orchestras in fragmented form. A grand pause precedes the secondary theme which emphasizes the tritone (Ex. 1.45).

Ex. 1.45. Ibid., second movement, secondary theme, bars 68–74.

Dazzling rhythmic crosscurrents are set in motion by imitative sequences of syncopated triple-note units, within and between orchestras. A short piano solo, followed by celesta and then by crescendo chords, is answered by fading timpani to end the exposition.

The development of main theme motif 1 is given to orchestra 2, as orchestra 1 and the percussion section continue playing syncopated chords. A diminuendo leads to an intricate web of pizzicato scale patterns in canonic imitation, supported by the harp, all in irregular metrical groupings. A short timpani iteration of the rhythm schema of main theme motif 2 marks the start of a *fugato* of that motif in the low strings of the two orchestras. This contrapuntal treatment serves as a transition to the recapitulation.

The return section follows the same form as the exposition. The coda, Allegro molto, is built out of main theme motif 2. The movement ends on its principal tone, a unison C.

Third Movement. This movement is an orchestral realization of "night music," first portrayed in the fourth piece from Bartók's *Out of Doors* for piano (1926).

According to the composer's elder son, Béla Bartók Jr., "My father captured the frogs' concert and other evocative sounds in the quiet of the [Hungarian] plain." Another critical comment on the piano piece seems appropriate as a general description of this movement: "Some kind of sobbing and vague, remote music, bird-music, star-music and the calm transcendental melody of the night's majestic hymn—everything one can imagine could be heard in these sounds. Without definitely striving to be crickets, birds, or stars, they portray a picture which is unearthly in its realism of the night, Bartók's night—this is a marvelous masterpiece of Hungarian nature poetry."

Theme 1 consists of falling thirds and rising seconds that are strikingly similar to the thirds and sixths in the first movement of the Brahms Symphony No. 4. Bartók's theme, however, is firmly rooted in Hungarian folk song—"dotted" rhythm and parlando (free) tempo—and in what seems to be a chromatically compressed transformation of a peasant mourning song (Ex. 1.46. Compare with the music example in the program notes to the first movement of the Concerto for Orchestra).

Ex. 1.46. Ibid., third movement, theme 1, bars 6–8.

Motif 1 from the first movement is heard, followed by theme 2—a twelve-tone melody in folk-song style. (Ex. 1.47).

Ex. 1.47. Ibid., third movement, theme 2, bars 23–27.

"Night sounds" lead to a reprise of motif 1, then the twinkling of celesta, harp, and piano with string tremolos that are based on a transformation of motif 1. Theme 3 is yet another motif 1 mutation, extended by means of its retrograde form (Ex. 1.48).

The diminution of the mutated motif is followed by an accelerando; theme 3 is then restated in quicker tempo, and an Adagio brings the reprise of theme 2 as the celesta, harp, and piano play accompanying roulades. They break into the final iteration of motif 1; violins 1 and 2 bring back theme 1, and the movement ends as it began—with the tinkle of the xylophone.

Ex. 1.48. Ibid., third movement, theme 3, bars 46–48.

Fourth Movement. The last movement is a rondolike suite of folk dances. It is linked to the first and third movements by motivic quotation and to the second movement by dance character. And it is the apotheosis of Slovak dance melody: Tempo giusto, syncopated rhythm schemata, and stress of the tritone (Lydian mode).

Theme 1 (Ex. 1.49) might represent a dance of the Bulgar bride, for the characteristically Slovak tonality is "married" to a Bulgarian rhythm (the Bulgarian peasants adopted as a national musical characteristic the *aksak* limping rhythms that the Turkish invaders brought to the Balkans centuries ago).

Ex. 1.49. Ibid., fourth movement, theme 1, bars 5–8.

Theme 2, played by the strings and accompanied by the timpani and piano, sounds like a bear dance (Ex. 1.50).

Ex. 1.50. Ibid., fourth movement, theme 2, bars 27–30.

Theme 3, antiphonally treated, would be appropriately designated as a *kolo* (round dance) for couples (Ex. 1.51).

Ex. 1.51. Ibid., fourth movement, theme 3, bars 53–56.

To borrow the title from a Bartók piano piece composed in 1908, theme 4 is perhaps a dance of the Slovak bachelors (Ex. 1.52).

Ex. 1.52. Ibid., fourth movement, theme 4,bars 74–76.

All the violas play theme 5, which has a Ruthenian (Ukrainian) *kolomyjka* (round dance) rhythmic pattern, derived from folk texts consisting of twelve eighth notes followed by two accented quarter notes, ♫♫♩ ♫♫♩ ♫♫♩ ♩ ♩. This infectious Ruthenian rhythm (the Ruthenians are eastern neighbors of the Slovaks) was adopted by the Slovaks, by Transylvanian Romanians, and, in shortened (thirteen-syllable) form, by Hungarian swineherds. Thus theme 5 could be labeled a *kánásztanc (*swineherd's dance), (Ex. 1.53).

Ex. 1.53. Ibid., fourth movement, theme 5, bars 88–89.

The Slovak bachelor's dance (theme 4) is heard again in the piano part as the strings play scalar passages in the Lydian mode.

Theme 6 seems to be a parody of a children's game song, and the use of parallel fifth intervals, that provide a pentatonic flavor to the melody, suggests Hungarian provenance (Ex. 1.54).

Ex. 1.54. Ibid., fourth movement, theme 6, bars 136–138.

The bear dance returns as repetitions of the "children's motif" are heard in violins 3 and 4 and viola 2. The pace grows fast and furious until a sudden switch to a moderate tempo, *espressivo*, brings the reprise of the fugue subject that opened the first movement. Now, however, the theme is expanded from chromatic to diatonic range—a compositional device invented by Bartók. A slower Adagio features the return of the "night music" motif from theme 1 of the third movement. The following Allegro, a reprise of the first theme from the fourth movement—inverted and in stretto canon—announces the return of the bride. Theme 1 is then repeated in its original form as the Bulgarized Slovak dance ends the work.

PIANO CONCERTO NO. 1 [12]

Between 1920 and 1924 Bartók composed only five works. And in 1925, nothing. A similar period of creative stagnation occurred between 1939 and 1943, before the composition of the Concerto for Orchestra. In both instances, world war with its political and economic problems, taxing concert engagements as a pianist, and poor health combined to inhibit the inspirational mood. As a less emotionally demanding outlet, Bartók turned to folk-music research, which mainly consisted of both music and poetic texts of the Romanian peasants.

In the case of the post–First World War period, Bartók's earlier works received widespread performances in Europe. He found himself the subject of much international commentary in the newspapers and in scholarly journals, to the extent that he was offered many opportunities to perform as composer-pianist. He gave concerts in England and on the Continent, and he was hailed in the press as a virtuoso of top rank. He included pieces from the standard repertory in his recitals and was constantly searching for suitable works that were off the beaten track. So far as appearances with orchestras were concerned, he said in a November 1925 interview: "I must compose a piano concerto. This is sadly lacking. This will be my next work." The urge to create had returned.

Almost a year later, on 12 November 1926, the draft of Bartók's First Piano Concerto was completed. And beginning in June of the same year he met his need for new recital pieces by composing his Piano Sonata, *Out of Doors*, and Nine Little Piano Pieces. Of equal significance was the preparation for publication of his monumental book, *Rumanian Carols and Christmas Songs (Colinde)*, completed in September, for the transcription and classification of this very unusual song repertory gave Bartók unique melodic and rhythmic source materials for his Piano Concerto.

According to the composer's comments and correspondence the Concerto is "bristling with difficulties . . . as much for the orchestra as for the audience." Indeed, in 1930 he intentionally equipped his Second Piano Concerto with "more pleasing thematic material [with] rather light and popular character of most of the themes."

There are underlying concepts in the First Concerto, however, whose clarification should help to understand and thus heighten enjoyment of this masterpiece. Perhaps the most important concept is structural—that is, the organization of the thematic material. Put another way, the Concerto would have been more aptly—if not uniquely—designated Toccata in E for Piano and Orchestra, for the work abounds in musical and technical features common to the keyboard toccatas of seventeenth- and eighteenth-century Italian composers such as Girolamo Frescobaldi, Azzolino Bernardino della Ciaia, Benedetto Marcello, Michelangelo Rossi, and Domenico Zipoli.

Apparently it was during his 1925 Italian concert tour that Bartók discovered and subsequently studied "with ever increasing eagerness" the music of certain old Italian masters. "I am deeply interested in them;" he wrote, "especially from the point of view of style. The austere, virile style of Frescobaldi and Rossi attracts me greatly. I have arranged for piano a number of their organ pieces. . . . I have been playing some of these." (They were first broadcast over Budapest Radio on 15 October 1926.)

Among the characteristic features of toccata style, which are similarly highlighted in the Bartók Concerto, is a chain of contrasting sections with tempos varying according to the emotional content. Other contrasts are obtained by alternating fugal writing with chordal and scalar configurations in a rambling improvisatory style. Daring chromaticisms, irregular phrases, and other unexpected passages give the toccata its strange yet powerful aura. The contrapuntal texture is freer and less dense than the later Bach style. Finally, emphasis is on rhythm and motivic borrowings from the popular pieces of the day.

The second concept, a Bartókian innovation "in reaction to Romantic exuberance," is treatment of the piano as a percussion instrument—that is, by attack of the keys and without use of the damper or sustaining pedal. To obtain added contrast, therefore, Bartók specifies pedal use here and there in the Concerto.

The third concept, also related to tone color, is sparse use of the brass (in certain instances, muted), prominence of woodwind colors, percussive string sounds (also Bartók inventions), and, above all, the special effects obtained from the percussion instruments individually, collectively, or integrated with the percussive piano.

First Movement. A short introduction opens the movement, in which two motifs are presented whose transformations provide almost all the material for the first and last movements. Motif 1 is based on repetition of a single note by the timpani (Ex. 1.55), and motif 2 is also based on repetition but now on a three-note unit played by the French horns (Ex. 1.56).

The exposition is initiated by the piano solo, accompanied by woodwind and string sonorities. The main theme, comprising motifs 1 and 2 as building blocks,

Allegro moderato

Ex. 1.55. Bartók, First Piano Concerto, first movement, motif 1, bars 1–3.

Ex. 1.56. Ibid., first movement, motif 2, R.N. 1.

is a direct borrowing from Bartók's transcription of della Ciaia's Sonata in G Major (Ex. 1.57).

Ex. 1.57. (a) Azzolino Bernardino della Ciaia (1671–1755), Sonata in G Major, second movement, bars 1–5, and (b) Bartók, First Piano Concerto, first movement, main theme, bars 38–44.

The solo continues with a kind of introductory passage based on a (Romanian) bagpipe motif, bits of which are tossed from oboe to clarinet to bassoon. Then the "toccata" begins with the solo playing motif 1 *in relievo* above double-stop configurations. The strings take over the motif as the piano hammers a chordal permutation of those configurations. A scale passage in octaves leads to six *sforzato* chords and a momentary stop.

The secondary theme is basically assembled from the first two bars of motif 2 and motif 1 respectively (Ex. 1.58).

Ex. 1.58. Bartók, First Piano Concerto, first movement, secondary theme, four bars after R.N. 12.

Contrast is achieved by change of dynamic level, but only for one statement of the secondary theme. Then the toccata-like passagework for the solo resumes, *forte*, with octaves and scales until a ritardando is reached.

The development, *in tempo*, begins with the main theme in the solo. A reprise of the chord configurations, scale passage in octaves, and *sforzato* chords—now eight in number—leads to another section that features the rhythm schema of motif 2 but in scalar form, in which the first clarinet and two bassoons play in contrary motion. This idea is developed briefly in stretto, imitatively.

The next developmental section begins with "Cell X" sonorities, a characteristic of Bartók's new tonal language, in which a chromatic tetrachord is divided into minor seconds. Here the resultant intervals are spaced an octave apart. The improvisatory treatment continues along the lines of Baroque keyboard toccata style: tempo changes in which thematic episodes are alternated with interludes based on such thorny pianisms as—in order of appearance—broken fourth chords plus *glissandi,* modal scale passages, arpeggios, a modified whole-tone scale figuration, canonic imitation of passagework in thirds, filled octaves, and, finally, four-voice chords.

The recapitulation is preceded by a transitional episode for the full orchestra, *crescendo e accelerando.* Tempo I is resumed as the woodwinds announce the return of the main theme. Before the completion of the theme, however, the piano interrupts with its transposed statement of the same material—that is, in stretto—in typical closing style of Baroque fugal forms. Another stretto takes place among the strings, with motif 1, as the solo repeats the main theme—now in highly dissonant minor seconds.

Horns, trumpets, and bassoon sound motif 1, the tempo slows briefly as the piano restates the main theme, and then a transition—similar to that in the exposition—is heard but the solo's sonorities are augmented from four-voice to five-voice chords that give the effect of tone clusters.

The piano is again assigned the secondary theme, which is developed after performance of a short passage of cluster chords.

The last episode is typical of Baroque toccata style: a completely unexpected solo passage of mellifluous thirds and triads!

The coda begins with an elongation of motif 2 from the introduction, played by the brass. As a motif 1 ostinato is taken up by the strings, the solo iterates the secondary theme. The timpani pounds motif 1, the winds enter with stretti of motif 2, and the movement ends with an orchestral bang on an unusual sonority: the simultaneous sounding of tonic and dominant fifths based on E, the principal tone.

Second Movement. This movement could be appropriately called Music for Woodwinds, Percussion, and Piano. The thematic material, organized in a ternary (ABA) form, has elements common to *colinde* (Romanian winter-solstice melodies).

The movement opens with an introductory dialogue between percussion and piano—perhaps a quotation from the so-called "Fate knocking on the door" motif in the first movement of Beethoven's Symphony No. 5—which plays a secco motif (Ex. 1.59).

Ex. 1.59. Bartók, First Piano Concerto, second movement, introductory piano theme, one bar before R.N. 1.

If there is an underlying program here, then in musical terms perhaps it could be related to the fate of the piano in twentieth-century music: is it an instrument of percussion (dry, xylophone-like timbre) or of string quality (pedaled, legato touch)? Theme 1, played by the piano, is lyrical, where it is treated as the upper voice in four-part chromatic counterpoint (Ex. 1.60).

The return of the percussive motif commences the transition section in which oboe, clarinet, and flute timbres are introduced. Theme 2, also lyrical but with pentatonic flavor, is played by the first clarinet as staccato major sevenths in the solo and rhythm patterns in the percussion serve as the accompaniment (Ex. 1.61).

The successive entries of English horn, first bassoon, and first oboe, in four-

Ex. 1.60. Ibid., second movement, theme 1, R.N. 3.

Ex. 1.61. Ibid., second movement, theme 2, R.N. 9.

part imitative counterpoint, are marked by augmentation of the piano ostinato to chords in fourths. When the first flute enters as a fifth polyphonic voice, the ostinato involves five-note clusters of seconds and thirds. The entry of horns 1 and 2 with sustained seconds marks the addition of an eleventh note (of the twelve tones that form the chromatic scale) to the solo cluster chords.

Now the apex of the movement is at hand, for the woodwinds and horns are treated instrumentally as a kind of double wind quintet. The subsequent textural thinning brings a reversal of the solo ostinato-fourth chords followed by major seventh intervals.

A short transition section, marked by pedaled piano, serves as a brief interlude to the return of theme 1 in the woodwinds, polyphonically treated, as the solo plays a secco transformation of the introductory motif.

A coda echoes the introductory dialogue between percussion and piano, momentarily interrupted by an "old piano style" pedaled solo passage and a stretto reprise of theme 2 by clarinet and bassoon. Percussiveness, however, reigns supreme as the fading dialogue continues, despite a half-hearted concession to the legato piano style—for the last bars of the movement have an instruction for the solo to use a *half*-depressed damper pedal!

Third Movement. A startling segue to a rhythmically transformed motif 1 from the introduction to the first movement is followed by glissandi ("A little bit tipsy"?) among the muted trombones. Ostinatos in the strings and woodwinds, played staccato, precede the main theme in the solo—all combining to produce a wild dance-like atmosphere (Ex. 1.62).

The secondary theme, rhythmically identical to the main theme, is constructed of major scale segments of E as principal tone (Ex. 1.63).

Toccata-like episodes, similar to first-movement procedure, follow. All are based on permutations of the secondary theme and are played by the woodwinds or muted trombones in a polyphonic texture. The solo is heard in the interludes and accompanying figurations, performing such pianisms as broken

Allegro molto

Ex. 1.62. Ibid., third movement, main theme, bars 5–14.

Ex. 1.63. Ibid., third movement, secondary theme, R.N. 6.

chord figures, scalar passages, tremolos, and repeated-note figurations.

A change in tempo brings a lyrical reprise of the secondary theme in the solo, its further development, and an accelerando that leads directly to a timpani solo.

The development opens with the division of the main theme between the timpani and the solo. Further fractionation results in a polyphonic mélange of woodwind figures and piano tremolos as the horns enter with a new theme that is essentially a variant form of preceding motifs. This new material is developed by the bassoons, then by the strings as the solo plays accompanying scalar configurations.

When the piano begins reworking the new theme the movement seems to take on the character of a large rondo form. A transition section, however, based on the secondary theme and terminating in a ritornando, is indicative of the sonata form of this movement.

The recapitulation is a compressed rewriting of the exposition, and it culminates with a reprise by the solo of motif 2 from the introduction to the first movement. A short coda ends with a bimodal Phrygian/Mixolydian cadence—a Bartókian harmonic innovation that yields a "neutral" tonality with E as the principal tone.

NOTES

1. The previous version of this essay appeared in the record album booklet published in 1981 by the Book-of-the-Month Club, Inc. (now Bookspan, 401 Franklin Avenue, Garden City, N.Y. 11530). The LP recordings (and optional cassette tapes) were originally produced by CBS Records and Vanguard Recording Society, Inc

2. The Introduction was written by Harold C. Schonberg for the mentioned booklet. Mr. Schonberg, long a senior music critic of the *New York Times*, is the author of many books, including *Lives of the Great Composers*, *The Great Conductors*, and *The Great Pianists*. He won the Pulitzer Prize in 1971.

3. My Notes on the Music, intended as a listener's guide for music lovers and students, appear as originally published, for the most part without source citations.

4. Recorded by the New York Philharmonic Orchestra, Pierre Boulez, conductor (CBS-44707).

5. Bartók, like Debussy, was fascinated by this exotic music and its possibilities for composition, as evidenced by No. 109, "From the Island of Bali," of *Mikrokosmos* for piano, and by the second movement of *Contrasts* for violin, clarinet, and piano (commissioned by Benny Goodman in 1938). This fascination apparently stems from structural features of gamelan music, such as five-tone scale and melodic intervals of seconds and fourths, which are also characteristic of "old" Hungarian folk music.

6. Recorded by Joseph Szigeti, violin, and Béla Bartók, piano. The Vanguard Recording Society monophonic recording—apparently no longer commercially available—was made during the Bartók-Szigeti joint recital at the Library of Congress in Washington, D.C., under the auspices of the Elizabeth Sprague Coolidge Festival, on 13 April 1940, twelve years after their first American performance of the work in New York (Pro Musica Society, Gallo Theater). Thus the recording is a living document of how Bartók wanted his composition performed and, moreover, of Bartók's amazing prowess as a concert pianist of the first rank.

7. Recorded by Isaac Stern, violin, and The New York Philharmonic Orchestra, Leonard Bernstein, conductor. The CBS recording apparently is no longer commercially available.

8. B♮ is H in German.

9. Same remark as to n. 6.

10. Sándor Rózsa, a highwayman, was a latter-day Hungarian Robin Hood.

11. Recorded by the New York Philharmonic Orchestra, Leonard Bernstein, conductor, CBS CD MK-44707.

12. Recorded by Rudolph Serkin, piano, and the Columbia Orchestra, George Szell, conductor. The CBS recording apparently is no longer commercially available.

2

Bartók's Fusion of National Styles[1]

The second stage in Bartók's stylistic development—which I refer to as Fusion of National Styles—was primarily the outcome of his methodical articulation of the true folk music of Hungary and of the national minority peoples and the resultant applications in his composed works. This period began in late 1905 with studies of Zoltán Kodály's first publication of autochthonous Hungarian folk songs. Continuing his investigations in 1906, Bartók made his own field recordings of folk music in Hungarian villages and, moreover, in linguistically Slovak territory. He found an incredible variety of old ecclesiastical or old Greek modes in both materials and, during the summer of 1907, the ancient pentatonic scale in the melodies of the Transylvanian-Hungarians.[2] Later on he collected Transylvanian-Romanian folk songs "with various, sometimes rather strange scales."[3]

> The outcome of these studies was of decisive influence in my work. . . . It became clear to me that the old modes, which had been forgotten in our music, had lost none of their vigor. Their new employment made new rhythmic combinations possible. This new way of using the diatonic scale brought freedom from the rigid use of the major and minor keys, and eventually led to a new concept of the chromatic scale, every tone of which came to be considered of equal value and could be used freely and independently.[4]

Bartók's new concept of the chromatic scale, which he designated "polymodal chromaticism," appears for the first time—in May 1908!—as the basic tonal language of his first Bagatelle and thereafter in the works he composed for piano solo:[5]

> Just as the two types of the minor scale can be used simultaneously [the ascending and descending forms of the melodic minor] two different modes can be used at the same time as well. . . . As the result of superposing a Lydian and Phrygian pentachord with a common fundamental tone, we get a diatonic pentachord filled out with all the possible sharp and flat degrees.[6]

In addition to the folk modes, Bartók found three kinds of prevailing rhythmic formations in eastern European rural music: parlando-rubato, a free, declamatory or recitative type (found in the second Elegy); tempo giusto, a more or less rigid type, in which change of bar may occur ("Bear Dance" from

Ten Easy Pieces); and the so-called dotted rhythm, where accentuated short values are followed by nonaccentuated long values ("Evening in Transylvania" from Ten Easy Pieces).

Another structural feature of eastern European folk music is the preponderance of four-section melodies, except for those three-section, Transylvanian-Romanian specimens which are "absolutely independent, even very characteristic formations."[7] "Old"-style Hungarian quaternaries show a remarkable type of transposition in which the second half of the melody is a fifth lower than the first half.[8]

Tone color is an important stylistic element in Bartók's piano writing. He considered the piano to be essentially a percussion instrument—somewhat similar to the hammered output of the Hungarian *cimbalom*—rather than a stringed one, and devised a special notation to indicate which way the piano was to be played.[9]

Above all, however, it was Bartók's supernal talent that enabled him to homogenize polyglot musical folklore and develop five innovative levels of complexity for its use in composition:[10]

(1) Genuine folk tunes are featured, and the invented additions are of secondary importance. In other words, the folk tune is the "jewel" and the added parts function as its "mounting"; (2) The folk tune and the invented material are treated equally; (3) The folk tune is presented as a kind of musical "motto," and the invented material is of greater significance; (4) The composition is based on themes which imitate genuine folk tunes; (5) The highest level is abstract composition in which neither folk tune nor its imitation is used, but the work is nevertheless pervaded by the "spirit" of folk music. Thus, for example, it might have Hungarian pentatonic turns, the Slovak Lydian tritone (that is, the augmented fourth degree), or other characteristics of eastern European rural music.

In September 1907, following his return from collecting folk music in Transylvania, Bartók began the composition of his First Violin Concerto (op. posth.) and his career as professor of piano at the Budapest Royal Academy of Music. Dedicated to his first love, the Hungarian violinist, Stefi Geyer, the main theme of the first movement is based on Bartók's "declaration of love" leitmotiv, D-F♯-A-C♯. No sooner had Bartók completed the work on 5 February 1908, than the beautiful young virtuoso terminated his courtship. Later that month the anguished suitor vented his innermost feelings in the first Elegy, during May in the last two of his Fourteen Bagatelles, op. 6,[11] and on 13 July in the "Dedication" of Ten Easy Pieces—all created from transformations of the leitmotiv.

TEN EASY PIECES

The original title of the collection was Eleven Piano Recital Pieces, since it included what later became the sixth Bagatelle.[12] Bartók completed the work

thus compiled in June 1908, and a contract for its publication by Károly Rozsnyai of Budapest was signed later that month. During the summer Bartók changed
the original title to Ten Easy Piano Pieces, in order to shift the sixth Bagatelle to
its eventual place, and added "Dedication" (composed on July 13) as the eleventh piece, perhaps to satisfy his contractual obligation. In 1945, Bartók described the work as follows:

> The Ten Easy Pieces—with a "Dedication" as an eleventh—are a complement to
> the Bagatelles. The former were written with pedagogical purposes, that is, to
> supply piano students with easy contemporary pieces. This accounts for the still
> more simplified means used in them.[13]

"Dedication": Analysis of this abstract composition reveals an ingenious
blending of motives from the First Violin Concerto (op. posth.) and structural
characteristics of "mixed"-style Hungarian folk song. The melody is an isometric quaternary with ABCD section structure. Each of the four melody-sections
consists of thirteen syllabic notes, that is, as if underlaid with folk text. There is
no time signature.[14] The first four bars—the prelude—contain the famous
leitmotif degrees, in augmented values, of the first bar of the First Violin Concerto. The repeated tetrachordal motif in the next four bars, A♯-C♯-E-F♯, is a
chromatic compression of the pentatonic motif, A-D-E-G, of the fifth bar of the
Concerto. All melody sections, interludes, and the postlude are polymodal collections, based on G, E, and D as fundamental tones, that combine Phrygian and
Lydian pentachords for the most part.[15]

"Peasant Song" (No. 1): The unisonal texture of this Level 4 folk-song imitation in Slovak style may well have been intended to underscore the monophonic character of east European rural music. The four-section, heterometric melody
is in the C♯-Dorian folk mode. Interest and variety are achieved by rhythmic
means: equal and unequal phrase lengths and different combinations of half-   ·
and quarter-note values in duple meter.[16]

"Frustration" (No. 2): An abstract composition, based on Slovak folk-song
characteristics, particularly the four-section, heterometric melody. Note the unusual pitch content of the first melody section: its incipit (bars 3–5) is the Lydian octave segment of the Dorian folk mode. The ostinato accompaniment,
however, illustrates the first systematic use of a unique tetrachordal motive that
pervades Bartók's oeuvre. Designated the "Z-cell" by American theorists,[17] the
cell consists of the first (fundamental tone or "tonic"), minor second, augmented
fourth, and fifth degrees of the Phrygian/Lydian polymodal pentachord. If we
tag such tetrachords with whatever designation will identify the fundamental
tone, the ostinato in bars 1–6, 15–18, and 21 (second half) is a D Z-cell; in bars
10–11, a G Z-cell; in bar 19, a C Z-cell; and in bar 21 (first half), an E Z-cell.
The D and F Z-cells accompanying the first half of the Dorian melody (bars 3–9) also

interlock to form an octachordal pitch collection of alternating half and whole steps—the well-known octatonic scale, which Bartók would later find among the Transylvanian Romanians and North African Arabs.[18] The resultant twelve-tone tonality of the combined melody and accompaniment is the product of a D Phrygian/Lydian polymode.

"Five-Finger Exercise" (No. 9): An abstract composition, with Slovak structural characteristics, that explores another tetrachordal motive–the so-called "Y-cell."[19] The cell consists of four whole steps or, in other orientations, the first four degrees of the Lydian folk mode, an octave segment of the Dorian folk mode, or a partition of the whole-tone scale. The first and third melody sections (bars. 5–8, 13–16) of the four-section heterometric melody have a repeated ♩. ♪ | ♩ rhythmic schema. Such repetitions, unknown in eastern European folk music material, stem from art-music sources, and they seem to be deliberately stressed in the repetition of the melody (bars 29–40). The Y-cell ostinatos are arranged in alternation of the two cycles of whole-tone pentachords and complete scales and, moreover, are concatenated to form chromatic octachords (as at bar 10) and octachordal polymodes (bars 43–48). In the case of the alternating pentachords, the ascending Y-cells in related bars outline an underlying C Z-cell framework, <u>C</u> D E F♯ + <u>D</u>♭ E♭ F <u>G</u> (bars 1–2).

"Sostenuto" (No. 4) and "Dawn" (No. 7): These abstract pieces are imbued with the spirit of impressionism and seem to have been created in the likeness of the sixth Bagatelle. In fact, their only connection with folk-music sources is modal chromaticism. "Sostenuto" exploits the leitmotiv as transitional triads (the fifth degree is missing), descending in thirds (bars 18–23) until it appears as a polymodal pentachord with a neutral third degree: A-C♮-C♯-E-G♯ (bar 25). The last four bars contain the opening theme (R.H., bars 2–5) transformed to the A whole-tone scale (L.H.). "Dawn" treats the leitmotiv as complete chords (beginning with bars 3–5), in minor alteration (bar 12), and as a consonant ninth chord in the last two bars. The whole-tone scale appears as a G whole-tone pentachord (bar 10) and, in the following bar, as a Y-cell, A-C♭-D♭-E♭.

"Evening in Transylvania" (No. 5) and "Bear Dance" (No. 10) are Hungarian folk-music imitations (Level 4) that have become famous repertory pieces. In 1931, Bartók transcribed them for orchestra as the first two pieces in Hungarian Sketches. No. 3, "Slovakian Boys' Dance," is a Level 1 transcription of a genuine hetrometric folk tune whose first half is C-Dorian (bars 1–10) and the second half, C-Aeolian (bars 11–19). No. 6, "Hungarian Folk Song," is a Level 1 transcription in C major. No. 8, "Folk Song," is a Slovak folk melody that was transformed into a Hungarian popular art song during the last century.[20] After the First World War, when the northern part of Hungary became Czechoslovakia, the art-song melody was adopted for the Slovak national anthem.

For Children

Bartók's next contract with Rozsnyai, dated 23 March 1909, was for "21 juvenile music pieces" to be titled *For Children*. The manuscript apparently was delivered to the publisher on or about that date. Based on Hungarian musical folklore, the collection was followed by a second set of twenty-one pieces, in accordance with a contract dated 23 June. On 6 December, Rozsnyai shipped the newly published copies of Ten Easy Pieces, Fourteen Bagatelles, and *For Children*, together with the following enclosure:

> Dear Professor Bartók,
> I was very glad to receive your cordial letter. I duly enclose the required pieces. I wish to emphasize that it would be better if the rules of classical harmony would be even more strictly observed than in the ones already published, without any modernization. I should not like to see a new trend in this undertaking but rather the beaten track on which you can continue working from time to time.[21]

When Bartók received this letter he had probably completed the forty-two pieces based on Slovak musical folklore for the last two volumes of *For Children*, yet publication was not achieved until 1911. Whether the postponement was related to Rozsnyai's criticism or the takeover of that company by another Budapest publisher (Rózsavölgyi és Társa) is uncertain. In 1931, No. XXXXII (No. 40, "Swineherd's Dance," in the revised edition) was transcribed for orchestra as the last piece in Hungarian Sketches for Orchestra. And in November 1944, Bartók responded to the request of his American publisher (Boosey & Hawkes) to "make some slight alterations" for copyright purposes. The next month he provided the music engraver with a "revised (improved)" copy of the original Hungarian publication.[22]

At lecture-recitals given by Bartók during the 1940–1941 concert season, his performance of pieces from *For Children* was prefaced by the statement that they were written "in order to acquaint the piano-studying children with the simple and non-romantic beauties of folk music. Excepting this purpose, there is no special plan in the work."[23] The following pieces selected for analysis, however, should make it quite apparent that he had another, unmentioned reason: to provide piano students with a melodious and uncomplicated introduction to the sound of his newly invented musical language.

Moderato (vol. 1, No. 26): The original form of this isorhythmic Transylvanian melody is limited to the first four degrees of the symmetrical Hungarian pentatonic scale: G-B♭-C-D. A number of variant or closely related melodies from that area have altered or expanded pitch collections, such as major or minor pentachords, a Mixolydian folk mode with lowered sixth degree, and one specimen where Mixolydian and Phrygian modes alternate to produce a peculiar "neutral" tonality (that is, with superposed major and minor thirds).[24]

The accompaniment begins in the G-Aeolian mode, with the raised seventh degree (the "color" tone of the modern harmonic minor) being added in bar 11. The repetition of the accompaniment has the lowered second degree (the Phrygian "color" tone, bars 22–23) and the raised sixth degree (the Dorian "color" tone, bar 27). In other words, this piece reflects the interaction of a simple pentatonic melody with a chromatic accompaniment, thus forming a ten-tone minor polymode.

Among other polymodal pieces in the first volume are No. 9 (D-Lydian/Aeolian eleven-tone polymode) and No. 18 (D-Lydian/Phrygian twelve-tone polymode). The latter piece is especially interesting with regard to its "international" melodic structure: G-pentatonic scale (G-A-B-D-E: the major or so-called Chinese form), with C as passing tone; uniquely characteristic, Hungarian "dotted" rhythm schemata; Ukrainian *kolomyjka* (round dance) syllabic structure (fourteen syllables in duple or quadruple meter, where the last two syllables are doubled values); Slovak heterometric four-section structure, in which the third melody section (bars 11–12) is a 6+6-syllable double section; and western European architectonic (AABA) form.

"Mourning Song" (vol. 2, No. 39): Bartók's treatment of the Slovak folk tunes comprising the second volume of *For Children* indicates his indifference to the conservative attitude of his publisher, for they show an increasing use of parallel fifths, unresolved dissonant chords, and polymodal chromaticism. Whereas the first volume ends with a brilliant dance piece in *kolomyjka* rhythm (No. 40), the second one concludes with this "Mourning Song," a dirge whose text reflects utmost despair:

> Down there, deep in the valley,
> A frightened black raven flies;
> Down there, deep in his grave,
> In blackness my father lies.

There may be extramusical significance in the punctuation of the accompaniment by the "declaration of love" leitmotiv in bars 2, 17, 22 (altered pentachord), 30–35, 45 (fifth degree omitted), and 51. The E-Phrygian/Lydian polymode provides a twelve-tone tonality, but the last melody section and the postlude (bars 43–53) are in the pure Phrygian folk mode. The piece ends *calando*, with the unaccompanied, almost undiscernible subtonic (D) as the final tone.

Two Elegies (op. 8b)

Bartók points to this opus as "a certain return to the old-style piano technique," indicating the tonality of No. 1 as D minor and No. 2, C♯ minor: "This information is addressed especially to those who like to pigeonhole all music they do not understand into the category of 'atonal' music"[25]

Grave (No. 1): As already mentioned, the first piece was composed in February 1908, soon after Bartók received Stefi Geyer's letter announcing the end of their relationship and several months prior to the composition of the experimental Fourteen Bagatelles. It is quite important for the reader to note that the only stylistic reversion in the first Elegy is in terms of the bombastic piano writing typical of Franz Liszt and other nineteenth-century virtuosos, and Bartók himself before 1908 (as in the Rhapsody op. 1). In point of fact, this musical memento of "Stefi Lost" inaugurates Bartók's new style of composition (Ex. 2.1).

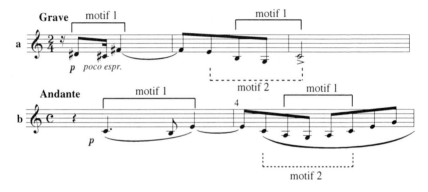

Ex. 2.1. (a) Bartók, first Elegy for Piano (1908), bars 1–3, and (b) Liszt, *Les Préludes* (1854), bars 3–4.

Ex. 2.1 illustrates the motivic relationship of Bartók's opening theme, indicated by "a," to that of Liszt's *Les Préludes*, indicated by "b." Bartók's theme (that is, the first melody section) combines two motifs—the trichord D♯-C♯-F♯ and the tetrachord E-B-G-C—which are derived from the two motifs comprising Liszt's theme. In other words, Bartók apparently transformed Liszt's germinal motif 1 (C-B-E) by way of transposition (D♯-C♯-F♯) and motif 2 (C-A-G-A-C) by reordering its notation to form Bartók's "declaration of love" leitmotiv (C-E-G-B). Based on C as the end tone of the first melody section (bar 3), the underlying structure of Bartók's theme is an octatonic hexachord within the frame of a Z-cell, C-C♯-D♯-E-F♯-G. Including B (the major seventh degree), the pitch collection represents an octachordal C-Lydian/Phrygian polymode, C-E-F♯-G-B/C-C♯-D♯-G.

The second melody section, transposed to F as the end tone (bar 7), contains the F Z-cell, F-F♯-B-C, now within the frame of the octatonic hexachord E♭-F-F♯-[ ]-A-B-C-[ ]. Here, too, the leitmotiv is provided by the addition of E, a non-octatonic degree. The third melody-section (bars 8–9) is the A octave-segment of the symmetrical Dorian folk mode. The placement of D as axis of symmetry underscores its main function as the fundamental tone, notwithstanding the position of A as end tone of the section.

The reader should note the intervallic structure: old-style Hungarian pentatonic orientation in terms of major seconds and minor thirds. The fourth melody section (bars 10–14) is similar to the kind of double section found in eastern European folk songs. The quaternary structure of this first part of the piece, the syllabic structure of the individual melody sections, and the parlando-rubato rhythm—delineated by irregular alternation of duple and triple meter—are other characteristics that point to the first Elegy as an abstract composition pervaded by the spirit of folk music.

Mention should be made that emphatic rendition of the C Z-cell, G♭-G-C♯-C, occurs in bars 39–52 and in the closing section (bars 85–95). A unique cadence is found in the last two bars, where the altered leitmotiv serves as a dissonant chord, D-F-A-C♯, resolving to a D minor-seventh chord as a "consonant" ending.[26] The two-part *fugato* that opens the fourth section (bars 53–71), perhaps an adaptation of the *fugato* form in Liszt's Piano Sonata in B minor,[27] is the first example of free, chromatic counterpoint as an outcome of polymodal structure. Another innovation by Bartók is the quartal harmony in bar 14, where the closing chord of the first section, B♭-E♭-A-D, is the vertical projection of the main degrees of the D-Phrygian folk mode. This bar, together with the preceding one, represents the ultimate in Bartókian polymodal chromaticism: twelvetone tonality resulting from superposed Phrygian and Lydian folk modes.

Molto adagio, quasi rubato (sempre improvisando) (No. 2): Almost two years elapsed until Bartók composed the second Elegy in December 1909. An agreement was signed with Rozsnyai for the complete work on 4 July 1910, and the publication appeared in 1911. Bartók alternately performed the two pieces well into the 1920s, when they were replaced in his repertory by the newer works of his "Synthesis of East and West" period (1926–1945). The entire composition consists of an introductory "motto" theme (bars 1–3) and its transformations or rhythmic permutations, all based on the A-Lydian/Phrygian polymode. In other words, this variation-like form is somewhat similar to a Level 3 transcription, where the invented material is of greater significance. The pentachordal theme, however, is a transformation of the "declaration of love" leitmotiv, in which a C♯ minor triad is encapsulated by the interval of a major seventh: A̲-G♯-E-C♯-A♯. If there is an extramusical connotation in the descending structure of the leitmotiv, perhaps it may reflect a subliminal "renunciation of Stefi": on 16 November 1909, some weeks prior to the composition of the second Elegy, Bartók married his sixteen-year-old pupil, Márta Ziegler. It is noteworthy that nine bars before the end of the piece Bartók introduces reverse (that is, descending) arpeggios—marked by a wavy line on the right side of a chord—alternating with ascending arpeggios that are indicated by placing a wavy line on the left side of the notation.

Two Romanian Dances (op. 8a)

Bartók's vast collection of Romanian folk-music material begins with four melo-dies he notated during November 1908, while on holiday in eastern Transylva-nia. Their three-section structure and certain characteristics related to old-style Transylvanian-Hungarian melodies impelled him to investigate further. During the summer of 1909 he collected hundreds of vocal and instrumental melodies from Romanian villagers in Bihar County (now Bihor, Romania) and composed the first of his Two Romanian Dances soon thereafter.

Allegro vivace (No. 1): The first dance is "based on original thematic mate-rial and not on folk tunes."[28] The piece, however, is a Level 4 transcription in which the thematic imitation is close enough to be considered a variant of an original folk tune. The rhythmic schema is a clone of a Romanian *drâmbă* (jew's-harp) dance-melody motif, ♫♫ | ♫ ♫♫, including its dronelike ac-companiment.[29] The downward tritone swoop on the last beat of the bar and the following bars is a borrowing from a Romanian jeering song.[30] There is also a simulation of the irregular repetition of bagpipe-type motifs (at bars 45–50) that characterizes the indeterminate melodic structure of such dance music. The in-novative aspect of the piece is the fusion of Bartók's newly won tonal language with rural folk-music section structure. Ex. 2.2 illustrates the harmonic applica-tion of the same Z-cell used in the melodic construction of the first Elegy (Ex. 2.1a) as the means to avoid commonplace I–V progressions characteristic of the Gypsy-styled, urban folk music disseminated in eastern Europe at that time.

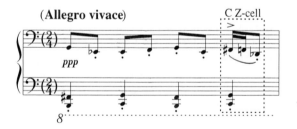

Ex. 2.2. Bartók, First Romanian Dance op. 8a, bar 3.

In terms of functional harmony, the C Z-cell serves here—and more em-phatically in the last bars of the piece—as a surrogate dominant seventh chord in the C-Phrygian/Lydian polymode, <u>C</u>-D♭-D-E♭-F-F♯-<u>G</u>-B. Certain motifs are cast in an impressionist mold: the two contrasting cycles of the whole-tone scale are represented by their segments in bars 47, 48, and 50. Indeed, a whole-tone scale is divided between the hands in bars 113–114, where an unusual cluster chord, E-F♯-G♯-A♯-B♯, serves as the accompaniment.

Poco allegro (No. 2): In 1910, when Bartók sought a companion piece to round out the opus, he turned to the vocal source melody of the first dance and borrowed its first melody section as a motto theme, in order to create a Level 3 composition (Ex. 2.3).

Ex. 2.3. *RFM*.ii., melody No. 456b. The instrumental version appears in *RFM*.i., melody No. 11a.

The motto theme, however, appears as the second subject (L.H.: bars 17–20), alternating with related thematic material (L.H.: from bar 5) of Bartók's own invention. The rhythmic schema (bar 11: ♪♩ ♪) serves as a pentatonic or modal interjection (for instance, at bars 69–72 and 110–113, respectively) in what otherwise is a G-Lydian/Phrygian polymode. Again drawing a parallel to functional harmony, the first half of the main theme (bars 17–18) is harmonized by the same C Z-cell found in the first dance (cf. Ex. 2.2), in which Db is a preceding grace note instead of an end tone. In the second half, the harmonic progression continues with the D Z-cell, D-G-Ab-Db (bar 19), and the G Y-cell, G-A-B-C♯ (bar 20). Thus, in Bartók's system of modal chromaticism, traditional IV–V–I progressions can be replaced in whole or in part by cellular equivalents.

THREE BURLESQUES (OP. 8C)

Bartók's growing reputation as pianist and composer—the outcome of his successful concert tours in Greater Hungary and abroad—gave him the incentive to expand his repertory with accessible recital pieces befitting his stature as a virtuoso, such as the Three Burlesques. Although the first piece of this opus was composed in 1908, the complete work remained unfinished till 1911. In 1931, the second Burlesque was transcribed for orchestra as the fourth piece in Hungarian Sketches.

"Quarrel" (No. 1): The first Burlesque, composed on 27 November 1908, is dedicated to Márta Ziegler, Bartók's first wife—then in her second year as his piano student at the Royal Academy of Music in Budapest. One of the drafts of this impressionist composition has an amusing entry that reads: "Please choose one of the titles: 'Anger because of an interrupted visit' or *'Rondoletto à capric-*

cio' or 'Vengeance is sweet' or 'Play it if you can. or 'November 27.'" The sketch version has other entries, such as "angrily" (bar 1), "with a weeping voice" (bar 60), and "sorrowfully" (bar 88).

The eight-bar introductory section, in unison, partially establishes C as the fundamental tone, by repetition of the cellular tritone G-Db as the last beat of each bar. The first section begins with the same melodic configuration but alternates with a different one (bars 9–14) whose first beat contains C-Gb, the fundamental tritone of the C Z-cell. Thus, by means of an innovative monophonic texture, the underlying harmonic foundation of the C-Phrygian/Lydian polymode is laid.

The C whole-tone scale introduces the second inversion Z-cell "dominant," D-Ab-G-Db (bars 22–25), the first inversion "tonic" Y-cell, D-C-Bb-Ab (bar 28), and the second inversion "subdominant" Z-cell, C-Gb-F-Cb (bars 26–29). The same scale and its other Y-cell segments are featured in the second section, in contrasting homophonic texture (bars 39–87). The reprise (bars 88–161) alternates homophonic with monophonic treatment of the thematic material, and the postlude (bars 162–176) iterates the introductory bars, ending with octave repetitions of the fundamental tone, C.

"A Bit Tipsy" (No. 2): The second Burlesque, composed in May 1911, is program music nearer the style of Richard Strauss (for instance, *Till Eulenspiegel's Merry Pranks*) than of Debussy. Its structural attributes, however, imitate those of eastern European peasant music, particularly the pentatonic organization of the melody. The first part of the ABA form consists of two heterometric quaternaries (bars 1–4, 5–17). The first quaternary has 7, 7, 7, 8 syllabic structure and ABAC section structure, ending on C as the fundamental tone of a Lydian/Phrygian polymode (bar 4). Although the visual appearance of the fourth melody section indicates a commonplace V–I cadence (R.H.: bar 4), the related acciaccatura triads provide the polymodal tritones C♯ and F♯ as sonic evidence that the quaternary ends on a "tonic" Z-cell, C♯-G-F♯-C. In the reprise, some acciaccatura triads are replaced by tetrachords (bars 48–51). What seems to be a Phrygian cadence in the last two bars of the composition is, after all, a V⁷–I ending but with a Bartókian twist: the last chord is the dissonant motif chord C-E-G-B!

Molto vivo, capriccioso (No. 3): The third Burlesque, created in 1910, was the centerpiece of the opus with regard to date of composition. The "capricious" theme (Ex. 2.4) and its L.H. accompaniment provide the structural elements for the scherzolike variation form. The leading motive is the trichord, Bb-Eb-Gb, superposed with its accompanying scalar hexachord, A-B-C♯-D-E-F, to form three pairs of minor seconds. These acciaccatura-like harmonic intervals, featured throughout the piece, foreshadow their chordal counterparts in the second Burlesque. The twelve-tone tonality is based on Eb as the principal tone of a Lydian/Phrygian polymode, Eb-F-G-A-Bb-C-D/Eb-E♮-Gb-Ab-Bb-C-Db.

Ex. 2.4. Bartók, Three Burlesques, op. 8c, for Piano (1908–1911), No. 3, bars 7–13.

An interesting example of cellular construction appears as a C Z-cell, C-G♭/ G♮-D♭, as the structural basis for a sectional variant (bars 151–160).

FOUR DIRGES (OP. 9A)

The fateful year of 1909 brought Bartók in contact with Romanian mourning songs whose "strange scales . . . absolutely unknown from modal music [cannot be] expressed as octave segments of the diatonic scale."[31] One of these nondiatonic formations—nowadays referred to as the octatonic scale—is represented by the heptachordal melody of a Romanian mourning song recorded by Bartók in July of that year (Ex. 2.5).

Daugh-ter, where is   your bride-groom now? He's been ta- ken to the grave - yard.

Ex. 2.5. *RFM*.ii, melody No. 628l, bars 1–4.

It would be difficult to overestimate the impact of this finding on Bartók's evolving tonal language. The melody verified for him the existence of octatonicism in folk song, a scalar peculiarity he had previously discovered in Liszt's Sonata in B Minor[32] and subsequently emulated in his own works, and he apparently memorialized the finding with the composition of the first Dirge.

Adagio (No. 1). The binary AB form has a quaternary AABC section structure. The first two melody sections consist of gapped, octatonic pentachords: G-[ ]-A♯-B-C♯-D and the same configuration transposed a whole tone upward (bars 2–8). The other two, nonoctatonic melody sections have C as their end tone (bars 12 and 14, respectively).

The accompaniment, opening the piece with the suggestion of B major (bars 1–2), is for the most part a succession of consonant intervals and triads. The overall effect is a dialogue between the accompaniment and the melody sections, resulting in an ambiguous (that is, without a fixed fundamental tone) twelve-tone Lydian/Phrygian polymode. Part B continues the dialogue in an unstructured, improvisatory manner, and the piece ends as it began—but now with the fundamental tone in place—in B major.

Andante (No. 2): This piece has a rounded (architectonic) structure, ABCA, and its melodic properties are related to the Transylvanian-Hungarian folk songs that Bartók collected in 1907.[33] The recurrent theme features the "flattened" form (that is, with augmented values) of Hungarian "dotted" rhythm: ♩♩|♩♩. Part A is an isometric (thirteen-syllable) double-section (bars 1–7, 8–14) based on characteristic Hungarian "old"-style pentatonic intervals: perfect fourths, minor thirds, and major seconds.[34] These intervals, however, are derived from the ascending form of the C♯ melodic minor scale. In part B, another double section, the theme is transposed to B♭ and extended in range to a nine-tone Aeolian/Lydian polymode (bars 15–21, 22–29). Part C consists of three heterometric sections, as if underlaid with ten, eight, and five syllabic texts (bars 30–34, 35–37, and 38–40). Although the accompaniment is an A♯ (=B♭!) diminished chord, their degrees, together with those of the theme, form a C-Phrygian/Lydian eleven-tone polymode, C-C♯-E♭-F-G-G♯-A♯/C-D-E-F♯-G-A. The theme in the reprise of part A (beginning at bar 40) is based on the symmetrical Hungarian pentatonic scale, C♯-E-F♯-G♯-B.

Assai andante (No. 4): The last Dirge represents an apparent—perhaps experimental—exploitation of complementary octatonic scales as an alternative means for creating a twelve-tone composition based on G as the common fundamental. The pitch collection of the first melody section, theme and its accompaniment, is based on the "Phrygian" form (beginning with a minor second and minor third) of the scale, G-A♭-B♭-B-C♯-D-E-F (bars 1–9). The second section opens with the complementary degrees of the "minor" form (beginning with a gapped minor tetrachord), G-[ ]-B♭-C-D♭-E♭-E-G♭ (bars 10–13). Thereafter smaller partitions of the complementary octatonic scales are juxtaposed as variants of the basic rhythmic motif, ♩ ♩|♩♩♩|♩.|.

SEVEN SKETCHES (OP. 9B)

In a statement written shortly before his death in 1945, Bartók refers to Seven Sketches—composed between 1908 and August 1910—as representative of the new piano style that first appeared in his Fourteen Bagatelles. The one exception is the fourth Sketch, that is similar to the Two Elegies with respect to "the 'old'-style piano technique [and] 'decorative' broken chords."[35] The varied styles of the present collection include the same mixed types previously met in Fourteen Bagatelles and Ten Easy Pieces, but the Sketches are closer to the Bagatelles as regards difficulty of piano technique.

"Portrait of a Girl" (No. 1): In view of its modest technical demands the first Sketch, composed in 1908, may have been Bartók's first musical impression of its dedicatee, Márta Ziegler, rather than the first Burlesque op. 8c. The theme is constructed from successive rhythmic patterns, ♪.♪♩ and ♫♫|♩. ♪|♪, that are not found in the peasant music of eastern Europe. The accompaniment features the motif chord, G-B-D-F♯ (bars 1, 3, 10, 13, etc.), and the whole-tone scale as a chain of inverted minor and major triads (bars 27–30). It is interesting from an extramusical ("Stefi" memento) aspect that the tonality is the twelve-tone G- Lydian/Phrygian polymode, yet the piece ends unambiguously with the motif-chord, D-F♯-A-C♯ (the original leitmotiv degrees), transformed into a functional V[7] chord for resolution to its tonic triad, G-B-D.

"Seesaw" (No. 2): One of Bartók's drafts of the second Sketch has the complete piece in the form of a spiral, in which the piano score is notated so that it undulates outward from the center of a sheet of ordinary paper. Instead of the title, a Latin caption appears in his handwriting, which can be translated as: "In everlasting memory of the hours 6, 7, 8, 9, 10, 11 p.m. 16 February 1909."

The descriptive title of this binary piece represents neither a minor (R.H.)/major (L.H.) bitonal struggle nor the alternate motion of a child's teeter-totter, but rather the dual nature of minor and major chords in a Lydian/Phrygian polymodal environment. Thus, the E minor trichord (R.H.: bars 1–4) represents an octave segment of the C-Lydian folk mode (a major scale with raised fourth degree), and the A♭ major tetrachord (L.H.: bars 1–4), an octave segment of the C-Phrygian folk mode (a minor scale with lowered second, third, and sixth degrees). The emphatic VII–I modal cadence and the abrupt change to unison texture in the last five bars also mark a change in tonality—to a C-Aeolian/Lydian polymode.

Lento (No. 3): The third Sketch, dedicated to Zoltán Kodály and his wife Emma, is dated August 1910. The whole-tone scale is treated in a somewhat experimental manner—along the lines of the Fourteen Bagatelles. It was Kodály, Bartók's closest friend, who introduced Bartók to the music of Debussy in 1907.

The AA_v form has a one-bar interlude (bar 10) and a four-bar postlude (bars 22–26), with C as fundamental tone of a Lydian/Phrygian polymode. The first part has the songlike character of a heterometric quaternary, and the thematic emphasis on the C whole-tone pentachord (bars 1–2, 4–5) and hexachord (bars 3–4)—each within the context of Lydian and Phrygian pitch content—underscores the close connection between Debussyian whole-tone collections and Bartókian modal chromaticism.

Non troppo lento (No. 4): As mentioned in my introductory remarks to Two Elegies and Seven Sketches, Bartók intended this piece and the Elegies to mark a certain return to the "old"-style piano technique. Indeed, the fourth Sketch is also elegiac in terms of rubato performance and stress of the motif chord, F-A-C-E (bars 1–3). The ABCD form is unusual with regard to the variegated substructure of the individual parts: a b | a b c d | a b c | a b. The connection with

Hungarian folk music is evident in the "dotted"-rhythm schemata that pervade the composition, particularly the "softer variety" in the theme (bars 1–3),[36] as well as in the octave segment of the pentatonic scale in the accompaniment of bar 13.[37]

The tonality is the C♯-Phrygian/Lydian polymode. It is interesting that the last bar ends with the "dotted"-rhythm schema A–E, accompanied by the fundamental chord, C♯-E-G♯. These four degrees are, of course, those of the motif chord and, with the addition of A♯, constitute the pentachordal motif chord that concludes the second Elegy.

"Romanian Folk Melody" (No. 5): Bartók collected the source melody in a Transylvanian village during July 1909 and sometime thereafter freely transcribed it as a Level 2 composition.[38] The original tune is based on an unusual scale, F-G-A-B-C-D-Eb, a Lydian mode with a Mixolydian seventh degree but invariably ending on the second degree, G.[39] Although this transcription replicates the ABC form, the melody, transposed to A as the fundamental (with B as the end tone), is a skeletal contraction of the original tune to a Lydian pentachord, A-B-D♯-E-F♯.

Each of the three repetitions of the originally monophonic folk song is harmonized by a different polymodal configuration. Part A (bars 1–12) is in the A-Dorian folk mode, with the Lydian augmented fourth, D♯, as a color tone. The added chromatic degrees in part B (bars 13–19) expand the tonality to an eleven-tone Lydian/Aeolian polymode. In part C (bars 20–38) the tonality is entirely major, as a Lydian/Mixolydian nine-tone polymode. The innovative cadence (bars 36–38) is actually a harmonic repetition of the characteristic Romanian ending on the second degree of the scale (A–B, bars 35–36). Bartók provides emphatic rendition of this peculiarity by the motion of a pentatonic fourth chord, B-E-A-D, to the major triad, B-D♯-F♯.

"In Walachian Style" (No. 6): Walachia was the designation given to Old Romania—the pre–First World War territory south of Transylvania—by its Slavic neighbors. The proper title of the sixth Sketch—a Level 4 composition based on the imitation of genuine folk melody—should perhaps be "In Transylvanian-Romanian Style," since the piece is fashioned from the same Romanian folk music material Bartók collected in 1909.[40] As in the case of the first Romanian Dance op. 8a, the melody is based on a specifically Romanian rhythmic schema, glissando, and bagpipe drone. Except for the held tones, however, the entire two-part composition is in unison. Variety is achieved by changes in melodic contour, modal chromaticism, and register.[41] The ten-tone polymode results from superposition of C-Lydian and C-Dorian folk modes.

Poco lento (No. 7): To the casual observer the last piece might appear to be an exercise in impressionist whole-tone polytonality. It is, however, a highly concentrated study of the two whole-tone scales within the context of poly-modal chromaticism, particularly with regard to their chord forms.[42]

Part A of this binary composition begins with the first half of the theme as an introduction (L.H., bars 1–2), in the guise of a B-Mixolydian pentachord, B-C♯-D♯-F♯-A, whose main degrees are sustained to form the B major triad. In the next bar, the repetition of the motif and its accompaniment (a stretto imitation of its altered self) reveals the possible polymodal content of the pitch collection, A-B-C-C♯-D♯-F♯-G, to be superposed A-Lydian and A-Dorian folk modes, with emphatic emphasis of the Lydian whole-tone tetrachord, A-B-C♯-D♯.

The second half of the theme (bars 4–5) partially verifies the presumed to-nality, since it commences with a whole-tone tetrachord, A-G-F-D♯ (the mirror inversion of the preceding Lydian structure), and is accompanied by the harmonic interval, F–C. But the resultant F major triad—a tritone removed from the preceding B major chord—adds Aeolian color to the pitch collection. Thus, with the fundamental tone A as axis of symmetry, a complete whole-tone scale is formed from two seemingly discrete tetrachords, D♯-F-G-A and A-B-C♯-D♯. The two entities are in fact organically related Y-cell octave segments of the A-Lydian/Aeolian polymode.

Part B highlights the two whole-tone scales as sustained pentachords, in par-allel motion at the interval of a major sixth (bars 17–22), alternating with unisonal transformations of a tetrachord derived from the theme, C-A-B-F♯ (bars 1–2). The climax is reached in bar 20, where the A and F♯ whole-tone pentachords are indirectly extended to complete whole-tone scales, thus expanding the tonality to the twelve-tone A-Lydian/Phrygian polymode. The piece ends with the men-tioned pentachords as simultaneities, perhaps the first example of so-called cluster chords.

ALLEGRO BARBARO

Allegro barbaro—often cited as Bartók's most famous and frequently per-formed work—was composed in 1911 but not printed until 1918 (by his new publisher, Universal-Edition of Vienna). Although the piece is a Level 4 com-position, similar in concept to the first Romanian Dance, it epitomizes the fu-sion of Hungarian, Romanian, and Slovak folk-music styles.

The arrangement of parts is quite unusual: A B C A$_v$ D E B$_v$, with a prelude, postlude, and several interludes. The quaternary substructure of part A (bars 5–30) is that of a Slovak folk song: heterometric double sections (alternating 5+5 and 7+7 syllabic structure), in which portions of the larger double sections (bars 13–15, 27–29) are expansions of the smaller ones by means of "Slovakian rhythm-contraction."[43]

The first half of the melody, E-G-A-B♯, is the tetrachordal form of the penta-tonic scale used by various peoples of central Asia; the second half, in so-called

Hungarian fifth transposition, is the "Old" Hungarian anhemitone pentatonic scale, A-B♯-D-E̱-F×.

Part B (at bar 34) has three important differences: there are two single sections, repeated to form a quaternary; the nine-syllable rhythmic schema is an artificial one, created from different halves of Slovak schemata that are occasionally met in Hungarian folk song; and both melody sections are created from the F-Lydian pentachord. Parts A and B, however, are based on the F♯-Phrygian/Lydian polymode.

A final characteristic worth noting is that the postlude of *Allegro barbaro* (from bar 200), that immediately follows the reprise of part B, features a return to the pure F-Lydian folk mode, in the form of unisonal octaves, leading to the same F♯ minor ostinato chords with which the piece began.

DANCE SUITE FOR PIANO (1925)

When in 1923 Bartók accepted a commission to compose a work in celebration of the fiftieth anniversary of the merging of Buda and Pest, he realized that he could personally memorialize the event by integrating Hungarian and other national folk-music styles. The outcome was the Dance Suite for Orchestra (1923), which he subsequently transcribed for piano, consisting of five dances connected by a recurrent ritornello (small repetition). The first dance marks Bartók's earliest invention of a "chromatic" theme, which "has some resemblance" to Arab chromatic folk melodies (Ex. 2.6).[44]

Ex. 2.6. Bartók, Dance Suite for Piano (1925), first dance, bars 1–5.

The 2/4 rhythmic schema of three quaternate eighth-notes ending with a bar of two quarter notes is typical of Ukrainian *kolomyjka* (round dance) melodies and was taken over by Transylvanian-Hungarians for their *kanásztánc* (hogherder's dance) melodies.[45] Note, too, that the arrangement of slurs is an ingenious adaptation of Romanian "shifted" rhythm, resulting in emphatic rendition of melodic intervals of a minor third, major second, and minor second.[46] So far as tonality is concerned, the melody begins with glissando from F to A, followed by repetitions of the X-cell (chromatic tetrachord) motif, A♭-A-B♭-C♭.

The complete melody (bars 1–14) and its simple intervallic accompaniment, G-D and F♯-E♭, identify the tonality of the first dance as a G-Phrygian/Lydian twelve-tone polymode, G-A♭-B♭-C-D-E♭-F/G-A-B-C♯-D-E-F♯.

NOTES

1. See pp. 4–5 for the explanation of this stage in Bartók's stylistic development.

2. Transylvania was Hungarian territory until its cession to Romania in 1920.

3. *RFM*.ii, 26.

4. *BBE*, 410. In view of the adaptation of these modes by the peasantry, such pitch collections are also referred to as folk modes.

5. Ibid., 367.

6. Ibid. With C as the fundamental tone the Lydian pentachord has D-E-F♯-G as modal degrees and the Phrygian pentachord has D♭-E♭-F-G.

7. *RFM*.ii, 13.

8. *HFS*, 22. It is interesting to note that *Allegro barbaro* has the order of fifth transposition reversed.

9. *BBE*, 288, 490. A comprehensive discussion of Bartók's ideas concerning piano playing, including the various touch-forms and their symbolic representation, will be found in *BM*, 13–14.

10. The five levels are an extrapolation of Bartók's remarks in *BBE*, 341–14, 350–52.

11. See *BBCO*, 45, 51.

12. The composition was intended to be the first in a series of "Little Piano Pieces."

13. *BBE*, 432.

14. *RFM*.ii, 43: "When no time signatures are used, the performance is parlando–rubato."

15. This analysis of Bartók's tonal language is based on his explanation that polymodal chromaticism consists of diatonic scales or scale portions filled out with chromaticized degrees which have "absolutely no chordal function; on the contrary, they have a diatonic-melodic function. This circumstance is clearly shown if the degrees are picked out and grouped into the modes to which they belong" (*BBE*, 376).

16. *BBE*, 128–33.

17. *MBB*, 71 n. 10.

18. It therefore appears that Z-cells represent a quartal harmonic system in Bartókian modal chromaticism, which has evolved from and has characteristics of the tertian system of functional harmony.

19. *MBB*, 70 n. 9.

20. No. 6 is an arrangement of *HFS*, melody No. 125, and the source melody of No. 8 appears in *SV*.ii, melody No. 585.

21. Quoted in the booklet to *Béla Bartók Complete Edition* (Hungaroton LPX 11394–95): 8.

22. Issued as forty Hungarian pieces in the first volume and thirty-nine Slovak pieces in the second one. A comprehensive discussion of the first edition, including Bartók's comments and the facsimile reproduction of the available source melodies, will be found in my notes to *Piano Music of Béla Bartók* (New York: Dover Publications, Archive Edition Series II, 1981), vii–xxi.

23. *BBE*, 427.

24. Ibid., 368–69.

25. Ibid., 432–33.

26. See *BBE*, 334–35, 371–73 for Bartók's comments on the consonant character of the modal seventh degree.

27. Bartók refers to this section of Liszt's masterpiece as expressing Mephisto's devilish irony (*BBE*, 452).

28. *BBE*, 432.

29. *RFM*.i, melody No. 648.

30. *RFM*.ii, melody No. 456b.

31. *BBE*, 363.

32. *BM*, 113.

33. *BBSE*, 77.

34. The intervallic relationship between the second Dirge and *Duke Bluebeard's Castle* is illustrated in *BBLW*, 71–73.

35. *BBE*, 432.

36. *BBE*, 76–77, 389.

37. *BBE*, 364: scale segment 4.

38. *RFM*.ii, melody No. 58e.

39. Ibid., 13.

40. See my remarks about Two Romanian Dances op. 8a, above.

41. The specific rhyhmic schema is derived from *RFM*.i, melody No. 607, and the glissando is a feature of *RFM*.i, melodies No. 58a–k.

42. The seventh Sketch as a model of "whole-tone polytonality" is discussed in H. A. Miller, *New Harmonic Devices* (Philadelphia: Oliver Ditson/Theodore Presser, 1930), 124–26.

43. The diminution of values, such as replacement of certain quarter notes by eighth notes. See *HFS*, 57–62.

44. *BBE*, 379.

45. *BBCO*, 68, 70.

46. A peculiarity of instrumental dance melodies in which a phrase is repeated so that the accentuated parts lose their accent during the repetition while the nonaccentuated parts gain one.

3

Second String Quartet: Stylistic Landmark[1]

When Béla Bartók completed his String Quartet No. 2, op. 17, in October 1917,[2] it marked the end of his quest for a new and distinctive mode of composition. This newly won means, attained only after more than a decade of preparation and experimentation, represents a unique contribution to chamber music repertory: the articulation of east European folk music and Western art music in the creation of abstract works. The folk category, however, more complex than its title would suggest, represents a Bartókian fusion of east European and Arabic peasant music styles. The art-music category, moreover, was conceived of by Bartók as being an amalgam of elements derived from the Baroque, Classical, and Impressionistic periods in music history.

It is interesting to observe the parallel between Bach and Bartók in terms of their sharing a trichotomous view of art-music content. The opening movement of the Baroque master's orchestral Ouverture (or Suite) No. 3 in D major, for example, demonstrates fusion of national styles: French overture, Italian concerto grosso, and German polyphony. The Second Quartet reflects contrapuntal texture, architectonic form, and nonfunctional harmony; for, as Bartók related to one of his biographers, he was constantly considering the possibility of "making a living synthesis of Bach, Beethoven, Debussy that would be valid for our own time."[3]

To begin with, Classical form—somewhat modified—constitutes the structural design of each of the quartet's three movements. The first movement, in nontraditional sonata form, has a motivic first theme (Ex. 3.1).[4]

Ex. 3.1. Bartók. Second Quartet, first movement, bars 1–4.

The first violin begins with a most unusual motif: sequential perfect fourths, E-A-D, linked to a D Z-cell, D-C♯/G♯-G♮. Such leaps of a perfect fourth are commonplace in Hungarian folk music, particularly in the "old"-style melodies (Ex. 3.2).[5]

Tempo giusto

Ex. 3.2. *HFS*, 258, melody No. 141, bars 1–2.

The Z-cell was the outcome of Bartók's grotesque transformation of the Austrian anthem, *Gott erhalte*, in his *Kossuth* symphonic poem (1903).[6] This cell, G-C♯-F♯-B♯, is a unique tetrachord consisting of juxtaposed tritones, used linearly to provide rudimentary motifs and vertically as chords (Ex. 3.3).

Ex. 3.3. Bartók. *Kossuth* symphonic poem, bars 393–96. The cellular structure is created by chromatic compression of the third and fifth degrees (E♮ and G♮, respectively) of the anthem's original major mode. Note Bartók's use of the C♯-minor key signature.

Z-cells pervade the first movement and are basic formations in the other two movements.[7] Thus, for instance, at R.N. 18 of the first movement the transposed Z-cell, E-A/B♭-E♭, appears as a prominent variation.

A fusion of Romanian dance-music style and Hungarian sequential fourths appears near the end of the movement (Ex. 3.4).

Ex. 3.4. Bartók, Second Quartet, first movement, four bars before R.N. 21.

The violins and cello imitate the dance-music style of a Romanian violin duo, in which the duo's first violin plays the melody. The second violin, with three strings and a flat bridge, is played with a loosely strung bow. Thus different triads in close position can be produced as the accompaniment (Ex. 3.5).[8]

Ex. 3.5. *RFM*.i, melody No. 426, bars 3–7.

The second movement, a rondo-variation form,[9] opens with an introductory section in which the repetition of interlocked tritones forms the first Z-cell, B-F/E-B♭ (bars 1–5), and the following succession of tritones forms the second Z-cell, E-B♭/A-E♭ (bars 5–6). The next bar concludes the section with a Phrygian cadence (E♭-D) that serves to establish D as the fundamental tone of the movement.

The first theme resembles the narrow-range, chromatic style of an Arab folk melody, including its ornamental tones and repetition of short motives (Ex. 3.6).[10]

Ex. 3.6. (a) Bartók, Second Quartet, second movement, bars 19–24, and (b) *BBSE*, 60, melody No. 38, bars 4–7.

The slow third movement begins with a short first theme that is based on permutations of the motif, ♩♩ ♩|♩ ♩ (at R.N. 1). A variation of the first movement opening theme includes the same Z-cell, D-C♯-G♯-G♮ (Ex. 3.7). And the structure of the third theme is in the style of a heterometric folk song (Ex. 3.8).

Ex. 3.7. Bartók, Second Quartet, third movement, second theme, R.N. 2.

Ex. 3.8. Ibid., third movement, third theme, R.N. 4. The quaternary heterometric section structure, as indicated by the virgules, is the textual equivalent of 6+7+7+6 syllables.

The polyphonic character of Bartók's writing is nowhere more apparent than in this quartet; in fact, much of the dissonance that prevails throughout originates from the interaction of wholly independent melodic lines. (These lines, it will be noted, are developed by means of contrapuntal devices such as canonic imitation, inversion, augmentation, and diminution). As Zoltán Kodály has remarked:

> Let us return to the dissonances. Bartók, who had pursued the development of modern harmony since *Tristan*, was an heir to Bach's harmonic world. Reger, too, in his opinion, professed that Bach still had a message for us, even after Wagner. The change in melodic style also inevitably influenced the harmonic world. The new connections between certain notes, which came about as a result of their "sequence" (their being played one after the other), also assumed a validity when they were sounded together. Chords that formerly we would have felt to be incomprehensible without their resolutions have now become satisfying.
>
> But most of the condemned dissonances spring from the melodies. Frictions and coarser events are brought about by the combination of two or more melodies. Bach's style is considered to have "not only passing notes but complete passing melodies and suspensions of not only a single note or chord but of complete melodic progressions."
> This is the secret of Bartók's dissonances as well.[11]

Between 1905 and 1917 Bartók collected and transcribed thousands of east European and Arabic folk melodies; indeed, he wrote scholarly studies concerning their properties. During this period he underwent an evolutionary kind of compositional apprenticeship which, together with his ethnomusicological activities, resulted in the complete absorption of the idiom of peasant music—to the extent that it became his musical mother tongue.

Notes

1. The first version of this study was published in the *American Music Teacher* 15, no. 2 (November–December, 1965): 30–32.

2. Bartók began its composition in 1915. He dedicated the work to the Waldbauer-Kerpely Quartet, who gave the first performance on 3 March 1918 in Budapest.

3. Serge Moreux, *Béla Bartók* (London: The Harvill Press, 1953), 92.

4. *LMBB*, 178.

5. *HFS*, 18.

6. *BBCO*, 24–25.

7. *MBB*, 93–103.

8. *RFM*.i, 16.

9. The variants are illustrated in János Kárpáti, *Bartók's String Quartets* (Budapest: Corvina Press, 1975), 191–95.

10. *BBLW*, 88.

11. *The Selected Writings of Zoltán Kodály*, ed, Ferenc Bónis, trans. Lili Halápy and Fred Macnicol (London: Boosey & Hawkes Music Publishers, Ltd., 1974), 90.

4

Impact of Italian Baroque Music on Bartók's Music[1]

At the beginning of the twentieth century, when Béla Bartók was a student at the Budapest Academy of Music, there was a growing public clamor for a Hungarian national anthem to replace the Austrian anthem (*Gott erhalte*) and for the Hungarian language to replace German in every aspect of national life. Bartók quickly became an ardent nationalist, concentrated on the study of Liszt's music, and in 1901 received the coveted Liszt Prize and glowing press reviews of his piano recitals.

With regard to composition, Bartók's autobiography refers to the period of 1900 to 1901 as one of stagnation. In 1902, the first Budapest performance of Richard Strauss's tone poem *Also sprach Zarathustra*, however, roused him as by a lightning stroke. He immediately plunged into the study of Strauss's scores; since this new music seemed to hold the seeds of a new way of composing.[2] He also recognized the Liszt influence on Strauss with respect to the symphonic poem and its structural feature of thematic transformation. Liszt, whose Hungarian Rhapsodies had brought him worldwide fame as the greatest composer of Hungarian music, was convinced that the Gypsy music on which they are based was the true Hungarian folk music. Bartók and the rest of the musical world thought so too. In 1903, therefore, Bartók's last year as a piano and composition student, he decided to compose a symphonic poem which would combine Liszt's Hungarianisms and Strauss's dissonant harmonic novelties. Carried along in the wave of desire for national independence that was sweeping Hungary, Bartók composed *Kossuth*, a symphonic poem inspired by the account of Louis Kossuth and the ill-fated Revolution of 1848 against Austria. Analysis of *Kossuth* discloses that part of its melodic material is based on thematic transformation from the first movement of Liszt's Hungarian Rhapsody No. 2. At the end of *Kossuth*, following a battle scene in which the Hungarian army is defeated, Liszt's theme appears in the form of a funeral march.[3]

Because of its sensational content as a parody of the Austrian national anthem, *Kossuth* propelled Bartók into the national limelight after its first performance on 13 January 1904. International recognition came in February, when the next performance was given in Manchester, England. Now a recognized composer as well as a piano virtuoso, Bartók devoted himself to composition during the summer and fall, at a villa in the northern part of Hungary that is now Slovak territory.

In October, he began work on his Rhapsody op. 1 for Piano and Orchestra (Ex. 4.1d), again turning to Liszt for direction. This time, aware that Liszt's Hungarian Rhapsodies represented a new musical form till then, Bartók adopted their two-part form of juxtaposed slow and fast movements. Liszt had been led to this form by the usual order of Hungarian rural and urban dances. Moreover, it appears that Bartók selected Liszt's Hungarian Rhapsody No. 13, a work that he had studied at the Academy of Music, as a specific model, for it contains Liszt's replication of a Gypsy-styled Hungarian art song (Ex. 4.1b). If we compare some available variants of Liszt's theme, it becomes apparent that it stems from an old art song composed by a dilettante from the educated Hungarian classes (Ex. 4.1a). These popular art songs or urban folk songs were disseminated in typically distorted style by city Gypsy bands, and the outstanding specimens were frequently adapted by Hungarian peasants (Ex. 4.1c).[4]

Ex. 4.1. Thematic sources in Bartók's Rhapsody op. 1 for Piano and Orchestra. (a) Károly Thern, in *Peleskei Nótárius* (1838), (b) Liszt, Hungarian Rhapsody No. 13, (c) Bartók, *HFS*, melody No. 74c (collected in 1907), and (d) Bartók, Rhapsody op. 1, bars 117–22.

Comparison of the two rhapsodies shows how thoroughly Bartók grasped the Liszt concept of thematic transformation. Another structural feature is an attenuated return to the main theme of the slow first movement, providing the work with classical architectonic form. Bartók's Rhapsody, which leans so heavily on concepts borrowed from Liszt and Strauss, represents a high point of his first stage of development. Because his compositions until 1905 are based on the prevalent Gypsy-styled national art music of the nineteenth century, Bartók's first stage of development can be referred to as a summary of Hungarian musical dialect.

Bartók's second stage of stylistic development was for the most part devoted to a fusion of national music styles. The impetus for the change was accidental: during that fateful summer of 1904, he overheard a nursemaid singing a folk-styled art song whose metamorphosis included modal structuring of the melody. Bartók, notating other songs in the girl's repertory, soon realized that he had chanced upon folk-music material uncontaminated by Gypsy or other urban influences, and he decided to investigate the peasant music of Hungary. In 1905, he met and established what was to become a lifelong friendship with Zoltán Kodály. And in 1906, after a summer of fieldwork, he and Kodály—each contributing ten transcriptions—self-published their Twenty Hungarian Folk Songs for Voice and Piano.

For approximately eleven years Bartók concentrated on recording music in the rural villages of then Greater Hungary, including the repertories of such minority peoples as Slovaks, Romanians, Ruthenians, Serbo-Croatians, and Bulgarians. And in 1913, he traveled to North Africa to record Arab peasant songs at the Biskra Oasis. It was Bartók's great talent that enabled him to homogenize polyglot musical folklore, beginning in 1907, and develop five levels of complexity:

(1) Genuine folk tunes are featured in a composition, and the invented material is of secondary importance. Put in other words, the folk tune is the "jewel" and the added parts function as its "mounting."

(2) In this level of construction, the folk tune and the invented material are treated equally.

(3) The folk tune is presented as a kind of musical "motto" and the invented material is of greater significance.

(4) The melody is composed in imitation of a genuine folk tune.

(5) The highest level is that in which neither folk tune nor its imitation is used but the work is pervaded by the atmosphere of folk music. Thus, for example, the music might have Hungarian pentatonic turns, Romanian bagpipe motif structure, Slovak modal features, and so on.

Since the collected material was almost exclusively monophonic and much of it pentatonic, new harmonic progressions were devised to avoid the stereotyped tonic-dominant sequences that were the hallmark of nineteenth-century dilettante composers of popular art music. In 1907, Bartók discovered the music of Claude Debussy, with its unusual harmonic progressions and innovative use of pentatonic and whole-tone scales, and he followed in the footsteps of the French master by incorporating stylistic features of his Impressionistic music. Moreover, with regard to formal design, Bartók adopted the progressive architectonic structures developed by Beethoven. The influence of Debussy and Beethoven can be determined at all five levels on which Bartók transmuted folk music into art music.

During this period of Bartók's fieldwork, transcription, and study of folk-music materials, he reached the point where their idiosyncrasies became his musical mother tongue.[5] Then he pondered the ways and means of incorporating a distinctive polyphonic dimension in his works. As he later stated in an interview, he leaned toward J. S. Bach's transcendent counterpoint as the goal.[6] But a number of factors served to postpone his contrapuntal quest: among them, and resulting from the process of fusing multinational musical folklore, was his development of a truly unique musical language.

Ex. 4.2 shows the opening bars of the first movement of Bartók's Dance Suite for Orchestra, which he composed in 1923 and transcribed for piano solo two years later.

Ex. 4.2. Bartók, Dance Suite, first movement, bars 1–5.

According to Bartók the theme resembles Arab folk melody, and it represents the first "chromatic" melody he invented.[7] In fact, the theme contains eleven of the twelve chromatic degrees, with G as the principal tone of the juxtaposed Lydian and Phrygian modes. In bar 15 (not shown) the closing chord is a simultaneity of the five tones comprising the G pentatonic scale (G-B♭-C-D-F). This unique procedure represents Bartók's innovative solution to composing with twelve tones based on a fixed principal tone. He designates the method as polymodal chromaticism, that is, the simultaneous use of Lydian and Phrygian modes in which the seemingly chromaticized degrees have no chordal function, only a diatonic-melodic function.[8] Since the Lydian mode is a characteristic of the Slovak folk song, the Phrygian mode a feature of Romanian peasant music of central Transylvania, and the anhemitone pentatonic scale a peculiarity of old Hungarian folk music, the fusion concept by means of a new tonal language is quite apparent. The Dance Suite is the last orchestral work composed in Bartók's second stage of development.

Other than the transcription of Slovak folk songs for voice and piano, in December 1924 Bartók devoted himself to folk-music studies and composed nothing until the summer of 1926. The end of World War I and the subsequent dismemberment of Greater Hungary in 1920, the preparation for publication of his monumental studies of Hungarian, Romanian, and Slovak folk music between 1921 and 1926, and the growing demand for his appearance as composer-pianist, to tour various European countries (beginning in 1922), contributed to this period of stagnation.

In retrospect, one could cite three circumstances that had a primary bearing on Bartók's resuming composition in June 1926, the year when he began his third and highest stage of development. First, the start of Stravinsky's concert career in 1924, as conductor and pianist, in which he performed his new works, the Concerto for Piano and Wind Instruments and the Second Piano Sonata. Stravinsky's contrapuntal treatments in these works, which he hoped would restore the ideals of Bach in contemporary music, received widespread attention.

Second, Bartók's concert tours in Italy: March 1925 in Milan, Rome, Naples, and Palermo; December in Trieste; and March 1926 in Bergamo, Cremona, and

Florence. These successful concerts apparently provided the impetus for his investigation of Italian music other than the works of Domenico Scarlatti.[9] The fortuitous acquisition of the keyboard works of Bach's Italian predecessors and contemporaries led to Bartók's mastery of their contrapuntal techniques, and thus more or less replaced the Bachian ideal as the polyphonic dimension in Bartók's ultimate goal, the synthesis of east European folk-music materials with Western art-music techniques.[10]

Third, Bartók's only work for piano and orchestra was the Rhapsody op. 1, the highlight of his earlier, discarded style of composition. He played it in Holland in October 1925 and in Germany in January 1926. He keenly felt the lack of a major work for piano and orchestra, with himself as soloist, that would be representative of his latest style. In an interview published in London in March 1926, Bartók indicated that he had devoted that winter to writing a pianoforte concerto that he had long had in mind.

Thus, in a tremendous burst of creative energy, Bartók composed his Sonata for Piano in June; *Out of Doors* for piano between June and August; Nine Little Piano Pieces, completed on 31 October; and the First Piano Concerto, brought to a close the next month. All these works bear the fruits of Bartók's study of early Italian contrapuntal style, that included the keyboard works of Benedetto Marcello, Michelangelo Rossi, Azzolino Bernardino della Ciaia, Girolamo Frescobaldi, and Domenico Zipoli. Another outcome of Bartók's study was the transcription of some of these works for piano, which he performed for the first time on Budapest Radio in October and November and which were published by Carl Fischer, New York, in 1930.

Style analysis of these transcriptions in terms of their morphological attributes could be the subject of a series of studies, particularly if comparison is made with even a limited number of works composed by Bartók beginning in 1926. The most significant attributes are those found in Frescobaldi's G-Major Toccata and della Ciaia's Canzone from his G-Major Sonata and their relationship to Bartók's First Piano Concerto, for such a revealing comparison provides adequate evidence of the impact of the earlier Italian style on Bartók's synthesized output which first emerged in 1926.

According to various sources, the keyboard toccata was born in Italy, perhaps in Venice during the first half of the sixteenth century, when the organist of St. Mark's Church was required to play improvisations. The form reached its zenith when Girolamo Frescobaldi (1583–1643) published his series of toccatas beginning in 1615. His Toccata in G Major consists of five sections in different tempos and treatments, based on cyclical pedal points. Ex. 4.3 illustrates the Lydian pitch content of the first three bars. In the remainder of the section Frescobaldi juxtaposes the other two G-major modes: Mixolydian and Ionian. The second section is based on the subdominant pedal point; the third section, on the subtonic, has an ingenious polyphonic texture including imitation and inversion. The fourth section follows a sudden change of key, with the supertonic as pedal point and alternation of the Aeolian and parallel Mixolydian modes.

Ex. 4.3. Frescobaldi, Toccata in G Major, first section, bars 1–3.

The first half of the fifth section (Ex. 4.4) illustrates Frescobaldi's use of chromatic motifs in the form of semitone tetrachords, B-C-C♯-D, A-B♭-B♮-C, and E-F-F♯-G, that are treated contrapuntally and based on the dominant (D) as the pedal point.

Ex. 4.4. Ibid., fifth section, bars 63–66.

Bartók uses such tetrachords as simultaneities in the first movement of his First Piano Concerto, where they are a cellular feature of his new musical language and are referred to by Bartók theorists as X-cells. Ex. 4.5 shows these chromatic cells, C-D♭-D♮-E♭ and G-A♭-A♮-B♭, which, similar to Frescobaldi's procedure, are based on a pedal point (D). Other similarities are Bartók's juxtaposition of modes (Mixolydian, Phrygian, and Aeolian) and contrapuntal treatments similarly based on a pedal point.

Ex. 4.5. Bartók, First Piano Concerto, first movement, four bars before R.N. 21.

The Canzone from the Sonata in G Major of Azzolino Bernardino della Ciaia (1671–1755) is more directly related to Bartók's First Piano Concerto (Ex. 4.6).

Allegro

Ex. 4.6. Della Ciaia, Sonata, second movement (Canzone), bars 1–5.

It is apparent that Bartók transformed the Canzone theme in terms of repeated notes and melodic contour to construct the main theme of his concerto (Ex. 4.7).

4.7. Bartók, First Piano Concerto, first movement, bars 38–43.

Another direct relationship is in the use of contrapuntal double-stop configurations as well as similar rhythm schemata.

As previously mentioned, Bartók had performed his Rhapsody op. 1 for Piano and Orchestra in 1926, prior to the composition of his First Piano Concerto that year. The first theme of the second movement from the Rhapsody (Ex. 4.1d) is a borrowing from Liszt's Rhapsody No. 13 (Ex. 4.1b), and the latter is a variant of a Gypsy-styled old Hungarian art song (Ex. 4.1a), that Liszt infused with characteristic Slovak rhythmic schemata, ♪♩ ♪ and ♫ ♩, and structural features.[11] In Ex. 4.8, Bartók's First Piano Concerto introduces the same Slovak rhythm schemata at R.N. 1.

Ex. 4.8. Bartók: First Piano Concerto, first movement, R.N. 1 and 3.

At R.N. 3, the rhythm is flattened, that is, without syncopation, the same procedure Bartók employs in the Rhapsody. It is relevant to the analysis of Bartók's compositional process that flattened forms of syncopated schemata rarely occur in Hungarian folk music other than in the "mixed" (that is, foreign-influenced) style. And what is more significant is that each schema is accentuated in "shifted rhythm," a characteristic feature that Bartók discovered in Transylvanian-Romanian dance melodies. Ex. 4.9 shows this type of rhythm in which accentuated units (designated by alphabetic letters in the illustration) are shifted so that they lose their emphasis; non-accentuated units thus gain emphatic rendition.[12]

Ex. 4.9 Bartók, *RFM*.i, melody No. 243v, bars 1–5.

Another use of Romanian folk rhythm is the numerous changes of time that occur in the First Piano Concerto. Such frequency of metrical alternation is a characteristic feature of Romanian Christmas carols (*colinde*) that Bartók collected from 1909 to 1917.[13]

Classical sonata form is the structural design of the Concerto, with contrasting main and secondary themes. The latter is pure Hungarian in style: pentatonic structure and eleven-syllable rhythm schema that are characteristic of "old" Hungarian folk songs (Ex. 4.10).

Ex. 4.10. Bartók, First Piano Concerto, first movement, bars 105–12.

The Concerto's development section has an interesting example of inversional counterpoint, where complementary whole-tone configurations suggest the influence of Debussy (Ex. 4.11).

In conclusion, this presentation has underscored the impact of seventeenth- and eighteenth-century Italian Baroque music on Bartók's music. It has been emphasized that Béla Bartók's compositions can be divided into three stages of stylistic development. The first stage, ending in 1905, represents a summary of Hungarian musical dialect, that is, composition based on Gypsy-styled popular

Ex. 4.11. Bartók, First Piano Concerto, first movement, R.N. 22.

art song as basic source material.

The second stage, ending in 1925, resulted from Bartók's discovery that the true Hungarian folk song resided in the peasant villages of pre–First World War Greater Hungary. He recorded, transcribed, and studied this music and that of the minority peoples, and it was his great talent that enabled him to assimilate the collected polyglot musical folklore and develop five levels of complexity for its use in composition. In the highest level he achieved a fusion of national music styles to the extent that even his abstract works are pervaded by the atmosphere or spirit of folk music.

The third stage, from 1926 to 1945, the year of Bartók's death, was devoted to achieving a synthesis of east European folk-music materials and Western art-music techniques of composition. His original idea was based on Debussy's harmonic concepts, Beethoven's structural innovations, and Bach's contrapuntal procedures. Although Bartók had studied, edited, or performed Bach's music for more than twenty years, he found the German master's style incompatible with his own Hungarian predilection for the variation principle and for his personal need for flexibility in fugal writing. Bartók therefore turned to the works of Bach's Italian predecessors and contemporaries for a distinctive polyphonic dimension in his work. In 1926, his quest was fulfilled: he composed his great "toccata cromatica"—the First Piano Concerto.

NOTES

1. The first version of this study was read at the Bartók Centennial Conference at the Teatro la Fenice (Venice, Italy, 1981) and at the International Conference on Bartók and Kodály at the University of Indiana (Bloomington, 1982). The first publication appears in György Ránki, ed., *Bartók and Kodály Revisited*, Indiana University Studies on Hungary 2 (Budapest: Akadémiai Kiadó, 1987), 183–97.

2. *BBE*, 409.

3. *BBLW*, 38.

4. See György Kerényi, *Népies Dalok* (Popular Songs) (Budapest: Akadémiai Kiadó, 1961), 211 n. 29.

5. *BBE*, 326.

6. Serge Moreux, *Béla Bartók*, preface by Arthur Honegger, trans. G. S. Fraser and Erik de Mauny (London: Harvill Press, 1953), 92.

7. *BBE*, 379.

8. Ibid., 376.

9. Published by Rozsnyai Károly, Budapest, in 1921.

10. See the specific works listed in *BBLW,* 256–59.

11. *BBE*, 128.

12. *RFM*.i, 45–46.

13. *RFM*.iv, 13–15.

5

History of Bartók's *Mikrokosmos*[1]

INTRODUCTION

Béla Bartók's *Mikrokosmos*, a collection of 153 progressive pieces and 33 exercises for the piano, has been attracting more and more attention since its publication in 1940. Indeed, more than fifty articles, books, and theses in whole or in part are devoted to a discussion of the work, particularly from the point of view of its objectives: first, to provide pianists with pieces suitable for concert use; second, to teach pianists, young or old, the technique and musicianship of the instrument from the beginning to a certain higher degree; third, to acquaint pianists with music written in different styles; fourth, to introduce piano students to folk music by means of graded transcriptions; and fifth, to serve as a reference book for composition students.

BACKGROUND AND DEVELOPMENT

Bartók's resumption of his concert career in the 1920s, expanded to an international scale, was perhaps the cause of his increased activity in the composition of piano music. Nineteen twenty-six was the year in which he wrote the First Piano Concerto, Sonata for Piano, *Out of Doors*, and Nine Little Piano Pieces and began the collection of piano pieces eventually called *Mikrokosmos*.[2]

Verification of 1926 as the year in which the *Mikrokosmos* originated can be found in two documents containing Bartók's handwriting. One, an offprint from Denijs Dille's biography of the composer,[3] contains Bartók's autographic additions and corrections to what is apparently the first published chronological catalogue of his works in which the *Mikrokosmos* is listed.[4] The other, "List of all noticed errors in piano score of Violin Concerto," is in part a request from Bartók to his publisher (Boosey and Hawkes, London) to change the entry concerning the *Mikrokosmos* (printed on the back cover of the score) as follows: "piano solo . . . last item: omit (1940), or substitute (1926–1939) for it."[5]

Which one of the 153 pieces comprising the *Mikrokosmos* was composed first is a matter of conjecture; the evidence, however, seems to indicate "Unison" (No. 137), and this can be quite conclusively attributed to having been composed in 1926. Bartók catalogued most of his manuscripts numerically, assigning the number 32 (printed with green crayon on the title page) to a thirty-one-page manuscript containing sketches and second (intermediary) drafts of Nine Little Piano Pieces, incomplete sketches of unidentified piano music, and one sketch each from *Out of Doors*, First Piano Concerto, and *Mikrokosmos*. The original Hungarian title on the cover page was written in pencil: kis zongoradarabok (little piano pieces); and above it, in bright blue ink:

9 Kleine Klavierstücke (Skizzen)
(einige Skizzen zu "Mikrokosmos"
"Im Freien" I. Klavierkonzert)

The entire manuscript was neatly written first in blue black ink with a narrow pen and later corrected in pencil. The twenty-fifth page contains a continuation of the second Dialogue (No. 2 of Nine Little Piano Pieces) on the first four staves. The remainder of the page consists of a sketch of "Unison" (*Mikrokosmos* No. 137) completed in two operations: first, an outline of the piece was written in the same color ink and the identical penmanship as that of the other pieces comprising the complete manuscript; then corrections, additions, and extensions were made in blue ink with a broad pen and with an autography considerably less neat in appearance. In fact, the revisions of the piece are identical in terms of ink, pen, and handwriting to those sketches contained in manuscript No. 49 ("Mikrokosmos Klavierstücke, Brouillon") that are the first drafts of *Mikrokosmos*.[6]

Logically, it appears that Bartók composed the preliminary (then unfinished) sketch to "Unison" as part of a collection of piano pieces intended for publication in 1926.[7] For one reason or another, perhaps because of his preoccupation with the composition of *Out of Doors* or the First Piano Concerto that same year, he decided to submit for publication under the title of Nine Little Piano Pieces those sketches he had completed, and he returned to the manuscript at a later date to finish the sketch of "Unison." Incidentally, this piece is not included in manuscript No. 49.

Mátyás Seiber suggested that Bartók's conception of *Mikrokosmos* as a title[8] or as a collection of pieces with a pedagogical purpose did not occur prior to 1933.[9]

> I possess no letter from Bartók myself on the subject of "Mikrokosmos," but I feel myself connected with this work in a small way of which I am rather proud. In 1933, I wrote a series of short piano pieces which were published by Schott, Mainz, under the title "Rhythmic Studies." The pieces dealt with various rhythmical problems like "Syncopation," "Shifting of Accents," Cross-Rhythms," etc., and were mainly devised for teaching purposes. As usual, after publication I sent a copy of it to Bartók, together with my "Easy Dances," published shortly before. Years later when I met Bartók again (I think it must have been in London in 1938) I asked him what he thought of my Rhythmic Studies. He congratulated me warmly, saying what excellent teaching material they were,[10] then continued: "In fact, I took up your idea and expanded it further: I am now working on a series of piano

pieces which deal not only with the rhythmic, but also with melodic, harmonic and pianistic problems." This series was to become the *Mikrokosmos.*

Bartók's unpublished lecture notes contain information in support of Seiber's contention. After referring to *For Children* (composed 1908–1909) as easy pieces written for piano students, Bartók said, "More than twenty years later I again turned to this problem. But now I approached the work with a very definite plan. My idea . . . is entitled Mikrokosmos."[11]

According to a statement made by Peter Bartók, his father's first reference to the title *Mikrokosmos* and his first assertion that the collection of pieces under that name constituted a piano method was made in 1936.

> I served as a "guinea pig" in my father's experiments with the *Mikrokosmos* in 1936, the first year I began piano study; in fact, he wrote the pieces faster than I could learn them. Then he composed the *Mikrokosmos* independent of any consideration of its suitability for me.[12]

A Bartók pupil showed me tissue proofs[13] in Bartók's autograph of several *Mikrokosmos* pieces which the composer presented to her during the 1936–1937 school year in Budapest. She said that Bartók referred to them as teaching materials from a collection called *Mikrokosmos.*[14]

One of Bartók's former colleagues at the Budapest Academy of Music disclosed that the composer asked for her assistance in the preparation of certain volumes of the *Mikrokosmos.*

> Since he had never taught beginners himself, the composer honored me repeatedly by asking for my suggestions concerning the musical and technical problems to be solved in the early grades. While we discussed sundry details of the pieces included in the first three volumes, what struck me most was not the systematic way in which be reached the solution of each problem, but his keen sense of responsibility towards the pupil whose progress he wanted to serve.[15]

On 9 February 1937, Bartók played the first performance of pieces from the *Mikrokosmos* at Cowdray Hall, London, and accompanied the violinist Zoltán Székely in the Bartók First Sonata for Violin and Piano and the Second Rhapsody for Violin and Piano.[16] He wrote to Székely less than a month before the concert: "A program loquacious enough! But at least these many flea-pieces are all 'manuscript.'"[17] A few days after the German occupation of Vienna in 1938, Ralph Hawkes flew to Budapest and met with Bartók:

> There was certainly no reticence on Bartók's part in agreeing to publish all his future works with us (Boosey and Hawkes). He had several manuscripts in preparation, such as the Sonata for Two Pianos and Percussion and *Mikrokosmos*, which were partly done.[18]

The Bartók file of the London office of Boosey and Hawkes, consisting of more than 200 letters and other documents, contains the correspondence between Bartók and Ralph Hawkes (and other members of the company) concerning the preparation of the *Mikrokosmos* for publication. The composer's letters were written for the most part from his home in Budapest and are dated from May 1938.[19]

The interchange of letters begins with an invitation from Hawkes to Bartók for the latter to appear at one of "the intimate little Concerts we give in our Organ Studio here in London."[20] Bartók's reply states, "Of course I am with pleasure at your disposal and would play at your concert some of my piano pieces from 'Mikrokosmos'"[21] Less than a week later Bartók sent the following program to Hawkes:

> From "Mikrokosmos" (piano pieces):
> Tale;/ Wrestling;/ Major seconds broken and together;/ Minor and Major;/ Theme and inversion;/ Boating;/ Burlesque rustique;/ Chords of the Fifth;/ From the Isle Bali;/ Merry Andrew;/ Five dances in "Bulgarian" rhythm.
> This takes approximately 20 minutes.[22]

The publisher's answer to the foregoing letter informs Bartók that the concert will be given at five o'clock in the afternoon on 20 June 1938.[23]

In what seems to be an office memorandum, the following statement appears: "Among his new works, the Studies for Piano 'Microcosmos' would be the most important for us."[24]

No further reference to the *Mikrokosmos* is made in the correspondence until early in 1939, the year in which Universal Edition released Bartók from his publishing agreement with them. On 6 March, Hawkes wrote to Bartók that Boosey & Hawkes was prepared to publish all the new works the composer had ready.

> Mrs. Hertzke, who called to see me the other day, tells me that you have a School for Piano in preparation. This work will, of course, be very interesting indeed but I do not recall that you told me anything about it when I had lunch with you.

Bartók's reply, sent from Basel on 9 March, states:

> That piano-school is nothing else than *first part of* the "Mikrokosmos";[25] In fact, it will be something like a school, with exercises, progressive order of the (very easy and easy) pieces. If you prefer to have it more similar to a School, I could add to it some changements.

The publisher then informed Bartók that a "strict Piano School in such a form" was not actually wanted, that the former wished to go ahead with the publication and not wait for the "absolute completion" of the composer's idea, and that individual pieces from the *Mikrokosmos* could be incorporated into a school at a later date.[26]

It seems likely that at this time Bartók discarded any ideas he might have had concerning the publication of the *Mikrokosmos* as piano pieces, per se, according to the following letter mailed from Budapest:

> *Mikrokosmos*. It is absolutely important to add still 20 or 30 very small and very easy pieces, to write them will not take much time. Besides, I want to transcribe most of the easier pieces for 4 hands, and to insert before some of the (easier) pieces presenting a new technical problem, a respective study (Fingerübung)— all that for pedagogical reasons. . . .[27]

The letter continues with a suggestion that certain pieces could be published with pictures "only if the pictures are very good and original" (such as that of a web in No. 142, "From the Diary of a Fly").[28]

Hawkes agreed with Bartók's proposals, particularly with reference to the use of sketches in illustration of the *Mikrokosmos*, voiced the opinion that publication might be possible in the early part of 1940, and suggested that if Bartók could not secure the services of an artist in Budapest he should come to London and confer with one there.[29] Bartók replied that he had "no occasion or possibility to come to England" before his next concert tour in November or December 1939, "so I can't see the gentleman you will choose for the sketches."[30]

In another letter, Bartók states that:

> I will send you a copy of the incomplete *Mikrokosmos* in a few days. I am very busy now in filling all the gaps still existent in it and have written ca 30 new pieces, but these are not yet copied. Now the whole work is almost complete.[31]

On 17 June 1939, Bartók wrote that he was sending the *Mikrokosmos* pieces whose order is "more or less pêle-mêle (given by haphazard)."

> The definitive order will be according to difficulty. My idea is to have them published in three volumes (you must not forget, there will be some 30 or 40 more of them!): I. the easiest pieces (intended for the 1. and 2. year), II. the less easier pieces, III. the more difficult ones. The I. volume should be printed in bigger characters (this is better for beginners) than the II. and III.[32]

After he received the *Mikrokosmos*, Hawkes engaged the services of an artist and sent several sketches to Bartók for approval.[33] The composer found them to be "too confusing for children" and suggested that they should be redrawn in terms of "the children's eyes." In the same letter he adds, "As for a new work, you know I want to score some of the Mikrokosmos pieces . . . I hope this will he ready perhaps end of Oct."[34]

Hawkes assured Bartók that the sketches would be improved and suggested that there be a preface of some kind in each of the four volumes planned for publication that would explain the various pieces and give an indication of the whole series. He enclosed an article about the *Mikrokosmos* written by his assistant, Dr. Ernst Roth (intended as advance publicity), for Bartók's review.[35] Bartók returned it with his insertions and wanted to know whether it was intended for *Tempo* (the Boosey and Hawkes periodical).[36] Hawkes replied that "the article on 'MIKROKOSMOS' is intended not only for general publicity purposes but also as a pamphlet to be issued with the works when they are published and I take it you approve of it."[37]

On 2 November 1939, Bartók informed Hawkes that the *Mikrokosmos*, consisting of 153 pieces, was ready except for the preface and the "footnotes" to some of the pieces.[38]

Three weeks later, Hawkes reported that he had received the complete *Mikrokosmos* manuscript and that he would write again within a few days concerning the progress made toward its publication. It was not until 9 December, however, that a rather lengthy letter was mailed in which the suggestion was made that the sketches planned as illustrations for certain pieces should be eliminated and that sales factors might necessitate the division of the first volume (containing sixty-six pieces) into two parts with a resulting publication of six volumes in all. The letter also noted errors in Nos. 8, 38, 66, 102, 120, 142, and 143 for Bartók's correction and stated that the composer's preface to *Mikrokosmos* did not give sufficient information or detail "and will be what we call 'sales resisting', unless it is done in a much more simple and easy manner . . . I am proposing to send you a revised preface at an early date which I think will meet this purpose." Hawkes further stated that a subtitle was required which would give an indication on the cover page as to the general contents of the series.

Bartók accepted Hawkes's proposals, requested that the publisher send subtitles in English which he, Bartók, would translate into Hungarian, and he corrected the noted errors.[39] Bartók's interesting comments concerning No. 142 ("From the Diary of a Fly") are worthy of inclusion here:

> No. 142: "jaj, pókháló!" means "Woe, a cobweb!" I wanted to depict the desperate sound of a fly's buzz when getting into a cobweb. Now, I don't know, if we use three languages for this explanation, the joke will be spoilt. Will you kindly decide, what to do here. We may leave out these words.[40]

The publisher then notified Bartók that future production problems concerning the publication of the *Mikrokosmos* would be handled by Dr. Roth and Mr. Stein of the London office, since he, Hawkes, was leaving for a three or four months' stay in America.[41]

The problem of selecting a suitable subtitle for the cover page was discussed by Roth in his first letter to Bartók: "'Progressive Pieces for Piano' or, what sounds very good in English 'Progressive Piano Pieces in Modern Idiom' or something of this kind." Roth further stated, "As far as the preface is concerned, we added a paragraph emphasizing the particular aim of your work," and he suggested that Bartók might "alter or rewrite it on similar lines."[42]

Bartók accepted the subtitle ."Progressive Pieces for Piano" but voiced his disapproval in no uncertain terms concerning the use of the word "modernity" in the paragraph that had been written by the company and inserted in his original preface to the *Mikrokosmos*:

> 2. In the English and French Preface, I have some slight remarks. But as for those parts about the "modernity" inserted by you, that is quite impossible to publish it in a Preface, signed by my name, where I am speaking, and giving hints and winks in my own name. I would never do that: to make excuses for the "modernity" etc.; besides I don't like the word "modern" at all! Think of it: in 20, or let us say in 40 years this work will cease to be "modern." And what does it mean "modern"? This word has no definite sens [sic], can he misinterpreted, misunderstood![43]

On 17 January 1940, Bartók wrote to Roth that the subtitle should be "Progressive Piano Pieces."

Bartók's plan to leave Budapest for the United States in March prompted Hawkes's urgent request to his London office to complete the engraving of the *Mikrokosmos* so that Bartók might correct the first proofs prior to his journey. Then, Hawkes suggested, if second proofs were not required by the composer, the final proofs could be sent to New York for printing and copies of the work placed on sale during Bartók's visit.[44]

In an effort to comply with Hawkes's wishes, Roth mailed proofs to Bartók as soon as they were completed—two volumes at a time—and requested that the composer "refrain from having second proofs sent to Budapest."[45]

Unaware of Roth's request (the mail service between London and Budapest was considerably delayed at this time), Bartók wrote to Leslie Boosey demanding second proofs of the fifth and sixth volumes of the *Mikrokosmos* since the first proofs had been sent without Hungarian titles and words. He enclosed explanatory remarks to certain pieces, in German, which were to be translated into English and French "but no Hungarian publication of them is necessary, every musician or even amateur of serious music has a thorough knowledge of these subjects."[46]

Roth answered the above with another request that the composer not ask for second proofs. Bartók yielded, "although reluctantly," and he insisted that the Hungarian titles and words missing from the first proofs be shown to " Hungarian-knowing people, the best would be the composer Mátyás Seiber."[47]

Bartók also wanted the explanatory notes to be on the same pages as their respective pieces (after each piece, or at the end of the page) in the first and fourth volumes of the *Mikrokosmos*.[48] In a postscript, however, he states that the notes could be printed as "Remarks" providing that an asterisk be inserted after the number of the respective piece. In another section of the same letter, he comments that the ten days it took him to correct the fifth and sixth volumes were not too much "for such complicated proofs," and he adds:

> I hope, you are not too much shocked by the additions I put into the proofs and by
> the few alterations (in some cases it appeared that in the Mss there are faults). In
> any case, take anything I have written into the proofs as my "last will," and disre-
> gard whatever contradictory you see in the Mss.[49]

Bartók's original plan to publish the first sixty-six pieces in one volume was
discarded by the company, who thought it would be more practical in terms of a
lower selling price per volume if the pieces were assembled into two books. The
composer could not understand why the division had to be made since the proofs
of the sixth volume contained almost as many pages (fifty-five) as those comprising vols. I and II (66, including the exercises and explanatory notes).

> It is a pity, that this division has been made: now, the first book gives a very poor
> impression; besides, the contents of those 60 pages are a real unity; they are meant
> for the first year of piano-studying. Now, every student will have to buy—after a
> few month's studying, the second book! Could not be changed this disposition?[50]

Roth replied that the first three volumes were to be priced lower than the last
three, and he asked Bartók to accept the division.[51]

In the meantime, additional proofs were sent to Bartók as soon as they were
engraved. The haphazard order in which they were mailed and the demands
made upon him to speed the proofreading were not to his liking, as evidenced
by the following statements made in his letter to Roth dated 18 February 1940:

> This is awful, this hurrying with the proofs; I am afraid there will be still many
> inconsequences: I have no opportunity/occasion to have here everything (6 books,
> exercises, notes, preface) at the same time and make the comparison.
>   This is a very complicated business, much more complicated than an ordinary
> score . . . I wonder why it is so important, to bring out these volumes until April.
> But if we do that, then the number of copies should be rather limited, in order to
> be able to correct every inconsequency and fault (resulting from this hurried work)
> in a very soon second edition.
>   I don't see any other possible way.[52]

On 5 April 1940, Roth reported to Hawkes that "we shall have finished copies by the 10th or 12th of April." Within the next two weeks the work was
placed on sale.[53]

THE MANUSCRIPTS

The *Mikrokosmos* manuscripts on file at the *PBA* have been assembled into
three classifications: sketches, intermediary drafts, and final copies. Compari-

son of the manuscripts and examination of the correspondence between Bartók, Ralph Hawkes, and Ernst Roth disclose what seems to have been the composer's procedure in the revision and correction of the *Mikrokosmos.*

The sketches, consisting of eighty pages, are written in blue ink on manuscript paper of various sizes and stave types. Deletions and insertions ranging from single notes to whole sections appear in profusion throughout the manuscript, and the scrawly autography seems to indicate a certain amount of feverish activity on the part of the composer to notate his musical ideas as rapidly as possible. Five pieces, all crossed out, and two exercises are contained in this manuscript which do not appear in the published volumes of the *Mikrokosmos.* Also, the sketch of "Unison" (No. 137) appears in the MS of Nine Little Piano Pieces.

There are eighty-two pages of intermediary drafts that are written in black ink on tissue masters composed of eighteen or twenty staves. There is in this manuscript, too, a considerable number of deletions and insertions but not to the extent that they appear in the sketches. On the other hand, the notation here is neat and precise. Titles are in Hungarian and German for the most part (some are in English), and almost all of the pieces contain timings, expression marks, and metronome indications. Twenty-two of the pieces are marked with Bartók's final numbers assigned to them in the published copies. However, the numbers were probably added after the final copies had been drafted, since the numerical designation of "Thumb Under" (No. 98) appears on a tissue master but not on its photographic reproduction.

Although the pieces in this manuscript seem to represent second drafts of the sketches, several can be found in more than one version.[54] For example, a preliminary draft of No. 46 is written so that the melody begins with the right rather than the left hand; Nos. 51 and 88 appear also in transpositions down a minor third and up a perfect fifth, respectively; and Nos. 111 and 142 appear as well in incomplete form. Two variants of No. 145a can be found—the piece consists of "a" and "b" parts which can be played separately as individual compositions or together as a piano duet—that do not appear in the published *Mikrokosmos.* The first part is in retrograde motion transposed down a major third, and the second one is a melodic inversion. No. 147 appears also in a simplified form without octaves and hand crossings. Finally, one of the canceled pieces of the sketches is in the intermediary drafts, but it too is crossed out.

According to his letter to Ralph Hawkes dated 13 November 1939, Bartók mailed a complete set of *Mikrokosmos* final copies to Boosey and Hawkes in London. This manuscript has not been available for inspection by the writer, but it is not unreasonable to assume that it does not differ appreciably from the final copy (59PFC1) on file at *PBA* in terms of revision or correction, since the latter manuscript is identical for the most part to the publication.[55]

It is likely that Bartók had at least two complete sets of photographic reproductions made from the tissue masters, correcting one set which he retained in his personal files (now in the *PBA*) and then completing the other for use by the engraver.[56]

Final Copy #1 consists of forty-nine pages of tissue proofs and twenty-one pieces written in blue ink on as many sheets of four-stave manuscript paper approximately six by nine inches in size.[57] The principal differences between this manuscript and the intermediary drafts are revised fingerings, additional English titles, and the insertion of numerals indicating the order of the pieces and exercises.[58]

Bartók proofread the third and sixth published volumes of the *Mikrokosmos* which are on file at the *PBA* under the designation 59PFC2.[59] His corrections, made in red crayon, extend to the addition of a dollar sign before the numerals "1.25" on the title page of vol. 3.[60] The *Mikrokosmos* was issued by Boosey and Hawkes in April 1940 in English and American editions printed from the same plates.[61]

TRANSCRIPTIONS

Bartók transcribed seven pieces from the *Mikrokosmos* (Nos. 113, 69, 135, 123,127,145, and 146) for two pianos (four hands) which were published by Boosey and Hawkes in 1947 under the title Seven Pieces from *Mikrokosmos*. Notations made on the cover page of the manuscript used as the engraver's final copy indicate that Bartók probably submitted the transcriptions for publication in 1944.[62]

Tibor Serly transcribed Nos. 139, 102, 108, and 142 for string quartet,[63] Nos. 128, 140, 117, 146, 151, and 153 for piano and string orchestra,[64] and Nos. 139, 137, 117, 142, 102, 151, and 153 for full orchestra.[65] The transcriptions for piano and string orchestra were performed first in March 1942 by Mrs. Bartók and some friends on the occasion of Bartók's sixty-first birthday.

> I set the Mikrokosmos for strings as a birthday present for Bartók at a party in my apartment. It was after hearing them that he paid me one of his rare compliments: "If I were a king I would make you my court composer." Perhaps that is what Bartók might have had in mind—to later expand the Mikrokosmos for orchestra.[66]

BARTÓK'S *MIKROKOSMOS* PERFORMANCES

Mention is made above of Bartók's first performance of pieces from the *Mikrokosmos*. He played twenty-seven pieces, which were divided into two groups as follows: Nos. 70, 81, 90, 78, 100, 62, 87, 84, 110, 91, 92, 73, 129, 131, 116, 124, and 122 in the order listed (nine minutes and thirty-nine seconds of playing time) and, after the intermission, Nos. 133, 126, 140, 142, 143, 147, 144, 145, 137, and 146 (ten and a half minutes of playing time).[67]

The composer played excerpts from the work on 7 May 1937, according to a letter he wrote to Mrs. Müller-Widmann,[68] and on 20 January 1938, played three groups of pieces for a BBC broadcast in London. In the order listed, the pieces performed were Nos. 125, 88, 130, 138, 120, 109, and 139 (eight minutes and thirty seconds); 53, 106, 94, 108, 132, 103, 114, and 123 (eight minutes and fifteen seconds); and 148–153 (eight minutes and forty-eight seconds).[69]

On 17 February, Bartók played five pieces from the *Mikrokosmos* (Nos. 140, 142, 144, 137, and 146) at a concert in Zurich, and a similar recital was played in Brussels and Antwerp.[70] Nos. 94, 108, 132, 103, 114, 125, 130, 120, 109, 139, and 148–153 were played at the Boosey and Hawkes Organ Studio in June of the same year.[71]

The first American performance of *Mikrokosmos* pieces was given by Bartók on 16 April 1940, at Juniata College, Huntington, Pennsylvania. Played in two groups, the first one consisted of Nos. 116, 129, 131, 68, 126, 102, 113, and 115; and the second, Nos. 140, 142, 144, 137, 133, 138, 109, and 148–153.[72] Three days later, Bartók played from the work at the Musical Arts Club in Chicago and a week later at the Curtis Institute of Music in Philadelphia.[73]

Bartók sailed for Hungary on 18 May, to settle his affairs before establishing residence in the United States. His farewell concert in Budapest on 8 October included ten pieces from the *Mikrokosmos* (Nos. 141, 128, 126, 102, and 148–153).[74]

After his return to New York on 30 October 1940, he prepared for the concert season of 1940–1941 several programs that included pieces from the *Mikrokosmos*. Certain of his programs combined a lecture on "Contemporary Music and Piano Teaching" with a recital in which he played seventeen pieces from the work: Nos. 40–42, 52–53, 62, 68–69, 73, 78, 82, 84, 87, 94, and 90–92.[75] Some programs consisted of Nos. 122, 128, 126, 102, and 148–153[76] or Nos. 140, 142, 144, 137, and 136.[77] Other recitals combined those groups.[78] Bartók also played duo-piano recitals with his wife, including transcriptions from the *Mikrokosmos*.[79]

In 1938 Bartók recorded Nos. 124 and 126 for English Columbia and in 1941 Nos. 94, 97, 100, 108–109, 113–114, 116, 118, 120, 125–126, 128–131, 133, 136, 138–144, and 147–153 for Columbia (American) Records.[80]

Transcriptions of Nos. 69, 127, and 145 for two pianos were recorded by Bartók and his wife for Continental Records in 1943.[81]

NOTES

1. The first version of this study was published in *Journal of Research in Music Education* 7, no. 2 (1959): 185–96.

2. See the style analyses in *BBMP*, 124–60.

3. Denijs Dille, *Béla Bartók* (Antwerp: Standaard-Boekbandel, 1939), 89–91.

4. A photostat copy of the pamphlet is on file at *PBA*. The date listed for the *Mikrokosmos* is 1926–1937.

5. *PBA* MS File.

6. The file number of this manuscript in the *PBA* is 59PS1. There is no apparent relationship between the other incomplete sketches in manuscript No. 32 (Nine Little Piano Pieces) and the *Mikrokosmos* as finally constituted.

7. He completed Nine Little Piano Pieces on 31 October 1926, in Budapest, and they were published by Universal Edition A. G. (Vienna) in 1927.

8. From the Greek: *mikros kosmos* (little world).

9. Mátyás Seiber, personal letter dated 9 October 1954. A pupil of Kodály and friend of Bartók, Seiber had emigrated to Britain.

10. Peter Bartók, in his personal interview on 28 July 1954, reported that his father taught him popular pieces composed by Seiber: "We played foxtrots, rhumbas, and so forth, as duets in which my father improvised a bass part."

11. *BBE*, 427.

12. Peter Bartók, personal interview, 28 July 1954. On the back cover of the jacket to the BRS recording of *For Children* (#919) he further states: ". . .the ink hardly dried on some when I started practicing them."

13. A *NYBA* designation for Ozalid-processed reproductions made from transparent masters.

14. Dorothy Parrish Domonkos, personal interview, 17 April 1955.

15. Margit Varró, unpublished paper read at the Wisconsin Conservatory of Music, 29 September 1950. Another unpublished paper, "Contributions to Béla Bartók's Biography," was presented to the Midwest chapter of the American Musicological Society in March 1949 and contains a similar statement.

16. *PBA* Program File.

17. *PBA* Correspondence File, letter dated Budapest, 12 January 1937.

18. Ralph Hawkes, "Béla Bartók: A Recollection by His Publisher," *A Memorial Review* (New York: Boosey and Hawkes, 1950), 17.

19. *PBA* Correspondence File.

20. Letter dated 29 April 1938.

21. Letter dated 8 May 1938.

22. Letter dated 13 May 1938.

23. Later changed to 3 P.M.

24. The document is undated and unsigned. The wording of the memorandum suggests that it was perhaps written by Ralph Hawkes. The reader will note that the *Mikrokosmos* is here referred to as "studies."

25. The italics are my insertion to indicate that the three words were not part of the original sentence but later added to it. Thus it seems reasonable to conclude that the *Mikrokosmos* in its present published form as a piano method was not Bartók's original

conception when he composed certain of its pieces.

26. Letter dated 6 April 1939.

27. Letter dated 17 April 1939.

28. Ibid.

29. Letter dated 25 April 1939.

30. Letter dated 3 May 1939.

31. Letter dated 13 June 1939.

32. Bartók also suggested that not all pieces should have sketches and that the illustrations should be in the first volume for the most part.

33. Letter dated 29 June 1939.

34. Letter dated 8 July 1939.

35. Letter dated 14 July 1939.

36. Letter dated 19 July 1939.

37. Letter dated 23 July 1939.

38. The manuscript was separated into two parts by the composer and mailed on the eleventh (Nos. 1–121) and fourteenth (Nos. 122–153, the exercises, and the preface and remarks) of November, according to his letter dated 13 November 1939.

39. Letter dated 18 December 1939.

40. Ibid. The words do not appear in the first edition of the publication.

41. Letter dated 20 December 1939.

42. Letter dated 2 January 1940.

43. Letter dated 7 January 1940.

44. Letter dated 15 January 1940.

45. Letter dated 19 January 1940.

46. Letter dated 21 January 1940.

47. Letter dated 2 February 1940.

48. Ibid. He was correcting the proofs to these volumes at the time. In the published copies of the *Mikrokosmos*, the explanatory notes appear on the last page of vols. I, II, and IV, and after the respective pieces in vols. III, V, and VI.

49. Ibid.

50. Letter dated 5 February 1940 and addressed to Roth.

51. Letter dated 15 February 1940.

52. The errors I discovered in the 1940 edition are listed in my essay "Errata in the *Mikrokosmos* Publication," *Piano Quarterly Newsletter* 16, (Summer 1956): 11, 24.

Corrections were made in the Winthrop Rogers Edition (n.d.) of the work, followed by Stuart Thyne's "Bartók's *Mikrokosmos*: A Reexamination"—consisting of detailed lists of "A. Self-evident Errors, B. Probable Errors, and C. Possible Errors,"—in *Piano Quarterly Newsletter* 27, no. 107 (1979): 43–46. The third printing of the *Mikrokosmos* is the "New Definitive Edition 1987," in which certain of Thyne's corrections are included. One of the unauthorized editorial revisions occurs in No. 144 ("Minor Seconds, Major Seconds") and is emended in *BBMP*, 172, n. 4.

53. Letter from Roth to Hawkes 23 April 1940.

54. Thus the manuscript consists of first and second intermediary drafts and is filed as archive code number 59PID1ID2 (the drafts cannot be separated without damage).

55. Exceptions are certain English and all French titles.

56. Tissue proofs of some pieces were given by Bartók to his pupils, Dorothy Parrish Domonkos and Wilhelmine Creel Driver.

57. Nos. 1–10, 13–16, 26–29, 38–39.

58. It will be noted that thirty-three pages of tissue proofs are missing from this manuscript. At the present time, their whereabouts are unknown.

59. I have been unable to determine whether Bartók corrected the other published volumes.

60. In the preparation of the final copy of Seven Pieces from *Mikrokosmos* (for piano duet), Bartók found errors in No. 145b which he had overlooked when proofreading 59PFC2 (he cut and pasted together the published versions of 145a and 145b as piece No. 6).

61. According to information contained in correspondence between Ernst Roth and Ralph Hawkes in February, March, and April 1940.

62. The notes are not in Bartók's handwriting.

63. In 1941. Published by Boosey and Hawkes under the title Five Pieces from *Mikrokosmos* and recorded on BRS 901.

64. In 1942. Unpublished.

65. In 1943. Published by Boosey and Hawkes under the title *Mikrokosmos* Suite and recorded on BRS 303.

66. Tibor Serly, in a personal interview, 21 December 1954. Unknown to Serly, Bartók had planned to score some of the *Mikrokosmos* pieces, such as the Six Bulgarian Dances (Nos. 141–153).

67. *PBA* Program File. The pieces are listed by title on the program, and the timings were noted by Bartók in pencil.

68. *Béla Bartók levelei*, ed. János Demény (Budapest: Művelt Nép Könyvkiadó, 1951), 123.

69. *PBA* Program File.

70. Ibid. (From a penciled notation in Bartók's handwriting. The dates are not listed.)

71. Letter dated 13 May 1938.

72. *PBA* Program File.

73. Ibid. (From a notation made by Bartók on scratch paper. The titles of the pieces are not listed.)

74. Ibid.

75. Given at Oberlin Conservatory, Mills College, University of Washington, and the University of Kansas City. The Mills College program also included Nos. 140, 142, 144, 137, and 146.

76. At the New Jersey College for Women, Swarthmore College, and Vassar College.

77. At the Detroit Institute of Arts, Stanford University, Wells College, and the University of Oregon. Nos. 148–153 were also played at Stanford, Wells, and Oregon.

78. At Oberlin Conservatory, Princeton and Brigham Young Universities, University of Washington, Reed College, and the Wilshire Theater in Los Angeles.

79. Nos. 69, 135, 127, and 145 were given their first American performance at Town Hall (New York City) on 24 November 1940. Nos. 123 and 146 were played at Amherst College on 23 February 1942.

80. Titles and numbers appear on the American Columbia (ML 4419) recording. The jacket lists thirty-five titles, but Nos. 122, 72, and 146 are not performed on the record.

81. Continental 4008 or Remington R19994.

6

Sixth String Quartet: Structure and Concept[1]

The melancholy thirteen-bar prefatory Mesto (Mournful) theme of the Sixth Quartet, that introduces the first three movements and is developed as the fourth movement of the work, has received much attention by Bartók scholars. Such terms as "motto theme," "idée fixe," "signature theme," and "ritornello" (recurrent prelude) have been used to describe the theme, indicating that the work heralds Bartók's direction away from arch form—the structural method of his two preceding quartets—and towards cyclic form as a means of achieving overall unity. The sketches of the work, however, and the documents relating to it, indicate that the development of the Mesto theme as the fourth movement was not part of the original plan. In fact, the work as first conceived consisted of four movements, each prefaced with the Mesto theme, with the last movement a fusion of Romanian dance music and Bulgarian *aksak* (limping) rhythmic schemata. The abandonment of this concept was a structural modification based on new expressive needs which arose after completion of the sketch draft.

BACKGROUND OF THE FOURTH MOVEMENT

At the end of July 1939 Bartók arrived in Switzerland to compose a new work for the Basel Chamber Orchestra. He completed the Divertimento for String Orchestra on 17 August and, a day or two later, began work on another commission, the String Quartet No. 6, for the New Hungarian String Quartet. The manuscripts indicate that his original intention apparently was a four-movement quartet, introspective in character, which would reflect the preparations for war that threatened to engulf western and eastern Europe but would close with a folk-styled dance movement to represent his longing for a peaceful solution among the contentious nations. Later that month, however, when the nonaggression pact between National Socialist Germany and the Soviet Union was signed, Bartók realized that his world was coming to an end. Thus, when he returned to Budapest and began making preparations to leave Hungary, he discarded the unfinished dance piece and replaced it with a brief, poignant "farewell" of infinite sadness.

The subsequently discarded dance piece, intended as the fourth movement and preceded by the first half of the Mesto theme (bars 1–45 in the printed score), has features which are in near relation to Romanian instrumental melodies and

Bulgarian *aksak* rhythmic schemata. The first theme, preceded by a short introduction, is based on Romanian-styled bagpipe motifs, usually played on a violin or peasant flute, and is somewhat similar to the motifs in the fifth movement of the Concerto for Orchestra (Ex. 6.1).

Ex. 6.1. Bartók, Sixth Quartet, discarded sketch of the fourth movement, introduction and first theme, bars 1–5. The suggested time signature is an editorial addition, since the Class *B* bagpipe motifs in *RFM.*i are mostly transcribed as sixteenths in 2/4 time, ♩ = ca. 160.

The contrasting second theme begins with twin-bar motifs in so-called Bulgarian rhythm that alternate with syncopated motifs in compound triple meter (Ex. 6.2). The sketch ends with several motifs in 6/8 and 2/4 time, as eighth- and sixteenth-note values, respectively.

Ex. 6.2. Sixth Quartet, discarded sketch of the fourth movement, second theme motifs.

Turning to the first movement of the printed score, the second theme provides the atmosphere of Hungarian folk music by the use of so-called dotted rhythm. This rhythmic peculiarity is a prominent feature of "old" and "new" styles of Hungarian folk music.[2] A typical schema is represented by short values, ♫ ♫. and ♫. ♫, or by their "flattened" (augmented values) form, ♩ ♪ ♪ ♩ and ♪ ♩ ♩ ♪.

The latter type appears in the first half of the second theme as cellular and noncellular motifs. The second half consists of a scalar formation in which a minor tetrachord is linked with a Y-cell (Ex. 6.3).

Ex. 6.3. Bartók, Sixth Quartet, first movement, R.N. 81. The Y-cells are tetrachords of complementary whole-tone scales.[3]

In the episodic material that follows, the upper and lower strings are engaged in an unusual, two-part imitative counterpoint, where X-cells and Z-cells are juxtaposed as well as articulated in a twelve-tone environment (Ex. 6.4). It is indeed worthy of note that Bartók's original concept was the articulation of the X-cells with four whole-tone tetrachords structured as arpeggiated French sixth chords, C-E-F♯-B♭, C♯-F-G-B, D-F♯-G♯-C, and E♭-G-A-C♯ (bars 127–130).

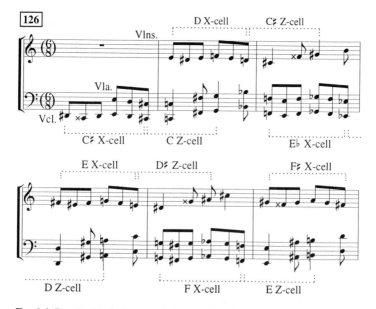

Ex. 6.4. Bartók, Sixth Quartet, first movement, R.N. 126.

The second movement, Marcia, is only the second example of that genre, the first being the March from *Mikrokosmos*, apparently composed in 1933 and first performed by Bartók four years later at Cowdray Hall, London.[4] He referred to the piece as "a march of primitive peoples" (Ex. 6.5).[5]

Ex. 6.5. Bartók, *Mikrokosmos* for piano (1926–1939), melody No. 147, bars 39–41.

The tonal representation of "primitive peoples" seems to be the juxtaposition of complementary whole-tone scale motifs in contrary motion. The upper staff shows emphatic rendition of the E whole-tone scale, E-D-C-Bb-Ab-F♯, and the lower staff reflects the complementary whole-tone scale, Eb-F-G-A-B-C♯. The combined pitch collections thus constitute a twelve-tone polytonal—not poly-modal!—tonality. The rhythmic schemata are related to those of the Rákóczi March, a nineteenth-century Hungarian instrumental piece in *verbunkos* (re-cruiting dance) style.[6] The use of cluster chords, cellular constructions, Roma-nian "shifted" rhythm, and the basic E-Phrygian/Lydian polymode contribute to the grotesque effect of the March.[7]

On 24 September 1938, Bartók completed *Contrasts* for violin, clarinet, and piano, whose first movement, Verbunkos, also features complementary whole-tone scales (Ex. 6.6).

Ex. 6.6. Bartók, *Contrasts* for violin, clarinet, and piano (1938), first movement, bars 1–2. The ascending Eb whole-tone scale is bracketed, and the descending tetrachordal par-titions of the complementary whole-tone scales appear in the lower staff.

Ex. 6.7 shows the *verbunkos*-styled first theme of the Marcia. Bartók alluded to the theme as an example of melodic chromaticism deliberately developed to a degree beyond that of any other contemporary music.[8] Analysis of the pitch collection discloses that it is an eleven-tone, B-Lydian/Phrygian polymode, B-C♮-D-E F♯-G-A/B-C♯-D♯-E♯-F♯-[ ]-A♯. It should be noted that the sketch draft indicates that the Marcia immediately follows the end of the first movement: the Mesto theme was a later insertion.

Ex. 6.7. Bartók, Sixth String Quartet, second movement, first theme, bars 1–4.

A most unusual variant of the theme occurs in bars 37–39, where octatonic scales appear in stretto and inversional counterpoint. The violins ascend in minor sevenths while the viola and cello descend at the same intervallic distance (Ex. 6.8).

Ex. 6. 8. Ibid., bars 38–39.

The third movement is "a grotesque, sardonic Burletta ('Burlesque'), which brings forth a whole arsenal of technical devices from Bartók's storehouse."[9] One of these unprecedented devices appears in bars 26–30, where the first and second violins alternate the playing of several degrees while the other instrument simultaneously plays them as flatted quarter tones. Another instance of Bartók's state of mind is the highly dissonant Lydian cadence, F-A-B-C, that ends the movement. As he wrote to his elder son, Béla Jr., on 18 August, from the Chalet Aellen in Saanen:

> The poor, peaceful, honest Swiss are being compelled to burn with war-fever. Their newspapers are full of military articles, they have taken defense measures

on the more important passes etc.—military preparedness. I saw this for myself on the Julier Pass; for example, boulders have been made into roadblocks against tanks, and such little attractions. It's the same in Holland—even in Scheveningen.— I do not like your going to Rumania—in such uncertain times it is unwise to go anywhere so unsafe. I am also worried about whether I shall be able to get home from here if this or that happens.[10]

Notes

1. This study is a revised version of my essay in *Tempo* 83 (Winter 1967–1968): 2–11.

2. *HFS*, 29–30. See *RFM*.v, where melodies No. 129–131 show the influence of both forms of Hungarian dotted-rhythm schemata.

3. See the discussion of cellular constructions in *MBB*, 69–72.

4. John Vinton, "Toward a Chronology of the *Mikrokosmos*," *Studia Musicologica* 8 (1966): 56.

5. *BM*, 155.

6. Ibid. See Bence Szabolcsi, *A Concise History of Hungarian Music* (Budapest: Corvina Press, 1964), 54–59.

7. *BM*, 155.

8. *BBE*, 380.

9. *BBLM*, 201.

10. János Kárpáti, *Bartók's String Quartets* (Budapest: Corvina Press, 1975), 244.

7

Genesis and Development of the Concerto for Orchestra

The first performance of Bartók's Concerto for Orchestra was given at the afternoon program of the Boston Symphony Orchestra, Serge Koussevitzky conducting, on 1 December 1944. In a perceptive review of the Concerto, the music critic reported that "I have more than a suspicion that it is highly personal, even autobiographical music. Yes, if a composition of transcendental musical art may be defined as one which, in its own way, is a summation of all that has gone before, then the Orchestra Concerto is a work of art, and a great one."[1]

Interpretation of the phrase "summation of all that has gone before" seems especially appropriate as an introduction to the background of Bartók's masterpiece, beginning with his own testimony at a Paris interview in March 1939:

> Debussy's great service to music was to reawaken among all musicians an awareness of harmony and its possibilities. In that, he was just as important as Beethoven, who revealed to us the meaning of progressive form, and as Bach, who showed us the transcendent significance of counterpoint. Now, what I am always asking myself is this: is it possible to make a synthesis of these three great masters, a living synthesis that will be valid for our own time?[2]

Another Bartók summation occurred during his second lecture at Harvard University in February 1943:

> The start for the creation of my "New" Hungarian art music was given, first of all, by a thorough knowledge of the devices of old and contemporary Western art music: for the technique of composition; and, second, by the newly-discovered rural music—material of incomparable beauty and perfection—for the spirit of our works to be created. Scores of aspects could be distinguished and quoted in regard to the influence exerted on us by this material: for instance, tonality, melody, rhythm, and even structural influence.[3]

As a footnote to Bartók's mention of folk-music influence, in a review of the Concerto performance in Liverpool on 27 October 1945, the critic stated that: "Whether we need, in order to understand the music completely, a knowledge of the background of that essentially Hungarian folk style, in which Bartók delved so unremittingly, and which is not a bit like rhapsodies of Liszt, is another matter."[4] In that regard, the meaning of "essentially Hungarian folk style" was clarified in Bartók's last essay, "Hungarian Music," where the term "New" Hungarian art music is replaced by "contemporary higher art music in Hungary." Bartók continues:

> Kodály studies, and uses as source, Hungarian rural music almost exclusively, whereas I extended my interest and love also to the folk music of the neighboring Eastern European peoples and ventured even into Arabic and Turkish territories for research work. In my works, therefore, appear impressions derived from the most varied sources melted—as I hope—into unity. These varied sources, however, have a common denominator, that is, the characteristics common to rural folk music in its purest sense.[5]

POLITICAL EVENTS IN HUNGARY: 1934–1940

In 1934, Bartók was granted a leave of absence from his teaching duties at the Academy of Music and transferred to the Academy of Sciences where he served as head of the newly organized publication subcommittee of the folk-music section. He began the systematization of Hungarian folk-music materials and, for comparative purposes, supervised the copying of folk-song publications of neighboring peoples.[6] Although the burdensome task of classroom piano teaching had been exchanged for scholarly research in comparative musical folklore, his newly acquired equilibrium was disturbed by political events during the following years, when the main objective of Hungarian foreign policy was revision of the 1920 Versailles Peace Treaty. The government's aspirations were strengthened when Britain's policy of appeasement was implemented by Prime Minister Neville Chamberlain's attempts to secure peace with Germany and Italy, at the expense of considerable concessions. Concluding that the Western Powers would not oppose cooperation with Germany, a pro-German Hungarian policy was initiated that not only led to a Nazi-type Arrow-Cross movement but to participation in Hitler's scheme of aggression aimed at the dismemberment of Czechoslovakia.

These events prompted the New Hungarian String Quartet to reorganize in 1937 and take up residence in Holland. The violist, Dénes Koromzay, recalled that:

> We were all unmarried and free, and moving to Holland wasn't too bad an idea, since the political winds were not exactly blowing our way in Hungary. In fact, the quartet was very badly located if we wanted to play concerts, because Germany was completely out of the question with its Nazi regime, and Naziism was spreading in Hungary too. Later, Bartók certainly had to leave Hungary. He was a most direct and outspoken man, and he made such strong anti-Nazi statements that he would have been among the first to be picked up by the Gestapo when the Hungarian Nazis eventually came into power.[7]

When in 1933 Boosey & Hawkes (London) became agents for Universal Edition, the association provided the publisher, Ralph Hawkes, with a direct connection with Bartók's music as well as information concerning the composer's refusal to allow his music to be broadcast in Germany:

> As soon as the *Anschluss* with Austria was proclaimed, I realized that both Bartók and Kodály were, so to speak, marooned in Budapest. Their works were published largely by Universal Edition, and as this house was obviously going to be "put in order" by Hitler's propaganda minister, these great composers, Aryan though they were, in view of their liberal and free attitude, would be in difficulty. A few days after the sensational news of the occupation of Vienna, I phoned Kodály in Budapest and said that I would immediately fly there to talk with him and Bartók. I arrived the next evening and met them both. There certainly was no reticence on Bartók's part in agreeing to publish all his future works with us. We talked about future plans and other forthcoming works far into the night. Thus, the foundation of Bartók's association [with Boosey & Hawkes] was laid."[8]

One of Bartók's plans related to the safe shipment of his compositions. On 13 April 1938, therefore, his letter to a Swiss correspondent requested that she give shelter to his manuscripts which he would bring to her at some future time. But the main thrust of the letter concerned his thoughts about emigration, in view of:

> the imminent danger that Hungary will surrender to this regime of thieves and murderers. The only question is—when and how? And how can I go on living in such a country or—which means the same thing—working, I simply cannot conceive. As a matter of fact, I would feel it my duty to emigrate, so long as that were possible. And I have my mother here: shall I abandon her altogether in her last years?—No, I cannot do that! So much for Hungary, where, unfortunately, nearly all of our "educated" Christians are adherents of the Nazi regime; I feel quite ashamed of coming from this class.[9]

Later that year, Bartók was advised that the Library of Congress had proposed a Bartók-Szigeti concert in April 1940, at the Elizabeth Sprague-Coolidge Festival in Washington. Of more immediate concern was the precarious economic situation, which apparently motivated Bartók and his wife to play two-piano concerts in Italy during the first two weeks in December. On the sixteenth, Bartók's mother died; illness prevented him from attending her funeral.

In addition to the Washington appearance, other concerts were scheduled for Bartók as pianist and lecturer by the New York office of Boosey & Hawkes. Thus, on 22 April 1940 he was at Harvard University for a lecture on "Some Problems of Folk Music Research in East Europe," in which he stated that:

> Eight or ten years ago, if we wanted to examine the Serbo-Croatian material, we found ourselves up against a few obstacles. The available material consisted of

about 4,000 tunes, for the most part in prewar transcriptions made by ear, without the aid of an Edison phonograph or gramophone. Subtleties of execution and grace-notes can scarcely be studied at all, since they are lacking in these rather amateur-ish transcriptions; but at least types and classes can be established.[10]

Among the attendees was Albert B. Lord, a Junior Fellow at Harvard, who informed Bartók that Yugoslav folk-music recordings were on hand at the university; a description of the collection, assembled from 1933 to 1935, would be mailed to Bartók; and that he should meet with other scholars interested in the musicological aspects of the collection, in New York.[11]

It is noteworthy that earlier in April, Columbia University voted to confer the honorary degree of Doctor of Music for Bartók's "distinguished service to the art of music." Bartók's concert appearances ended at the University's McMillan Theater on 1 May, with a gala performance of his works—an event that provided the opportunity for discussions about a future position at the University. The music department then initiated a request for a research scholarship beginning in the fall for Bartók to examine Harvard's collection of Yugoslav folk music recordings, with the expectation that the material would throw new light on Homeric problems. Also at this time, Boosey and Hawkes concert management was arranging for another, more extensive tour of the United States by Bartók during the 1940–1941 season.

Following his return to Budapest, Bartók and his wife began preparations to take up residence in New York. He was completely beside himself due to the red tape he met in his attempts to expedite departure from Hungary. The obstacles he encountered began with permission of the Hungarian War Minister to leave Hungary before passports could be issued, followed by filing of visa applications with, in turn, the American, Portuguese, Spanish, French, Swiss, and Italian consulates. Since it was necessary for Bartók to purchase the boat tickets in advance of procuring the necessary visas, the unavoidable delays that ensued reached the point where it was uncertain whether the journey could be undertaken.

THE EXILE IN AMERICA: 1940–1945

Although Bartók and his wife Ditta eventually arrived in New York on 30 October, their baggage, including his folk-music collections, had been left behind in Lisbon. Fortunately, the six large trunks landed at the port later on.[12] Thereafter, in 1941, the first link can be traced in the chain of events that was directly related to the composition of the Concerto for Orchestra. While Bartók was working at Columbia University, his colleague, Professor George Herzog, provided him with commercial recordings of Dalmatian two-part chromatic folk melodies. As he later remarked, during his 1943 lectures at Harvard University, he was impressed by the "unity, higher development and unusual effect on listeners" of the pieces.[13] The replication of this Dalmatian folk-music style in the second movement of the Concerto was the outcome of his transcription and study of these recordings.

A second important event was a letter from his London publisher, Ralph Hawkes, in April 1942:

> I believe that you would be interested in composing a series of concertos for solo instrument or instruments and string orchestra. By this I mean piano and string orchestra, solo violin and string orchestra, flute and string orchestra, etc., or combinations of solo instruments and string orchestra. I have in mind the Brandenburg Concertos by Bach, and I believe you are well fitted to do something on these lines.[14]

At that time, however, Bartók was completely involved with the Yugoslav materials, including a highly technical introductory study, for publication by the Columbia University Press. Moreover, as he replied to Hawkes on 3 August:

> I am ill since the beginning of April. And the doctors cannot find the cause, in spite of very thorough examinations. Fortunately, I can continue my work at Columbia University. I only wonder how long this can go on in this way. And whether it is perhaps a general breakdown? Heaven knows. Just before my illness I began some composition work, and just the kind you suggested in your letter. But then, of course, I had to discontinue it because of lack of energy, tranquillity and mood—I don't know if I ever will be in the position to do some new works.[15]

The overall structural concept and title of the Concerto, especially the plan of its second movement, indicate the extent to which Bartók was motivated by his publisher's ideas. The third occurrence was the broadcast of the NBC Symphony Orchestra on 19 July, when Arturo Toscanini conducted the Shostakovich *Leningrad* Symphony No. 7. According to Bartók's son, Peter,

> During the first part of the work which I believe was supposed to signify the advance of the German army, my father became aware of numerous repetitions of a theme which sounded like a Viennese cabaret song. My father was surprised to hear such a theme used for such a purpose in such great abundance.[16]

A variant of the same tune appears as the *interrotto* theme in the fourth movement of the Concerto. According to the Hungarian conductor Antal Dorati, Bartók showed him the music soon after its completion and said:

> The big, overblown *Leningrad* Symphony of Shostakovich is no good. While I was doing my piece, suddenly I thought of the *Leningrad*. It made me very angry. I put that anger into the Concerto—and then laughed at the Russian work.[16]

The next circumstance was concurrent with Bartók's preparation of his Yugoslav material for publication, when he worked on his monumental collection of Romanian folk music in the hope that the New York Public Library would serve as the publisher. In the first volume of instrumental melodies, which includes a chapter on folk dance and its choreography, one of his conclusions concerns bagpipe dance tunes. These melodies, seemingly of indeterminate structure, are actually composed of shorter or longer motifs strung together in a way recognizable by the dancers. The motifs and their imitations on violin and peasant flute were extracted, classified, and tabulated by Bartók as an appendix to his study. An outcome of this work was his idealization of bagpipe motifs as the thematic basis of the Concerto's Finale.

After he completed the second volume of Romanian folk music in December 1942, Bartók began to prepare a series of lectures to be given at Harvard. In March, however, following the third lecture, he had a sudden breakdown which was aggravated by the Public Library's rejection of his Romanian material because of the high cost of publication. He was deeply troubled by the apparent failure of his doctors to diagnose his illness, and he was unaware that he had incurable leukemia. Although he was convinced there was no hope of recovery, he found the strength to work on his collection of Turkish folk music, for he had the impression that the Public Library might accept a smaller, less-complicated publication project. Then, in May 1943, while Bartók was still hospitalized, Serge Koussevitzky, conductor of the Boston Symphony Orchestra, called on Bartók and offered a grant of $1,000 to write an orchestral composition. On the thirteenth, Ditta Bartók's letter reports that:

> plans, musical ambitions, compositions are stirring in Béla's mind—a new hope, discovered in this way quite by chance, as if it were incidentally. One thing is sure: Béla's 'under no circumstances will I ever write any new work' attitude is gone. It has been more than *three* years now.[19]

And so the last and most important link in the chain of events was forged. A special grant from the American Society of Composers, Authors, and Publishers enabled Bartók to convalesce during the summer in a small cottage at Saranac Lake, New York. He brought his Turkish field sketchbook for reference purposes in the preparation of the fair-copy draft of his book on Turkish folk music from Asia Minor. On 20 July, Ralph Hawkes wrote to Bartók, asking whether any new compositions were under way. The 31 July response included a long description of the illness and the various medical diagnoses:

> I feel better when I have periods of lower fever. But, on the whole there is no perceptible change! Now about the doctors . . . they are groping about in the darkness.[20]

On 15 August, Bartók turned to composition of the Concerto, using the Turkish field sketchbook for the purpose, and apparently began with the third movement, Elegia. The work was completed two months later.

The Concerto and Its Diverse Sources

In 1944, Bartók prepared his analytic essay, "Explanation to Concerto for Orchestra" as the program note for the Boston Symphony premiere of the work at Boston's Symphony Hall on 1 December. The previously mentioned Bartók quest for synthesis of Bach's counterpoint, Beethoven's progressive form, and Debussy's innovative harmony is implied in the program note. The following extracts may be construed as illustrative examples, beginning with the question of counterpoint: the "virtuoso" treatment in the *fugato* sections of the development of the first movement, played by the brass instruments, and the fugue in the development of the fifth movement.

In regard to structure: the first and fifth movements are written in a more or less sonata form. The less traditional form of the second movement consists of a chain of independent sections which could be symbolized by the letters ABCDE. This is followed by a kind of "trio"—a short chorale for brass instruments and side drum—after which the five sections are recapitulated. And the form of the fourth movement—"Intermezzo interrotto"— could be rendered by the letter symbols ABA—interruption—BA.

As for Debussy: The structure of the third movement likewise is chain-like; three themes appear successively. These constitute the core of the movement, which is enframed by a misty texture of rudimentary motives. In another analysis of the movement, bars 10 to 18 are described as follows:

> A mysterious sonority appears, trembling in the strings, arpeggiated by clarinet and flute alternately, and played by the harp alternately glissando and as a chord. As it persists without change, forming the background for a slow chromatic melody in the oboe, this sonority tends to become acceptable as mere atmosphere—an outdoor atmosphere, surely—and to lull any efforts to reduce it to familiar chords or scales. At such a moment we may see Bartók as the worthy heir of Debussy.[21]

Ex. 7.1, the second Dirge from Bartók's Four Dirges op. 9a for Piano, illustrates the first, pentatonic antecedent of the Concerto's Introduzione first theme. The pentatonic base of the Dirge, C♯-E-F♯-G♯-B, is extended to a minor hexachord—that is, neither Aeolian nor Dorian, by the addition of the second degree, D♯. In 1931, Bartók arranged the piece as the third movement in his Hungarian Sketches for Orchestra.

The Prologue theme from *Duke Bluebeard's Castle*, composed in 1911 (Ex. 7.2), is constructed of the symmetrical pentatonic scale, F♯-A-B-C♯-E. This type of pentatonicism, a characteristic of old Hungarian folk song, was discovered by Bartók in 1907 during his fieldwork in Transylvanian-Hungarian villages.

The *Introduzione* (Ex. 7.3) has the same configuration, but the repetition of the theme is extended (bar 14) to an Aeolian hexachord by the addition of D.

Ex. 7.1. Bartók, second Dirge, bars 1–7.

Ex. 7.2. Bartók, *Duke Bluebeard's Castle*, op. 11, bars 1–17.

Ex. 7.3. Bartók, Concerto for Orchestra, Introduzione, bars 1–16.

In February 1943, during his second lecture at Harvard University, Bartók discussed the tonal influences of folk-music material on his works:

> We found the five most common modes of the Middle Ages, and besides these, some others absolutely unknown from modal music. None [of the latter] can be expressed as octave segments of the diatonic scale."[22]

He notated two nondiatonic pitch collections whose construction incorporates partition of discrete octatonic scales. In other words, as a pentachord of alternating whole and half steps, G-A-Bb-Cb-Db, and a hexachord of alternating half and whole steps, G-Ab-Bb-Cb-Db-Eb, respectively.

A pentachordal type of octatonic construction, transposed to F as principal tone, appears in melody No. 631, a funeral song, in the second volume of Bartók's Romanian folk music publication. In the first movement of the Concerto, the same pentachordal pitch collection, F-G-Ab-Bb-Bᵗ, occurs as motif 1a of the first theme (Ex. 7.4).

Ex. 7.4. (a) *RFM*.ii, melody No. 631, bars 1–2, and (b) Concerto for Orchestra, first movement, R.N. 76.

Three of the five dances in the second movement have structural relationships with Serbo-Croatian folk music. The theme of the first dance, played by two bassoons, and its apparent source of inspiration may have been the kind of rhythm patterns and four-bar phrasing of a Serbian *kolo* (national round dance) shown in the violin piece Bartók recorded during 1912 in southern Hungary (Ex. 7.5).

Ex. 7.5. (a) *YFM*.i, p. 457, melody No. 4, bars 1–4, and (b) Concerto for Orchestra, second movement, theme 1, bars 1–4.

The influence of Dalmatian accompanied folk song on Bartók's thematic invention is apparent in the second movement. He transcribed a commercially recorded Dalmatian part song, performed by two voices in major seconds, that is preceded by an instrumental prelude played by two *sopels*.

> In Dalmatia, besides the "normal" part singing, there is an extremely peculiar kind of "two-part" singing—in major seconds. . . . Listening to those records, one may hear the major seconds sometimes "degenerate" into minor thirds. . . . In the instrumental preludes, for technical reasons the melody played by two sopels (a kind of oboe) is inverted to minor sevenths instead of major seconds. These minor sevenths are never changed into any other interval.[23]

The clarinets emulate the traditional *sopel* duet of parallel minor sevenths (Ex. 7.6), and the trumpets, performing their melody in major seconds, take on the role of Dalmatian folk singers (Ex. 7.7).

Ex. 7.6. (a) *YFM*.i, p. 63, bars 1–3, and (b) Concerto for Orchestra, second movement, theme 3, R.N. 45.

Ex. 7.7. (a) *YFM*.i, p. 63, bars 1–4, and (b) Concerto for Orchestra, second movement, theme 5, R.N. 90..

The repetition of the five dances is interrupted by a short chorale for brass choir, thus providing the movement with a large ternary structure. If Bartók intended this chorale trio as a programmatic insertion, then perhaps it can be related to a religious feature of village life that Bartók encountered during his fieldwork in Transylvanian-Romanian villages. According to his observations, there was a recurring order of dances during Sunday recreations, that differed in number, genre, and choreography.[24]

The elegiac third movement was played during the recessional of his Budapest funeral.[25] While the somber themes are of course suitable for that kind of ceremonial purpose, the additional material "a misty texture of rudimentary motives"—suggests a different mood, namely, Bartók's so-called night music. Apparently the first appearance of this impressionist genre occurs in Musiques Nocturnes, the fourth movement of *Out of Doors* for piano, composed by Bartók in 1926. According to Bartók's elder son, Béla Bartók Jr., "The Night's

Music perpetuates the concert of the frogs heard in peaceful nights on the Hungarian Great Plain" during Bartók's visits to his sister's home in Békés County.[26] Aside from the rudimentary motives found in the full score, and whether they reflect a concert of frogs, crickets, or bird calls, the core theme has structural attributes found in Bartók's collection of Hungarian, Romanian, and Slovak folk songs, especially those with four melody sections and AABC form. But only nondiatonic funeral songs in the Romanian corpus have a certain similarity to the chromaticism in Bartók's melody. As a case in point, Ex. 7.8 shows certain characteristics in common between the rubato core theme and a Transylvanian-Romanian funeral song sung by a young peasant woman in November 1917. Both melodies consist of essentially isorhythmic sections, that is, with a rhythmic schema of equal eighth notes as well as of nondiatonic pitch collections. The folk song is based on an octatonic pentachord, Fb-G-Ab-Bb-Cb, and the core theme is built of chromatic scale segments.

Ex. 7.8. (a) Concerto for Orchestra, third movement, core theme, R.N. 62, and (b) *RFM*.ii, melody No. 628a.

In the opening and closing sections of the third movement—bars 10–18 and 99–111, respectively—arpeggiated configurations are played by the flute, clarinet, and harp. The similarity between these configurations and those in Bartók's opera, *Duke Bluebeard's Castle*, op. 11, is shown in Ex. 7.9. The operatic excerpt is from the section when the sixth door has been unlocked and opened by Judith, Bluebeard's wife, and she sees a Lake of Tears whose mute and lifeless waters were brought by sorrowful weeping.

In the first draft of Bartók's explanation to the fourth movement, he struck out the first three words, "The only programmatic," and confined his remarks to the formal structure. Perhaps he felt that his "Intermezzo interrotto" title—an Italian construction meaning "interrupted interlude"— was self-explanatory, in view of the parodic third theme. Ex. 7.10 shows the first theme, in B major,

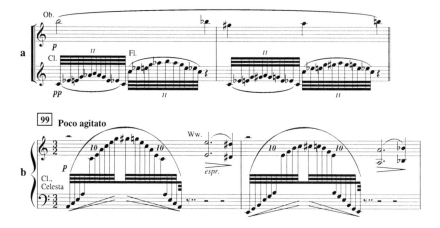

Ex. 7.9. (a) Concerto for Orchestra, third movement, bars 12–13, and (b) *Duke Bluebeard's Castle*, R.N. 99.

with which the movement ends, and its source melodies. Although the rhythm pattern is Bartók's invention, generated by the alternation of 2/4 and 5/8 time, it is related to the 7/8 schema of the Slovak folk melody that apparently stems from the widespread Hungarian popular art song "Szeretnék szántani" (I should love to plough), whose melody has been traced back to 1834 (Ex. 7.10).[27]

Ex. 7.10. (a) Concerto for Orchestra, fourth movement, first theme, bars 3–7, (b) Kerényi, *Népies dalok* (Popular songs), p. 25, bars 1–4, and (c) *SV.*i, melody No. 84b.

It is noteworthy that the theme not only begins with E, the fourth degree of the scale, but that the same tone is sustained in the accompaniment. The continuous repetition of the tetrachord, E-F♯-A♯-B, implies the E-Lydian mode, because of the emphatic rendition of the tritone E-A♯. The Lydian mode, a distinctive Slovak characteristic, is not found in Bartók's Hungarian material.

The second theme, on the other hand, is based on a Hungarian art song, composed in 1926 by Zsigmond Vincze for his operetta, *A hamburgi menyasszony* (The Hamburg Bride). The sentimental text begins with: "Hungary, how beautiful, most beautiful you are." It has been suggested that the theme represents an idealization of the operetta melody by the self-exiled composer, on account of the text.[28] It seems likely, moreover, that Bartók was aware of a variant relationship between the operetta melody and his own transcription of a Hungarian folk song.[29] A different interpretation, suggested to me by an attorney of the Hungarian Performing Rights Society,[30] was the possibility of an underlying political allusion: the art song had been used as the musical slogan of a Hungarian irredentist movement, to rally support for the return of Transylvania to Hungary. Subjective opinions aside, Bartók's theme represents the transformation of an art song in *Magyar nóta* style, that is, with characteristics of Hungarian national melodies. As a case in point, Ex. 7.11 shows the harmonization of the operetta melody, where the commonplace progression is from A-melodic minor to the relative C-major tonality (bars 1–4). Bartók's transformations of the melody begin with Mixolydian modes (bars 42–46) and close with complementary octatonic partitions of the chromatic scale, G-A-B♭-C-D♭-E♭-F♭ (bars 46-47) and G-A♭-[ ]-B-D♭-D-E (bars 48–50). The harmonization consists of a chain of perfect fifths reminiscent of Debussyian harmony, together with a more or less similar type of chord progression that was commonplace in American popular tunes during the 1940s.

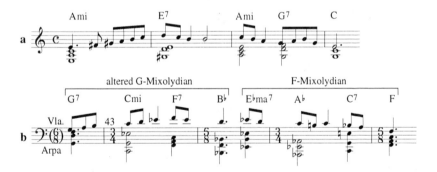

7.11. (a) Zsigmond Vincze, *A hamburgi menyasszony,* "Szép vagy, gyönyörű vagy," bars 29–32, and (b) Concerto for Orchestra, fourth movement, theme 2, bars 42–46.

Ex. 7.12 displays the third theme and its antecedents. The original source is Danilo's song "Maxim's" from the first act of Franz Léhar's operetta, *The Merry Widow.* Bartók, however, arrived at his parodic invention by way of the third theme in the first movement of the Shostakovich Symphony No. 7 (*Leningrad*). According to the Russian composer's program note, "this theme, which governs the middle passage of the movement, presents the spirit and essence of those harsh events when our peaceful and pleasant life was disrupted by the ominous force of war."

And then the corks go   pop, We dance and nev - er   stop,

7.12. (a) Concerto for Orchestra, fourth movement, theme 3, bars 79–83, (b) Shostakovich, Symphony No. 7, op. 60 (1941), first movement, and (c) Lehár, *The Merry Widow*,
No. 4 ("Maxim's").

In another, more detailed recollection, Peter Bartók stated that:

> In 1942, the Shostakovich Symphony was broadcast with great fuss about the
> event; the score came from Russia by microfilm, it was an important work, etc.
> My parents and I listened to the broadcast. During the part of the work which I
> believe was supposed to signify the advance of the German armies, my father
> became aware of numerous repetitions of a theme which sounded like a Viennese
> cabaret song. This part of the symphony was also referred to as the great cre-
> scendo. As the theme came again and again, we counted the repetitions, and
> the number of times it occurred was quite high, I believe several dozen. My
> father was quite surprised to hear such a theme used for such a purpose in
> such great abundance. It was only after my father's death that I first had a
> chance to hear the Concerto. I noticed this theme alternating with another
> very beautiful one. That the connecting bits represent laughter is only the
> product of my fantasy, as well as the assumption on my part that there should
> be any connection between our having heard the Shostakovich symphony
> during the war and the presence of the theme in the Concerto. Nevertheless,
> one thing is certain: my father was not quoting the symphony—he was quot-
> ing from a cabaret song.[31]

The parodic episode following the end of the theme includes shrieking
laughter in the woodwinds and strings, and trombone glissandos that sound
like the braying heehaws of a donkey. It is noteworthy from the theoretical-
analytical viewpoint that the glissandos consist of two tritones, B-F and E-B♭,
whose juxtaposition forms a Z-cell tetrachord (Ex. 7.13).

In the development section of the fifth movement, the art of the fugue is
merged with the spirit of the dance. While the fugue is a polyphonic form of
Western art music, the spirit of the dance is represented by Bartók's transformation of a unique style of eastern European instrumental folk music, originated
by Transylvanian-Romanian bagpipers who performed ad libitum at village
dances. The structure of this music results from the improvisation of twin-bar

Ex. 7.13. Concerto for Orchestra, fourth movement, Z-cell motif, bar 90.

motifs, for the most part consisting of eighth and sixteenth notes in quick tempo.

Ex. 7.14 shows the opening of the fifth movement and its source of the composer's inspiration: a Romanian *ardelenescu* (meaning "Transylvanian"). This round-dance genre, transcribed by Bartók during March 1913, illustrates the way bagpipe motifs follow one another in seemingly haphazard manner throughout the performance. Bartók was the first scholar to discover such dance music, which he designated as "Romanian bagpipe motifs in indeterminate form." As the bagpipe eventually disappeared, the genre was taken up by flute and violin performers, sometimes with an accompaniment of consecutive fifths, which were strummed on an ordinary guitar fitted with two strings.

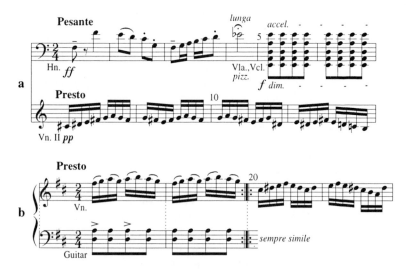

Ex. 7.14. (a) Concerto for Orchestra, fifth movement, bars 1–11, and (b) *RFM.*v, melody No. 161c, bars 12–15, 20–21.

Ex. 7.15 shows the exposition closing theme and, following below, possible sources of its second motif, beginning with its similarity to the melody of *El cumbanchero*, a Latin American song hit composed, performed, and widely broadcast in the United States during 1943. The comparison was suggested by the music director of WQXR, the *New York Times* radio station, during the International Bartók Conference held at the University of Indiana in 1982.[32] Assuming that the remarkable similarity is not happenstance, perhaps Bartók considered the Latin American melody just as worthy of adaptation as the Hungarian operetta melody underlying the second theme in the fourth movement. In that event, when the closing theme serves as the subject of a monumental fugue in the development, the second motif is varied by the addition of acciaccaturas, that is, very short ornamental grace notes, such as those notated by Bartók in transcribing certain Transylvanian-Romanian bagpipe motifs. There are, however, other possible antecedents where the melodic construction of repeated notes followed by the interval of a minor third occur, such as the motif played by the clarinet in *Duke Bluebeard's Castle*, when the seventh door—the last one—opens.[33]

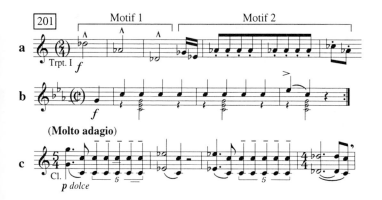

Ex. 7.15. (a) Concerto for Orchestra, fifth movement, R.N. 201, (b) Rafael Hernandez, *El cumbanchero* (1943), and (c) Bartók, *Duke Bluebeard's Castle*, two bars after R.N. 121.

The last two music examples are intended to address a query posed by William Austin, in regard to the two endings of the fifth movement that appear in the Concerto pocket score:

> To publish these alternative endings is surely strange. If the original ending is a bit too abrupt or the revised ending a shade too bombastic for my taste, why should the composer direct me to choose between them? I should like to have only the one <u>he</u> preferred, or else, perhaps to have liberty to compromise between the two.[34]

In my view, the original ending is stylistic, and the alternative ending is sarcastic, apparently composed to satisfy Koussevitzky's request for an extended, more striking closure of the Concerto. In fact, a letter from the editor of Boosey & Hawkes, dated 15 March 1945, reports that:

I had a most pleasant meeting with Koussevitzky this morning. He asked me to tell you how happy he is with the new ending and that he will play the Concerto "many times" next season. He will repeat it in New York among others.[35]

Did Bartók share the conductor's happiness? There is circumstantial as well as analytical evidence to the contrary, beginning with an extract from Bartók's piano reduction of the Concerto full score.[36]

The score, which Bartók prepared for rehearsal purposes, was commissioned by the American Ballet Theater, but the production was later canceled. It was not until 21 January 1945 that Bartók informed his publisher that the piano reduction was ready, except for the last two pages, and that they probably would be mailed on 1 February. It is noteworthy that the last page is not only undated but that only the original ending is notated as the closing bars of the Concerto. It is also significant that construction of the last four bars is based exclusively on the F-Mixolydian mode, F-G-A-Bb-C-D-Eb. Moreover, the juxtaposed arpeggiated and harmonic triads in contrary motion form a modal cadence: C-minor, D-minor, Eb-major, and F-major, where the final chord is perfect, that is, the fundamental tone, F, is in the uppermost voice (Ex. 7.16).

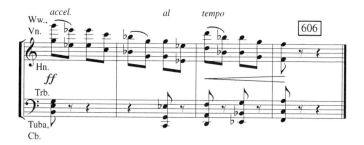

Ex. 7.16. Concerto for Orchestra, fifth movement, original ending, bars 603–606.

The last two bars of the alternative ending—arranged as a condensed form of the full score—reveal an unusual if not most uncharacteristic orchestral melange of polymodal and polyrhythmic constructions and, moreover, highlight an allusion to the *interrotto* section of the fourth movement. The woodwinds and strings play an eighth-note septuplet of triads in the F-Lydian mode—a major scale with an augmented fourth, beginning and ending with the fifth degree in the uppermost voice, thus creating an imperfect cadence. The horns play a swooping glissando of sixteenth-note intervals in the F-Mixolydian mode—a major scale with a lowered seventh—also ending on the fifth degree in the upper voice. The trombones are given polyrhythmic glissandi, chromatically notated as a sixteenth-note triplet and quintuplet. These glissandi seem to be an intentional reprise of the braying heehaws played by the trombones in the parody of the Shostakovich Seventh Symphony in the Concerto's fourth movement (cf. Ex. 7.13). Thus, when compared to the modal cadence of the original ending, the sonic effect as well as the construction of the last two bars of the alternative ending give the impression of an authentic dominant-tonic cadence based on stylized noise (Ex. 7.17).

Ex. 7.17. Concerto for Orchestra, fifth movement, alternative ending, bars 624–625.

Following the first New York performance of the Concerto by the Boston Symphony Orchestra on 10 January 1945, Olin Downes reported that:

> Koussevitzky did [Bartók] a notable service by his performance, which was of extraordinary spirit and virtuosity. There were places where the whole string choir had to be so many Heifetzes; when the whole orchestra, singly and en masse, did feats of derring-do. Repeatedly Dr. Koussevitzky led Mr. Bartók from the wings and finally left him on the stage with the applauding audience.[37]

After such an acclamation, why did the conductor nevertheless feel the need for a superfluous "feat of derring-do" and ask Bartók to revise the original ending? And, by the same token, why did the composer accede to that request? I suspect that Koussevitzky was troubled by the reception of the Boston audience at the premiere performance, which was reported as less demonstrative: "The composer came to the stage to acknowledge the applause, of which there was a heartening volume."[38] So far as Bartók's posture is concerned, perhaps he felt obliged to satisfy his patron's request, but only as an alternative Koussevitzky coda.

NOTES

1. *Boston Globe*, 2 December 1944.

2. Serge Moreux, *Béla Bartók* (London: Harvill Press, 1953), 91–92.

3. *BBE*, 363.

4. *Liverpool Post*, 28 October 1945.

5. *American Hungarian Observer* (New York), 4 June 1944. Reprinted in *BBE*, 395.

6. József Ujfalussy, *Béla Bartók* (Budapest: Corvina, 1971), 299.

7. Claude Kenneson, *Székely and Bartók* (Portland, Ore. Amadeus Press, 1994), 178:

8. *A Memorial Review* (New York: Boosey & Hawkes, 1950), 16–17.

9. *BBE*, 267.

10. Ibid., 186.

11. *YFM*.i, xx–xxi.

12. *BBE*, 297.

13. Benjamin Suchoff, "Notes on the Music," *Béla Bartók. A Celebration.* The Classics Record Library (Camp Hill, Penn.: Book-of-the-Month Club, Inc., 1981), 6.

14. Ibid.

15. Ibid.

16. Ibid.

17. Ibid.

18. *BBCO*, 115.

19. Suchoff, "Notes on the Music," 6.

20. *PBA* Correspondence File.

21. William Austin, "Bartók's Concerto for Orchestra," *Music Review* 18, no. 1 (February 1957): 33. It seems prescient that Bartók refers to the movement as a "lugubrious death-song."

22. *BBE*, 363.

23. *YFM*.i, 72.

24. *RFM*.i, 33.

25. Bartók was originally buried in Ferncliff Cemetery in Westchester County, New York, on 28 September 1945.

26. Béla Bartók Jr., "Remembering My Father, Béla Bartók," *New Hungarian Quarterly* 7, no. 22 (Summer 1966): 203.

27. Other variants are found in Bartók's collections of Hungarian, Slovak, and Yugoslav folk music.

28. György Kroó, *A Guide to Bartók* (Budapest: Corvina Press, 1974), 231.

29. *HFS*, melody No. 304, collected by Bartók in 1906. See also *BBCO*, 156–57.

30. During one of my meetings in Budapest as successor-trustee of Bartók's New York estate.

31.*BBCO*, 157–58.

32. Ibid., 240 n. 23.

33. Ibid., 65–66.

34. Austin, "Bartók's Concerto for Orchestra," 17.

35. *BBCO*, 194.

36. See *PBA* 80TPFC1.

37. *New York Times*, 11 January 1945.

38. *Boston Daily Globe*, 2 Deceember 1944.

8

Some Observations on Bartók's Third Piano Concerto[1]

In the correspondence between Bartók and his publisher, Ralph Hawkes, a letter to the composer, dated 22 August 1940, contains what is apparently the first mention of the Third Piano Concerto:

> I do not know whether you have developed any ideas for new works during the last few months, quite possibly not, but would like to remind you of your promise of the orchestral version of the Two Pianos and Percussion work, also to advise you that I shall expect the Third Piano Concerto by the summer of 1941. My reason for saying this is that you will be wanted as soloist with this work for the New York Philharmonic during its Centennial Season 1941–42.[2]

Although Bartók scored the Concerto for Two Pianos in December, 1940, he did not perform it until January 1943—his last public appearance as pianist. As for the Third Piano Concerto, composed during the summer of 1945 in Saranac Lake, New York, he was destined never to hear this, his last work, for death terminated his labors as he attempted to complete the scoring of the last two pages of the fair copy. The last seventeen bars were left blank, with the exception of the piano part and the first timpani roll. Tibor Serly, composer and Bartók disciple, reconstructed these bars on the basis of the skeleton version in the composer's sketch. Ralph Hawkes's "great expectation" of 1940 was finally realized on 8 February 1946, when the premiere of the Concerto was given by György Sándor with the Philadelphia Orchestra conducted by Eugene Ormandy.

Turning to the manuscripts,[3] the sketch (*PBA* 84FSS1) consists of nineteen pages, in penciled notation for the most part. The final copy (*PBA* 84FSFCI) comprises sixty-two leaves of transparent master sheets written in black ink. Serly's reconstruction, as can be seen from the photograph of the sketch, consists principally of the completion and voicing of the skeletal chord structures indicated in the sketch,[4] and the addition of chromatic passages for the woodwinds in the last five bars.

Regarding publication, Mátyás Seiber made the reduction for two pianos.[5] The publisher's prefatory note, which appears in the reduction and in the full score, refers to the use of different type sizes as the means by which Bartók's markings can be distinguished from those added by Serly, Ormandy, Kentner, and Stein. In the full score, at least, as a comparative survey of the manuscripts will reveal, this typographic procedure is not always clear. It should be noted that bass clef signs are missing from both staves of the piano part in bar 27 of the first movement, full score. A more serious inadvertency is the omission of the *ritard.* sign at bar 279 of the third movement, in both publications.

The reader will observe the appearance of the word *vége* (Hungarian for "end") after the last bar of the sketch. Bartók also wrote the word in at the end of the uncompleted final copy. Agatha Fassett has reported that Bartók was aware of his fatal illness more than a year before the composition of the Concerto.[6] Perhaps *vége* was intended as a signpost in the event that he could not complete the scoring. Or perhaps that unique entry (not to be found in his other manuscripts) had epitaphic significance—an indication that the Third Piano Concerto was to be considered his last composition.[7] The slow movement, marked Adagio religioso, opens and closes with what in essence is a dirge, in imitation of east European peasant music style, and perhaps it is not too fanciful to hear in this a mourning song for the composer's impending death? There is a remarkable resemblance in terms of configuration and pentatonic structure between the first theme (Ex. 8.1) and the melody of the second Dirge (Ex. 8.2).

Ex. 8.1. Bartók, Third Piano Concerto (1945), second movement, bars 1–8.

Ex. 8.2. Bartók, Four Dirges op. 9a, for Piano, No. 2, bars 1–7.

There is also a definite textural kinship between the piano part at the close of the Adagio religioso (Ex. 8.3) and the first of the Four Dirges (Ex. 8.4).

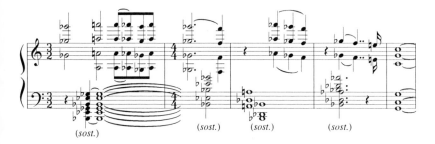

Ex. 8.3. Bartók, Third Piano Concerto, second movement, bars 130–134.

Ex. 8.4. Bartók, Four Dirges No. 1, bars 10–14.

The second theme of the Adagio religioso (Ex. 8.5), stated in the form of a piano solo, has frequently been referred to as a chorale. The propriety of such a designation seems evident when a comparison is made with *Mikrokosmos* No. 35, Chorale (Ex. 8.6).

Ex. 8.5. Bartók, Third Piano Concerto, second movement, bars 130–134.

Ex. 8.6. Bartók, *Mikrokosmos* for piano, No. 35 (Vol. 1), bars 1–6.

NOTES

1. The previous publication of this revised essay appears in *Tempo* 65 (Summer 1963): 8–11.

2. *PBA* correspondence files.

3. The following alphanumeric designations, formerly listed with the prefixal *NYBA* during my tenure as curator of the New York Bartók Archive, were later changed to *PBA* (Peter Bartók Archive). See *BBLW*, 219.

4. The chord construction of the first beat in bar 759 of the sketch, however, is markedly different from that of the final copy and published versions.

5. Mátyás Seiber, expatriate Hungarian composer living in London, was a Bartók colleague and consultant to Boosey and Hawkes, Ltd.

6. See Agatha Fassett, *The Naked Face of Genius: Béla Bartók's American Years* (Boston and New York: Houghton Mifflin Company; Cambridge: Riverside Press, 1958), 300. Reprinted as *Béla Bartók—the American Years* (New York: Dover), 1970.

7. A parallel can be found on p. 67 of Bartók's draft preface to *RFM*.iii, in the form of this equally unique entry: "Torockó, _____ New York,
                            1908 nov.   1945, márc. 30."

9

Folk-Music Sources in Bartók Works[1]

In 1904 Béla Bartók, a recent graduate of the Budapest Academy of Music, tasted the first nectar of success as a composer: his symphonic poem *Kossuth* received its premiere in Budapest in January and its next performance in Manchester, England, in February. This work, based on a Richard Strauss *Ein Heldenleben* model but with rhythmic and ornamental features in the Lisztian style of what was then considered to be Hungarian folk music, created a sensation in Hungary. At that time public opinion demanded things Hungarian in every sphere of life—Bartók himself was fanatical in that respect—as a manifestation of the national struggle toward independence from Austrian rule.[2] The sudden leap to fame of the twenty-three-year-old composer was surely the prime generative force that led to the creation of the Rhapsody op. 1 for Piano and Orchestra (1904), whose style is patterned after Liszt's Hungarian Rhapsodies but employs original themes.[3]

Bartók then turned from Strauss to the analysis of Liszt's works, in his search for a basis on which to construct his own style, and quickly decided that too much of Liszt's invention was "certain formal imperfections, the mechanical repetition of certain parts, the so-called Liszt-sequences . . . for the most part merely conventional ideas—Gypsy music."[4] And this music, as Bartók later wrote, was popular art music composed by Hungarians of the upper middle class and almost exclusively performed by city Gypsy bands.[5]

During the summer of 1904, while Bartók was working on his compositions in a small village, he heard a Székely servant girl, Lidi Dósa, singing a song which revealed to him the special characteristics of Székely music. The Székely, a Transylvanian-Hungarian people, performed melodies which have structural elements of centuries-old Hungarian peasant song, particularly the characteristic symmetrical form of the pentatonic scale, G-Bb-C-D-F (Ex. 9.1).

Ex. 9.1. *HFS*, melody No. 313.

The next year Zoltán Kodály's first publication of Hungarian peasant songs in the Budapest journal *Ethnographia*, followed by his doctoral dissertation on the verse structure of Hungarian folk song in 1906, convinced Bartók that the genuine Hungarian folk music is the product of peasant communities, untouched by nineteenth-century European influence and therefore a more truly national melodic source for creating the sought-for new style of Hungarian composition. And he set out, beginning in 1906, to collect Hungarian musical folklore by means of recordings and on-the-spot transcription by ear.

Bartók's fieldwork resulted in the collection and transcription of thousands of vocal and instrumental melodies, and he studied their structural attributes for typological purposes. Blessed with a figuratively supernal musical ear, Bartók immediately detected foreign influences in Hungarian village music, as well as stylistic differences, and he extended his field trips to those Hungarian-controlled areas containing Slovak, Romanian, and other minorities.[6]

The end of World War I and the subsequent dismemberment of Greater Hungary in 1920 prevented Bartók from further collecting in the mentioned areas which were now foreign territory. He therefore concentrated on publishing the results of his morphological studies, along the lines of his first book-length study of the Bihor County Romanians.[7] His attention focused on such aspects as scale type and permutations, rhythmic schemata, variation forms, performance peculiarities, and instrumental color. The fruits of his many years of laborious transcription and analysis were published during his lifetime and posthumously, consisting of more than thirteen thousand carefully transcribed instrumental and vocal melodies, which he collected from Arab, Bulgarian, Gypsy, Hungarian, Romanian, Ruthenian, Slovak, Turkish, and Yugoslav rural informants.[8]

There was another, equally significant outcome with respect to Bartók's ethnomusicological efforts: the assimilation of peasant music idiom so completely that he was able to forget all about it and use it as his musical mother tongue.[9] Put in another way, he was able to grasp the spirit of hitherto unknown peasant music and make this spirit (difficult to describe in words) the basis of his works.[10] This difficulty led him to further state that neither peasant melodies nor imitation of peasant melodies are found in his abstract music but it is pervaded by the atmosphere of peasant music.[11] It is the illustrated description of this "atmosphere" that is presented below, in the stepwise approach that Bartók himself has for the most part delineated:[12] the inherent meaning of Bartók's terminology implies hierarchical processes in terms of the composer's craft.

Figure 1 displays the five levels in which folk-music sources appear in Bartók works. The first level features the folk tune as a kind of musical jewel, in which the accompaniment and such added materials as introduction and interlude comprise the mounting; that is, the composed parts are of secondary importance. The accompaniment, moreover, may be derived from the melodic structure or freely invented.[13] And one specific purpose of this kind of setting is appreciation: to acquaint the public, especially music students, with "the simple and non-romantic beauties of folk music."[14] Moreover, as Zoltán Kodály stated, "Whether for chorus or piano, the accompaniment should always be of such a nature as to make up for the lost fields and village."[15]

Level Five: folk music	spirit or "atmosphere"
Level Four: folk tune	imitations
Level Three: folk tune	serves as a motto
Level Two: folk tune	and accompaniment equated
Level One: folk tune	is treated as a "jewel"

| pentatonic scale, ♪♩.♩ rhythm | Lydian mode, ♪♪ ♪ or ♫♩ patterns | nondiatonic scales, bag-pipe motifs | half cadence, chromatic compression | *kolomyjka* dance rhythm | additive 5/8, 7/8, and 9/8 rhythm | narrow-range chromatic melodies |
| Hungary | Slovakia | Romania | Yugoslavia | Ruthenia | Bulgaria | Arab |

Figure 1. Metamorphic stages in Bartókian transmutation of folk music into art music.

Ex. 9.2 illustrates a simple accompaniment in which the folk tune is doubled in the accompaniment.

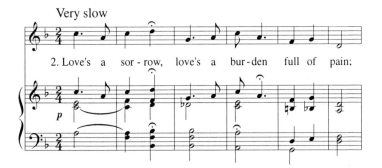

Ex. 9.2. Bartók, (Ten) Hungarian Folk Songs for Voice and Piano (1906), No. 7, bars 1–6. Nos. 11–20 were composed by Zoltán Kodály.

A concomitant purpose—the creation of a new piano style "stripped of all unessential decorative elements, deliberately using only the most restricted technical means"[16]—resulted in the derivative harmonization of a Hungarian folk song in 1908, which he had collected the preceding year. The melody is pentatonic, one of the characteristics of old Hungarian folk-music style that dates back perhaps a millennium (Ex. 9.3).

The setting avoids the "trite dominant-tonic cadence" and ends on a seventh chord: "In the pentatonic scale . . . there is no dominant at all in the commonly-accepted harmonic sense of the word. Four of the five degrees, that is, the fun-

Tempo giusto

Ex. 9.3. *HFS*, melody No. 7a, bars 1–4.

damental tone, third, fifth and seventh are almost equal in their weight. The fourth degree generally appears as a passing tone, and the seventh assumes the character of a consonance."[17]

The use of nonfunctional chord progressions to harmonize the melody is a stylistic borrowing from Debussy's music. This procedure illustrates the second level, in which the accompaniment achieves parity with the folk tune (Ex. 9.4).

Ex. 9.4. Bartók, Fourteen Bagatelles for Piano, op. 6 (1908), No. 4, bars 1–4.

Ex. 9.5. (a) *RFM*.i, melody No. 11a, (b) Bartók, second Romanian Dance op. 8a for Piano (1910), bars 16–19.

Level 3 transcriptions employ the folk tune only as a motto: the added material is of primary importance. In this case, too, the impression must be of complete unity between the original melody and the composed version. Ex. 9.5

shows how Bartók transformed a Transylvanian-Romanian *mărunţel* (couples dance).

The fourth level is the imitative one: thematic material is created in folk-tune style. During a New York radio broadcast in 1944, Bartók, referring to No. 5 from Ten Easy Pieces for Piano (Ex. 9.6), stated that: "'Evening in Transylvania'" is an original composition . . . with themes of my own invention, but the themes are in the style of the Hungarian-Transylvanian folk tunes."[18] The original title of this piece, "Este a Székelyeknél" (Evening with the Székely villagers), provides a clue as to a possible folk-tune source (Ex. 9.7).

Ex. 9.6. Bartók, "Evening in Transylvania," No. 5 from Ten Easy Pieces for Piano (1908), bars 1–8.

Bartók invented the melody after he returned from his first field trip in April 1907, among the Székely villages in then Hungarian Transylvania, where he discovered the special characteristics of the old style of Hungarian peasant music: pentatonic system, nonarchitectonic quaternaries, and isometric (same number of text syllables) in each of the four sections. His later research led him to the conclusion that such characteristics are typical of "the oldest known materials in old Hungarian peasant music, not to be found among any other races—even neighboring races—except as obvious imports."[19]

"Evening in the Village" has the identical characteristics: the pure pentatonic scale, E-G-A-B-D, nonrounded quaternary (ABCD) section structure, and the text line equivalent of eight syllables in each section. A possible source melody is the one Bartók collected from an eighty-year-old man in the village of Csíkrakós (Csík County). The characteristics are the same, except that the melody is a rotation of the pentatonic scale, A-C-D-E-G, and F appears as a passing tone (Ex. 9.7).

As mentioned above, the fifth and highest stage is reached when abstract works are created that are pervaded by folk-music idiom or atmosphere. According to Bartók's explanation, his original works reflect the influence exerted by the newly discovered rural folk music, in terms of tonality, melody, rhythm, and structure.[20] An outstanding example is the Dance Suite for Orchestra (1923) he composed for the Budapest jubilee festival-concert in celebration of the fiftieth anniversary of the unification of Buda, Pest, and Obuda to form the Hungarian

Ex. 9.7. *BBSE*, p. 124, melody No. 123.

capital.[21] The composition consists of five dances that reflect the influence of Arab, Hungarian, Romanian, and Ruthenian folk music. In the first dance, the opening theme combines narrow-range, chromatic Arab melodic style with Ruthenian *kolomyjka* dance rhythm, 2/4 ♫♫ | ♫♫♫ | ♫♫♫ | ♩ ♩ (Ex. 9.8).

Ex. 9.8. Bartók, Dance Suite for Orchestra, first movement, bars 1–5.

Whether folk-music sources are borrowed, imitated, or assimilated, Bartók emphasizes that their use in the creative process is as difficult—if not more so—than composition based on original themes: it is not the source itself that is of primary importance but the molding of the material. In other words, folk music as a source of inspiration for the creation of art music will attain significance only if the transplantation of musical folklore is the work of a great creative talent.[22]

NOTES

1. This essay was published in *"Weine meine laute . . ." Gedenkschrift Kurt Reinhard*, ed. Christian Ahrens et al. (Laaber: Laaber-Verlag, 1984), 197–218.

2. Zoltán Kodály, "Bartók the Folklorist," in *The Selected Writings of Zoltán Kodály*, ed. Ferenc Bónis, trans. Lili Halápy and Fred Macnicol (London: Boosey & Hawkes Music Publishers, Ltd., 1974). See also *BBE*, 399, 409.

3. The themes are given in *BBE*, 404–5.

4. Ibid., 452.

5. Ibid., 206–7. At that time Hungarian urban music consisted of folk-song imitations, *verbunkos* (recruiting music) styled dance pieces, and other melodies in the public vogue.

6. He also made a short trip to the Biskra Oasis in Algeria to collect *mărunțel*Arab

music.

7. Published by the Romanian Academy in Bucharest. See *BBE*, 527–55, for a detailed bibliography of Bartók's ethnomusicological writings. See also *BBGR*, 49–121.

8. Bartók additionally analyzed an even greater number of melodies from the published transcriptions of other collectors.

9. *BBE*, 341.

10. Ibid., 333.

11. Ibid., 344.

12. Ibid., 348–53.

13. Bartók's folk music collections mainly consist of monophonic specimens.

14. *BBE*, 427.

15. Preface to Twenty Hungarian Folk Songs for Voice and Piano (Budapest: Rozsnyai Károly, 1906).

16. *BBE*, 432.

17. Ibid., 371–73. Bartók refers to the so-called Hungarian anhemitone scale, a symmetrical construction in which the second and sixth degrees are missing, for example, D-F-G-A-C or G-B♭-C-D-F.

18. *BBCO*, 92.

19. *HFS*, 23.

20. *BBE*, 363.

21. *BBLW*, 100.

22. *BBE*, 347.

10

Ethnomusicological Roots of Béla Bartók's Musical Language[1]

During the formative part of Bartók's career as composer, including the first two student years at the Royal Academy of Music in Budapest (1899–1901), his musical language was typical of late nineteenth-century romanticism. The emphasis was on Brahms as the model and hardly if at all related to those characteristics of national popular music that were the stylistic hallmarks of Hungarian and Slavonic composers.[2]

Beginning in 1902, however, the emphasis changed direction. Caught up in the wave of resurgent national longing for Hungarian independence from Austrian rule, young Bartók became an ardent nationalist. In a letter to his mother, dated 23 September 1903, he declared this credo: "Everyone, on reaching maturity, has to set himself a goal and must direct all his work and actions toward this. For my part, all my life, in every sphere, always and in every way, I shall have one objective: the good of Hungary and the Hungarian nation. I think I have already given some proof of this intention in the minor ways which have so far been possible to me."[3]

One of these ways was Bartók's parodic treatment of *Gotterhalte,* the Austrian national anthem, in his first major work, the *Kossuth* Symphonic Poem, completed on 18 August 1903. Its first performance, on 13 January 1904, created a sensation in Budapest and literally catapulted the young genius, then twenty-two years old, into instant fame. The local press hailed him as the "Hungarian Tchaikovsky," and the work was programmed for its first English performance the next year.

The musical content of *Kossuth* is imitative of Liszt's Hungarianisms, as are the other works Bartók composed from 1902 to 1905.[4] Indeed, this period can be appropriately referred to as his summary of urban Hungarian musical dialect, since all those works are based on Hungarian popular art song or their imitations as source material. It should be emphasized that Bartók and his predecessors—and the rest of the musical world!—erroneously assumed that such music, for the most part composed by amateurs from the educated classes and disseminated with typical distortions by city Gypsy bands, was the true Hungarian folk music.

Characteristic tonal features of Gypsy-styled music are the so-called Hungarian scales, each containing two different augmented seconds (Ex. 10.1). These scales, as Bartók later stated, "are entirely unknown to Hungarian peasant music."[5]

Ex. 10.1. *HFS*, 55. (a) Minor form of the Hungarian Gypsy scale, with augmented fourth degree, and (b) Phrygian form, with minor and augmented second degrees.

The second musical expression of Bartók's credo grew out of a fortuitous occurrence during the summer of 1904, while he was working on his Rhapsody op. 1 at a rural villa in the northern (Slovak) part of then Greater Hungary.[6] He overheard a Székely maid[7] singing Hungarian popular art songs with such significant differences from the original sources as three-section melody stanzas replacing the characteristic Hungarian quaternaries, transformation of heterometric melody sections into isometric ones, and Dorian and Aeolian folk modes instead of the harmonic minor scale (Ex. 10.2).[8]

Ex. 10.2. *HFS*, melody No. 313. Because of its structural differences, Bartók placed the melody in the miscellaneous category (Class *C*) of Hungarian folk songs.

Bartók decided to investigate further:[9]

> I set out in 1905 to collect and study Hungarian peasant music unknown till then. It was my great good luck to find a helpmate for this work in Zoltán Kodály, who, owing to his deep insight and sound judgment in all spheres of music, could give me many a hint and much advice that proved of immense value. I started these investigations on entirely musical grounds and pursued them in areas which linguistically were purely Hungarian. Later I became fascinated by the scientific implications of my musical material and extended my work over territories which were linguistically Slovakian and Rumanian.

His other investigations resulted in published studies of Arab peasant music (1917), Turkish folk music (1976), Slovak folk songs (1959, 1967), Yugoslav folk music (1978), and a substantial number of smaller essays on various ethnomusicological subjects.[10] Between 1906 and 1925 he devoted countless hours to the meticulous transcription of thousands of recorded vocal and instrumental melodies, for the most part transposed to G as final tone in order to determine certain relationships.[11] It was this singularity of purpose, combined with supernal talent, that enabled Bartók to literally homogenize his polyglot folklore material and absorb its characteristic elements to the point where they became his musical mother tongue. Thus it appears quite appropriate to designate this second, twenty-year period as his fusion of national music styles.

And it is the characteristic aspects of melodic organization (the various elements of melodic contour and section structure), rhythm structure (tempo, metric structure, and rhythm schemata), and timbre (including folk-instrument imitations and performance peculiarities) that constitute the essence of Bartók's musical language. In the following presentation a representative selection of those aspects is given in chronological order of the ethnic areas investigated by Bartók.

HUNGARIAN SOURCES

Melodic Organization

When Bartók collected Transylvanian-Hungarian folk songs in Székely villages in 1907, he was exhilarated by the discovery that he had chanced upon a melody type unknown till then (Ex. 10.3).[12]

Ex. 10.3. *HFS*, 21. Parlando means free rhythm, in which the bars mark only structural articulation and are irregularly unequal.

The tonal organization of this "old"-style Hungarian folk song is its characteristic central Asian type of anhemitone-pentatonic scale: a symmetrical structure consisting of the first, minor third, fourth, fifth, and minor seventh degrees (with G as the fundamental note: G-B♭-C-D-F). There is no tonic-dominant relation, and the melodic contour has frequent leaps in fourths.[13] In Bartók's published collection of Hungarian pentatonic folk songs, about half the melodies appear in his compositions from 1906 to 1931 (*HFS*, 219–39, 330–32).

Pentatonicism is a characteristic element of Bartók's style, rooted in his Magyar cultural heritage, and exemplified with telling effect as the harmonic means in Bagatelle No. 4 from Fourteen Bagatelles op. 6 for Piano (1908).[14]

New-style Hungarian folk melodies apparently came into being at the beginning of the nineteenth century. Although they have the same four-line stanza
structure and, in many instances, the same pentatonic turns as the old-style melodies, there is a marked difference in content structure. The new style is architectonic (AABA and ABBA) and the old style consists of such free sectional arrangements as ABCD and ABBC. An ingenious old-style imitation is seen in
No. 5, "Evening in Transylvania," from Ten Easy Pieces for Piano (1908). New-
style melodic construction is found in No. 6, "Hungarian Folk Song."

Rhythm Structure

Hungarian folk song provided Bartók with two unique sources of rhythm to
draw from: parlando-rubato and the so-called dotted rhythm. The former is a
feature of old-style melodies, without regular time signatures (Ex. 10.3; see
also the second Burlesque from Three Burlesques op. 8c for Piano (1911). Dotted rhythm occurs in both old and new-style folk songs, in combinative patterns
containing an accented short value followed by a nonaccented long value (Ex.
10.2, bars 3 and 5; Ex. 10.3, bars 4, 6–8).[15]

Both styles of folk song have other attributes in common: variable *tempo
giusto* (strict or rigid rhythm), in which, for example, pairs of quarter-notes
adjust themselves to the length of the underlying text syllables, and avoidance
of the *arsis* (upbeat) in melody beginnings. Variable *tempo giusto*, an exclusively Hungarian peculiarity, is illustrated by the solo violin part in the first
movement of the Rhapsody No. 2 for Violin and Piano (1928), R.N. 7–8.

SLOVAK SOURCES

Bartók's Slovak folk music material, containing about twenty-five hundred
melodies, was collected intermittently between 1906 and 1916. In addition, he
studied and classified more than two thousand Slovak melodies and about thirty-
five hundred Czech and Moravian melodies published between 1880 and 1926.[16]

His analyses indicate that these materials fall into three groups: autochthonous melodies; direct adoptions from the Hungarian material or Hungarian-
influenced original structures; and the more extensive group of uncommonly
varied types, for the most part related to the Moravian material and to a lesser
extent to melodies of Czech and German origin.[17]

Melodic Organization

A striking feature of the larger group is frequency of occurrence of the Lydian
mode—a major scale with augmented fourth degree—that is completely missing from Bartók's Hungarian material. Ex. 10.4a shows the original form of a
svadobná (wedding song) melody, collected by Bartók in April 1915, constructed
of a G-Lydian pentachord, G-A-B-C♯-D. Example 10.4b, a variant he collected

in a different village in July of the same year, extends the range to a heptachord with the seemingly Mixolydian seventh degree (F♮ instead of F♯).[18]

Ex. 10.4. (a) *SV*.i, melody No. 318a and (b) variant No. 318b.

In point of fact, the heptachord is a rotation of the ascending form of the D melodic minor scale and therefore represents an octave segment, with G as principal tone, of a nondiatonic scale (Ex. 10.5).[19]

Ex. 10.5. Nondiatonic Slovak folk mode, based on G as an octave segment of the D melodic minor scale.

The old-style Hungarian folk songs are for the most part pentatonic or have chromatic alteration of the pentatonic scale. In the latter case, the pitch collection of *HFS* melody No. 40 is G-A-B-C-D-E♭-F.[20] A hexachord of the same pitch collection occurs in *YFM*.i, melody No. 21b, and *RFM*.iv, melody No. 73m.

Rhythm Structure

Slovak melodies show an extraordinary variety of metric and rhythmic schemata, asymmetrical three-bar phrases are commonplace, and in 2/4 the notes are invariably eighths and quarters, frequently as ♪♩ ♪ and ♫♩ schemata.[21]

The emphatic rendition of these patterns are apparent in the first movement of the First Piano Concerto (1926).

A characteristic feature of certain four-section isometric[22] Slovak folk songs is designated by Bartók as Slovak rhythm contraction. The outer two lines are in three-bar groups, (2/4) ♩ ♩ | ♫ ♩ | ♩ 𝄾 | ♩ ♩ | ♫ ♩ | ♩ 𝄾 |, and the inner ones are in two-bar groups in which syllabic uniformity is maintained by contraction of note values, ♫♫ | ♩ ♩ | ♫♫♫ | ♩ ♩ |. There are also a number of Hungarian folk songs that show the influence of this Slovak peculiarity, such as *HFS*, melody No. 185, and No. 87 (Variations) from the *Mikrokosmos* for piano (1926–1939). No. 8 (Slovak Song) from the Forty-four Duos for Two Violins (1931) is an arrangement of a genuine folk song that contains Slovak rhythm-contraction.[23]

ROMANIAN SOURCES

There are more than three thousand melodies in Bartók's Romanian folk-music material, collected between 1908 and 1917 in then Hungarian, now Romanian Transylvania. His studies of this extensive collection and others from the same area as well as from Old Romania indicate that all these materials, unlike the musical folklore of the Slovaks and Ruthenians, have no reciprocity with Hungarian folk music (with the exception of some Székely influence in certain Romanian folk songs).

Bartók discovered that Transylvania could be divided into music-dialect areas, each with remarkably discrete regional characteristics. There was little evidence of folk-style imitations, art songs, and urban-Gypsy music; the poetic texts had pagan features; and his wide-ranging tour of remote peasant villages gave him the impression that he had been transported back to the Middle Ages.[24]

Melodic Organization

It would be difficult to overestimate the impact of Romanian musical folklore on Bartók's tonal language. Mention is made above of one type of nondiatonic folk mode in the Romanian *colinde*. Ex. 10.6 shows the configuration of some other types.

Ex. 10.6. (a) *RFM*.iv, melody No. 12e, and (b) *RFM*.iv, melody No. 639a.

Another nondiatonic folk mode, E-F-G-A♭-B♭-C, will be found in *colinde* melody No. 12bb. The epic text, of pagan origin, was set by Bartók as the libretto for his *Cantata profana* (1930) he reworked the "heathen" scalar configuration as the opening and closing bars; and with the diatonic folk modes, he developed and transformed both tonal sources for purposes of dramatic symbolization in the text.[25] These nondiatonic folk modes are in near relation to the octatonic scale, an octachordal, symmetrical collection of alternating semitones and whole tones.

Characteristic features of Romanian peasant dance melodies are two- or four-bar bagpipe motifs, generally pentachords in range, that are repeated without any plan or order.[26] The fifth movement of the Concerto for Orchestra is based on a transformation of such bagpipe motifs.

Rhythm Structure

In a discussion of *tempo giusto* Bartók states: "What mostly interested us in the rigid rhythm kind were the changes of measure. I had fully exploited these possibilities already in my earliest works, and later perhaps even with some exaggeration."[27] It is in the Romanian *colinde* that he first observed both regular and irregular change of measure as a characteristic feature of rural folk song. The former has regular alternation of 5/8 with 3/8 and 3/4; 3/8 with 2/4 and 3/4; and so forth; the latter shows such irregular meters as 2/4, 3/4, 4/4 and 3/8, 5/8, 2/4. The Fourth Dialogue from Nine Little Piano Pieces (1926) is an interesting example of both kinds of change of measure.

Timbre

During the first decade of the twentieth century, the bagpipe—probably the only instrument used for village dances in earlier times—became obsolescent in Transylvania and was replaced by the shepherd's flute (*fluer*) and the violin. In the northern part of the territory, the violin was accompanied by a two-stringed guitar tuned to the fifth, D-A. This interval, an imitation of the drone and middle pipe of the bagpipe, was plucked (without plectrum) in alternating accented and unaccented eighths as an ostinato rhythm.[28] When the violin simultaneously played A-E as a double-stop, the result was the fifth chord D-A-E.[29] It is precisely this chord and in the same ostinato rhythm pattern that serves as the accompaniment to the bagpipe motifs in the fifth movement of the Concerto for Orchestra, thus providing the means for re-creating the tonal color and the spirit of rural Transylvanian dance style.

Ruthenian Sources

The Ruthenians, a tribe of Ukrainian people, inhabit former Hungarian territory that borders Slovakia to the east and Transylvanian Romania to the north. Bartók collected Romanian folk music in that area in 1909 and, two years later, about a hundred instrumental and vocal Ruthenian melodies.

Rhythm Structure

The *kolomyjka* is the most characteristic Ruthenian dance music, and its infectious four-bar rhythm schema, ♫♩♩ | ♩♫♩ | ♫♩♩| ♩ ♩ ,was taken over by Hungarian hog herders and Romanian shepherds for their vocal and instrumental melodies.[30] Example 10.7 is a Ruthenian folk-song melody that Bartok arranged in 1931 as No.10 (Ruthenian Song) in Forty-four Duos for Two Violins.

Ex. 10.7. Ruthenian folk-song melody. The underlying folk text has fourteen syllables.

One of the differences between the instrumental transcription and the Ruthenian melody is the former's use of characteristic Hungarian dotted rhythm, 4/4 ♩. ♪ ♪ ♩., in *tempo giusto*. There is a striking difference in scalar structure, where the tonality of the transcription is E-Phrygian, ending with a tritone configuration, G♯-D-E. The folk song also shows the same type of tritone configuration, B-F-G, but its structure is based on a G-Mixolydian mode with an altered sixth degree (E♭), a "strange" scale that occurs in Bartók's Hungarian collection (*HFS*, melodies no. 276b and 280).

In the first movement of the Dance Suite for Piano (1925), the opening theme (Example 10.8) represents Bartók's first invention of a chromatic melody in Arab peasant music style.[31] The rhythm stems from the Ruthenian *kolomyjka*.

Ex. 10.8. Bartok, Dance Suite for Piano (1925), opening theme, bars 1–5.

BULGARIAN SOURCES

Bartók made his first contact with Bulgarian peasant music on 1 March 1912, in southwestern Transylvania (now part of Romania), during a field trip to collect Romanian folk music. Although he had made a preliminary transcription of seven Bulgarian folk songs it was not until 1935 that he revised them "with the greatest possible accuracy."[32] The new transcriptions were a necessary adjunct to the preparation for publication, beginning in 1932, of his Romanian collection: he discovered that about 5 percent of the latter—almost exclusively instrumental and *colinde* melodies—were in a peculiar asymmetrical rhythm that he later designated as "Bulgarian" rhythm.[33]

Rhythm Structure

Bulgarian rhythm consists of groups of binary and ternary units (sixteenths or eighths) within the measure, in quick *tempo giusto*. The organization of these units in specific rhythm schemata is a characteristic feature of Bulgarian folk dances: Thus, for example, the *pajdushko* is 2+3 units in 5/16 or 5/8, and the *rŭchenitsa* is 2+2+3 units in 7/16 or 7/8. In the *Mikrokosmos* for piano (1926-1939), No.150 (Bulgarian Dance [3]) is a *pajdushko* and No.149 (Bulgarian Dance [2]) a *rŭchenitsa*.

The melody of *Mikrokosmos* No.113 ("Bulgarian Rhythm [1]") may have been borrowed from a Bulgarian folk song (or a variant thereof) as the prototype (Ex. 10.9) but restructured by Bartók as a *pajdushko* instead of the original *daichovo horo* dance rhythm of 2+2+2+3 units in 9/16 or 9/8 .

Ex. 10.9. "Song of the Ferryman," No. 8 in *Südslawische Volkslieder*, ed. Heinrich Möller (Mainz: Edition Schott, n.d.). This reprint was first published in *Bulgarische-makedonische Volkslieder*, Sofia, 1926.

Yugoslav Sources

It was also during March 1912 that Bartók made another field trip in the Banat region, this time to a neighboring Serbian village where he recorded twenty-one vocal and instrumental melodies.[34] During the next two decades he acquired, analyzed, and tabulated approximately 5,400 published and unpublished melodies which had been collected by various Yugoslav ethnomusicologists between 1859 and 1935.[35]

Melodic Organization

The Yugoslav folk-music material is for the most part comprised of narrow-range melodies, most frequently constructed of the first four, five, or six degrees of a diatonic major or minor (or some other variety) scale with the second degree as final tone. The unique characteristic of ending on an imperfect (that is, half) cadence infiltrated the folk-music material of neighboring Romanian and Bulgarian territories to such an extent that Bartók designated this peculiarity as a "Yugoslav" cadence.[36]

The second movement of the Concerto for Orchestra presents five melodies in Yugoslav dance style, followed by a chorale tune in B major that ends on the dominant (F$\sharp$ major) as a Yugoslav cadence.[37] An earlier use of this type of half cadence appears in *Mikrokosmos* melody No. 51.

Timbre

In the same movement, Bartók emulates a peculiar type of Dalmatian folk song. The clarinets (third dance, at R.N. 45), substituting for the traditional *sopel* (a kind of folk oboe) prelude, play their duet at the unusual but characteristic interval of a minor seventh. The muted trumpets are given the role of Dalmatian folk singers, that is, as a duet in major seconds—the inverted form of minor sevenths-—to follow the *sopel* prelude.[38]

ARAB SOURCES

In March 1906, Bartók was in Spain, as accompanist for the concert tour of the young Hungarian violinist, Ferenc Vecsey. He had the opportunity to make an evening excursion from Cadiz to Tangier on the African coast and found himself in an Arab tavern listening to the singing of Arab songs. The performance made an indelible impression; indeed, so impactfully that, six years later, he was able to identify Oriental influence in the folk songs of the Transylvanian-Romanians (such as the augmented second interval in Ex. 10.6a). He therefore decided to investigate Arab peasant music in the field, and in June 1913 traveled to Arab villages in the Biskra district of central Algeria.[39]

Melodic Organization

It was not until 1917 that Bartók published his study and transcriptions of the collected Arab material. All the melodies are based on a genuine chromatic system in which the single degrees generally are at a half-tone distance from each other and have no interrelationship except to a fixed fundamental tone.[40] Rural melodies are narrow range: five, six, or at most seven half tones, corresponding to a compass of about a fourth. Urban melodies (that is, influenced by or imported from the city music of the Arabs) have a greater range; some of them are in constructions similar to Western major and minor scales.[41]

Mention is made above ("Ruthenian Sources") of the Arab peasant music style in the opening theme of the Dance Suite for Piano, that is probably based on narrow-range Arab vocal material. The instrumental repertory includes certain urban-influenced dance tunes played by a γeița (a kind of folk oboe) whose construction produces a nondiatonic scale (Ex. 10.10).[42] This instrumental approximation of the plagal octatonic scale, so carefully notated by Bartók (including his measurements of the related tone-hole spacing, and so forth), is the complete form of the octatonic segments he discovered among the Transylvanian-Romanians (cf. Ex. 10.6) later that year and again in the spring of 1914.

Ex. 10.9. North African Arab γeița octatonic scale.

In 1908, in the first four bars of his innovative sixth Bagatelle, Bartók experimented with a hexachordal octatonic scale segment, B-C-D-D♯-E♯-F♯, thereby following in the footsteps of Liszt (for example, the Sonnetto 104 del Petrarca from the second book of *Années de pélerinage*). In 1920, perhaps secure in the knowledge that octatonicism is a tonal peculiarity of Western art music as well as Eastern musical folklore from widely divergent sources in terms of geographic location and cultural difference, Bartók composed his remarkable Eight Improvisations on Hungarian Peasant Songs for Piano (op. 20) in which diatonic folk tunes interact with octatonic constructions.[43]

TURKISH SOURCES

Bartók's last field trip to collect folk music occurred in November 1936, as part of an official invitation to visit Ankara, the capital city of Turkey, lecture on folk music, and participate in an orchestral concert of Hungarian music. A brief illness cut short the collecting work, but he nevertheless managed to record significant examples of vocal and instrumental pieces performed by nomadic peoples of Asia Minor.[44]

Timbre

After Bartók completed the major part of his Turkish transcriptions in May1937, he initiated steps to obtain a joint Turkish-Hungarian publication. He interrupted these proceedings during July and August, however, in order to compose the Sonata for Two Pianos and Percussion. It seems reasonable to conjecture that Bartók's timbral impression of his visit to the Turkish village of Çardak is vividly portrayed in the Sonata, particularly in the first movement, in approximation of the village drummer who "beat that drum [a bass drum called *davul*] with terrific energy with a wooden drumstick, and I really thought at times that either his big drum or my eardrum would break. Even the flames of the three flickering kerosene lamps jumped at every beat."[45]

In 1944, Bartók summarized his outlook upon rural music and its part in the development of his style of composition by referring to Hungarian rural music, folk music of the neighboring peoples of Eastern Europe, and his research work in Arabic and Turkish territories as having provided him with impressions, derived from the most varied sources, which appear in his works: "melted—I hope—into unity."[46] And it is this unity or, rather, synthesis of Eastern folk-music materials with Western art-music techniques that brought Béla Bartók international recognition as an outstanding composer of the twentieth century.

NOTES

1. This study is a revised version of my article published in *The World of Music* 29, no. 1 (1987): 43–65.

2. For example, the Hungarians Liszt and Erkel; the Bohemians Smetana and Dvorak; and the Russians Mussorgsky and Rimsky-Korsakov.

3. *BBL*, 29.

4. Piano Quintet, Rhapsody op. 1 for Piano and Orchestra, Scherzo for Piano and Orchestra, op. 2, and Suite No. 1 for Orchestra, op. 3.

5. *HFS*, 55.

6. This territory was turned over to Czechoslovakia after the First World War, following ratification of the Treaty of Trianon in 1920.

7. The Székely are an enclave of Hungarian-speaking people in southeastern Transylvania (now part of Romania).

8. See Bartók's remarks in *HFS*, 63, 77.

9. *BBE*, 409–10. He began the collection and recording of Slovak folk music in 1906, Romanian folk music in 1908, Ruthenian (that is, Ukrainian) folk music in 1911, a few specimens of Serbian and Bulgarian folk songs in 1912, Arab peasant music in 1913, and Turkish folk music in 1936.

10. See the bibliography in *BBE*, 527–55, and the listings in *BBGR*, 135–64.

11. *YFM*.i, 13–14, 27–28.

12. Ex. 10.3 is a skeleton form (without ornamental tones) of *HFS* melody No. 21.

13. Comparison of Ex. 10. 2 and Ex. 10. 3 clearly reveals the former's inherent pentatonicism. Bartók's comments on pentatonicism are given in Benjamin Suchoff, *Bartók's Mikrokosmos: Genesis, Pedagy, and Style* (Lanham, Md, and London: Scarecrow Press, 2002), 58.

14. *BBLW*, 62.

15. *BBCO*, 106–7.

16. *SV*.i, 38, 61–62.

17. See *BBSE*, 178, with regard to the second group and *BBE*, 128–29 and 130–33, for remarks on the other groups.

18. Melodies No. 316a. and b. in *SV.*i, 38, 61–62, where variant b. appears as the main theme (Allegro non troppo) in the second piece of Three Rondos on Folk Tunes for Piano (1927).

19. Bartók provides other examples of nondiatonic scales in *BBE*, 363.

20. *HFS*, 18.

21. *BBE*, 128.

22. Having the same number of syllables in each text line. See *SV.*i, melodies No. 186–88, 246–52, 329–45, and 393–97.

23. See Bartók's comments concerning this rhythm peculiarity in *BBSE*, 182–83 and 263 n. 15.

24. *BBE*, 119–20.

25. *MBB*, 241–49.

26. *RFM.*i, 50–51.

27. *BBE*, 386.

28. *RFM.*v, 28–30.

29. Ibid., melody No.154b.

30. Bartók's remarks concerning the influence of Ruthenian folk music on the folk music of neighboring countries will be found in *BBSE*, 187–89.

31. *BBE*, 379.

32. *YFM.*i, 451.

33. Bartók's use of this designation resulted from his investigation of the findings by the Bulgarian ethnomusicologist, Vasil Stoïn (1880–1938) and his detailed analysis of more than eight thousand Bulgarian folk melodies Stoïn published between 1928 and 1934. See *BBE*, 40–49, *RFM.*i, 43–44, *RFM.*iv, 31–32.

34. The transcriptions are published in facsimile in *YFM.*i, 453–71. Melody No.7, a *zaplet* dance piece, is the source tune for No. 39 (Serbian Dance) in Forty-four Duos for Two Violins.

35. Excepting Bartók's Serbian material, none of these melodies were transcribed from recordings. See *YFM.*i., xx–xxi, 18, 27.

36. *YFM.*i, 59–60.

37. *BBCO*, 139–41, 146.

38. See Bartók's remarks on Dalmatian part singing in *YFM.*i, 72.

39. *BBSE*, 29.

40. *BBE*, 377.

41. *BBSE*, 31–32.

42. Ibid., 56, scale No. 29.

43. *MBB*, 204–6, 213–29.

44. *TFM*, 29–30. A part of the vocal melodies is in near relation to the old Hungarian material, particularly with regard to syllabic and pentatonic structure.

45. *BBE*, 141.

46. *BBE*, 395. He died the next year, on 26 September, in New York City.

11

Approaching Bartók's Principles of Composition

POLYMODES, MODES, AND SCALES

On 19 January 1945, following negotiations with a New York music publisher, Bartók drafted an introduction for a "carefully revised" edition of his early piano works: Fourteen Bagatelles op. 6 (1908), Ten Easy Pieces (1908), Two Romanian Dances op. 8a (1908, 1910), Two Elegies op. 8b (1908, 1909), and Seven Sketches op. 9b (1908–1910).[1] His introduction specifies the following intrinsic principles of composition manifest in the listed works:

- A new piano style stripped of all unessential decorative elements, deliberately using only the most restricted technical means.
- A new trend of piano writing that accentuates the percussive character of the piano.
- The absurdity of using key signatures in certain kinds of contemporary music.
- The erroneous attribution of bitonality or polytonality to the first Bagatelle and other works.
- The tonality of selected pieces are given, in order to avoid misunderstanding. "This information is addressed especially to those who like to pigeonhole all music they do not understand into the category of 'atonal' music."[2]

In one of his lectures at Harvard University during February 1943, Bartók described polytonality as "the use of different diatonic keys in music of two or more parts, each part in a special key."[3] In the first Bagatelle, his use of four sharps in the upper staff and four flats in the lower one illustrates the absurdity of categorizing the music as atonal, that it is not a mixture of C♯ minor and F minor but simply a Phrygian-colored C major.[4] In point of fact, his euphemistic analytical remarks apparently were intended to avoid mention of the first Bagatelle as an early example of polymodal chromaticism—a unique Bartókian principle of composition that he explained for the first time at Harvard.

> As the result of superposing a Lydian and Phrygian pentachord with a common fundamental tone, we get a diatonic pentachord filled out with all the possible flat and sharp degrees [C-D♭-E♭-F-G and C-D-E-F♯-G]. These seemingly chromatic degrees, however are totally different in their function from the altered chord degrees of the chromatic styles of the previous periods. A chromatically-altered note of a chord is in strict relation to its non-altered form; it is a transition leading

to the respective tone of the following chord. In our polymodal chromaticism, however, the sharp and flat tones are not altered degrees at all; they are diatonic ingredients of a diatonic modal scale.[5]

Thus Bartók's first Bagatelle represents a C-Phrygian/Lydian eleven-tone polymodal construction in which the missing Lydian degree, D♮, indirectly brings out the essential Phrygian color degree, D♭ (Ex. 11.1).

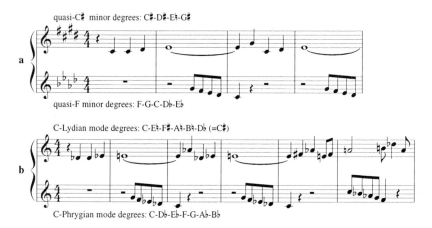

Ex. 11.1. Bartók, Fourteen Bagatelles op. 6 for Piano (1908), No. 1, (a) bars 1–4 and (b) bars 1–6 (without key signatures), with chromatically altered degrees to illustrate the polymodal C-Phrygian/Lydian eleven-tone construction.

With regard to modal types, Bartók mentions them as the five most commonly used modes of the art music of the Middle Ages (Ex. 11.2).[6] In view of their importance and function in his arrangements and abstract works, Bartók specialists refer to them as folk modes.

Ex. 11.2. The five folk modes in Bartókian polymodal chromaticism.

It is important to note Bartók's qualifying statement about the use of polymodal chromaticism in his musical language.

For instance, you cannot expect to find among our works one in which the upper part continuously uses a certain mode and the lower part continuously uses another mode. So if we say our art music is polymodal, this only means that polymodality or bimodality appears in longer or shorter portions of our work, sometimes only in single bars. So, changes may occur from bar to bar, or even from beat to beat in a bar.[7]

In addition to the folk modes is the old Hungarian pentatonic scale that Bartók discovered during July 1907, during his fieldwork in remote Székely villages of then Hungarian Transylvania (Ex. 11.3).[8]

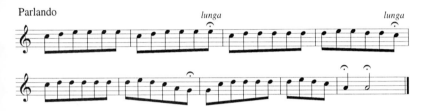

Ex. 11.3. Székely folk-song melody. Its symmetrical pitch collection, A-C-D-E-G, represents the typical pentatonic structure of archaic Hungarian folk music.

Another type of pitch collection that appears in Bartók's folk-music collections and abstract compositions is the so-called octatonic scale,[9] an eight-note symmetrical configuration with alternating half and whole steps or whole and half steps. In the case of polymodal chromaticism, based on a single (i.e., common) fundamental tone, there are two complementary octatonic scales. Ex. 11.4 compares the "Phrygian" and "minor" forms with their related Hungarian Gypsy scales.

Ex. 11.4. Comparison of (a) octatonic and (b) Hungarian Gypsy scales.

While the Gypsy scales—each with two augmented seconds—are commonplace in Hungarian urban folk music, Bartók's rural folk music collection has few examples of tunes with one augmented second and none with two such intervals.[10] Comparison of octatonic and Gypsy scales, especially those with the characteristic Phrygian (minor second) degree, may have sparked Bartók's in-

terest in the potential of octatonicism as a principle of composition.[11] The pitch
collection of a Romanian mourning song he collected in 1909, sung in unison
by two girls, consists of an octatonic pentachord (Ex. 11.5).

Ex. 11.5. *RFM*.ii, melody No. 6281. The text relates the sorrow of a mother about the
death of her daughter.

Bartók found other octatonic pitch collections during his 1913 fieldwork in
rural Arab areas of northern Algeria. In an instrumental performance played on
a peasant oboe (γeita), he heard the complete scale, F-G-Ab-Bb-Cb-Db-Dᵥ-E.[12]
Then, in 1916, he composed his Suite op. 14 for Piano, in which the second
movement features the emphatic rendition of the C-octatonic scale (Ex. 11.6).[13]

Ex. 11.6. Bartók, Suite op. 14 for Piano, third movement, bars 27–32.

There are two early Bartók works in which he used octatonic and whole-tone
pitch collections for the first time. In the third movement of the Sonata for Violin and Piano (February–August 1903), partitions of the octatonic scale appear
in the retransition to the tonic key (bars 363–366), followed by configurations
of the Bb whole-tone scale (bars 372–374).[14] The *Kossuth* symphonic poem (2
April–18 August 1903) has the same types of pitch collection that Bartók employs to tonally describe the battle between the Austrian and Hungarian armies
during the Hungarian insurgency of 1948. The parodic treatment of the Austrian

anthem is accomplished by chromatic compression of its first two diatonic bars into an octatonic scale partition (Ex. 11.7).[15]

Ex. 11.7. (a) Austrian anthem, bars 1–4, and (b) Bartók, *Kossuth* symphonic poem, bars 318–322.

The next variation of the anthem is thematic extension in range to partitions of the B♭ whole-tone scale (Ex. 11.8).[16]

Ex. 11.8. Bartók, *Kossuth* symphonic poem, R.N. 35.

INTERVALLIC CELLS

Ex. 11.9 illustrates the outcome of chromatic compression of the "Franz den Kaiser" motif. The resultant pitch collections are paired tritones, B♯-F♯-C♯-G (bars 394 and 396) and B♭-E-B♮-F (bars 398–401 and 402–404). The motif may be analyzed as juxtaposed minor seconds a tritone apart, it marks the first appearance of a characteristic (double-tritone) tetrachord in Bartók's tonal language, and it is commonly referred to as a "Z-cell."[17] In the eighth Bagatelle (op. 6, for piano) Bartók replaces traditional triads with Z-cells.[18]

Ex. 11.9. Ibid., R.N. 33.

Ex. 11.8 shows the next variation of the motif as a transposition and diatonic expansion to a whole-tone pitch collection, B♭-C-D-E-G♭-A♭. The emphatic rendition of a partition of this scale, played by the tuba, forms a characteristic "Y-cell" tetrachord in Bartók's tonal language.[19] Furthermore, the chromatic compression and diatonic expansion of melodies is another unique Bartókian principle of composition.[20] Thus, as notated in Ex. 11.10, the transformations of the "Franz den Kaiser" motif produce octatonic and whole-tone variations.

Ex. 11.10. *Gott erhalte* motivic variants.

In March 1911, when Bartók reached his thirtieth birthday, he began work on the score to the one-act mystery play, *Duke Bluebeard's Castle*, which had been written the previous year by the Hungarian poet Béla Balázs. The action, limited throughout to dialogue between Bluebeard and his latest wife, Judith, takes place in the cavernous hall of Bluebeard's castle. Judith, searching for light to dispel the gloomy atmosphere, persuades her reluctant bridegroom to hand over the keys to the seven locked doors in the hall. As she opens each door, she is horrified at the sight of a torture chamber, an armory, a treasure chamber, a flower garden, and the landscape of Bluebeard's vast domain, all drenched with blood. Whenever there is an allusion to blood in the libretto, Bartók's symbolic representation is the interval of a minor second, in melodic as well as harmonic form.[21] The juxtaposition of these intervals as a chromatic tetrachord transforms them into a rudimentary motif or X-cell.[22]

Ex. 11.11 illustrates the musical atmosphere when Judith opens the first door and sees the blood-encrusted torture instruments. The flute trill, B-A♯, representing blood, is combined with the brass half notes, A–G♯, at the moment when the stage direction indicates that Judith is to react with horror. Bartók's opera thus marks the first emphatic rendition of X-cell motifs in his musical language.

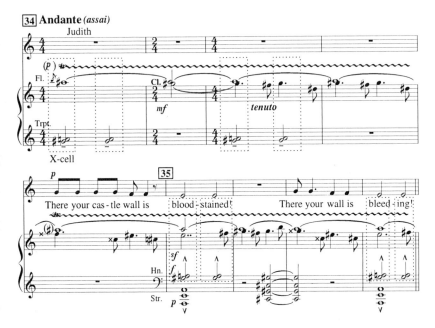

Ex. 11.11. Bartók, *Duke Bluebeard's Castle,* op. 11, R.N. 34.

RHYTHM

In his last Harvard lecture, Bartók begins with the statement that his rhythm formations are similar to those in Eastern European rural music: mainly based on the *arsis* principle—without upbeats. He continues with an explanation of the three kinds of rhythm widespread in that rural area:

> First is the *parlando-rubato*, that is, free, declamatory rhythm without regular bars or regular time-signatures. Its nearest equivalent in Western European art music may be found in recitative music; Gregorian music probably had a similar rhythm [Ex. 11.12]. Second is the more or less rigid rhythm, with regularly set bars, generally in 2/4 time. In certain types, change of measure may occur—which leads in some cases to seemingly complicated rhythms [Ex. 11.13]. The third kind of rhythm is the so-called "dotted" rhythm especially characteristic for certain types of Hungarian rural music. Our dotted rhythm is a combination of the following three rhythmic patterns: ♪ ♩., ♩. ♪, and ♩ ♩. [Ex. 11.14]. Among these, the first one, with an accentuated short value and a nonaccentuated long value, is the

most important. It is this rhythm pattern which gives that well-known rugged rhythm to many Hungarian pieces.[23]

Ex. 11.12. Bartók, *For Children*, Part II: Slovak Melodies, No. 23, bars 8–17.

Ex. 11.13. Bartók, *RFM*.iv., melody No. 62t, bars 1–6.

Ex. 11.14. *BBE*, 385: music example No. 21.

An asymmetrical rhythm found in certain of Bartók's compositions is the one he refers to as the "so-called Bulgarian rhythm."

It appears that the most frequent Bulgarian rhythms are as follows: 5/16 (subdivided into 3 + 2 or 2 + 3); 7/16 (2 + 2 + 3—the rhythm of the well-known *rŭchenitsa* dance); 8/16 (3 + 2 + 3); 9/16 (2 + 2 + 2 + 3); and about sixteen other less common rhythmic types.

When I first saw these unfamiliar rhythms, in which such fine differences are decisive, I could hardly imagine that they really existed. But then I seemed to remember that in my own collection of Romanian material I had come across similar phenomena. . . . Since then I have thoroughly revised my phonograph recordings, and it turns out that about five per cent of the Romanian material is also in so-called Bulgarian rhythm. For the present all we know is that it is best known and most widespread on Bulgarian soil. For this reason . . . we may rightly call it Bulgarian rhythm.[24]

During 1932, Bartók's revision of his Romanian material, excluding the Colinde (carols and Christmas songs), disclosed a small number of Bulgarian rhythms among the instrumental dance pieces and a few specimens in the vocal part of the collection. Apparently at that time he decided to study and classify Bulgarian folk-music publications (Ex. 11.15).[25]

Ex. 11.15. Vasil Stoin, *Chants populaires de la partie centrale de Timok à la Vita* (1928), melody No. 1450 as classified by Bartók.

The rhythmic difference between a Romanian *colindă* melody in Bulgarian 10/16 time (*RFM*.iv, melody No. 86a) and its variant (ibid., No. 86c) in 6/8 is shown in Ex. 11.16 and Ex. 11.17, respectively.

Ex. 11.16. *RFM*.iv, melody No. 86a.

Ex. 11.17. *RFM*.iv, melody No. 86c.

Other prevalent rhythm schemata in Bartók works were derived from his Slovak folk-song collection. He found that the rhythm of the oldest melodies "is nearly always *tempo giusto*, 2/4, and the notes are nearly always quarters and eighths; frequent forms are ♪♩♪ or ♫♩."[26] These forms, together with ♩ ♩, are permuted by the performers to produce a substantial number of variants in

Bartók's Slovak folk-song material. Ex. 11.18 is a partial tabulation of schemata derived from isometric melodies based on syllabic number of their text lines.

Five-syllable	Six-syllable	Seven-syllable	Eight-syllable

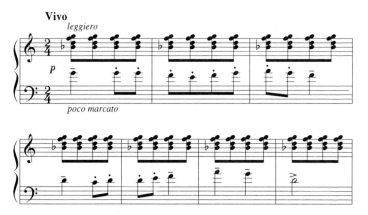

Ex. 11.18. *SV.*i, selected rhythm schemata from Table Ia, 731–48. A small number of melodies with texts of higher syllabic structure (9–15) are included in the table.

Two years after Bartók had begun his Slovak fieldwork, he selected a pentatonic folk-song melody from the collection as the theme of his fifth Bagatelle for piano (Ex. 11.19).

Ex. 11.19. Bartók, fifth Bagatelle for piano (1908), bars 5–11. The source melody is *SV.*ii, melody No. 692a, variant schema (August 1906).

MELODY

The first, simplest type of melodic construction is based on the symmetrical Hungarian pentatonic scale that Bartók discovered in Transylvania (then part of Greater Hungary) in 1907. Ex. 11.21a, a dotted-rhythm melody collected in 1908, shows the pentatonic scale based on G as principal tone, G-A-Bf-C-D-F. Ex. 11.21b, collected in 1909 during Bartók's fieldwork in a Transylvanian-Romanian village, has the same scale and dancelike rhythm.

Ex. 11.20. (a) *BBSE*, 124, melody No. 120, bars 5–8, and (b) *RFM*.ii, melody No. 565, bars 1–4. The·profuse ornamental tones are excluded for comparative purposes.

In Bartók's second Dirge for piano, structural features of the pentatonic scale, such as frequent leaps of perfect fourths and sequences of major seconds and minor thirds, are employed to create an original theme (Ex. 11.21).[27]

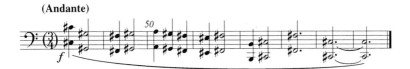

Ex. 11.21 Bartók, Four Dirges op. 9a for Piano (1909–1910), No. 2, bars 48–55.

The pentatonic introduction to Bartók's opera, *Duke Bluebeard's Castle*, is an expressionist, four-section theme (Ex. 11.22).

Ex. 11.22. Bartók, *Duke Bluebeard's Castle*, op. 11 (1911), bars 1–17.

The first theme in the Introduzione of Bartók's Concerto for Orchestra is an extended variant of the pentatonic theme that opens Bartók's opera (Ex. 11.23).[28]

Ex. 11.23. Bartók, Concerto for Orchestra (1943), first movement, bars 1–6.

In his third Harvard lecture, Bartók describes his innovative device in which his chromatic melodies are extended in range to any diatonic scale or mode.

> You know very well the extension of themes in their value called augmentation, and their compression in value called diminution. These devices are very well known, especially from the art music of the seventeenth and eighteenth centuries. As you will see, such an extension will considerably change the character of a melody, sometimes to such a degree that its relation to the original, nonextended form will be scarcely recognizable. We will have mostly the impression that we are dealing with an entirely new melody. And this circumstance is very good indeed, because we will get variety on the one hand, but the unity will remain undestroyed because of the hidden relation between the two forms.[29]

In his lecture notes, he points to the Music for Stringed Instruments, Percussion, and Celesta as an example of extension in range. Ex. 11.24 shows the fugue subject, played by the violas, that opens the first movement. Each of the four sections consists of a partition of the chromatic scale, based on A as the principal tone. In terms of polymodal construction, the scalar degrees represent juxtaposed pentachords of the A-Phrygian mode, A-Bb-C-D-E, and the A-Lydian mode, A-B-C#-Eb(=D#)-E. On the other hand—in terms of intervallic cells—the arrangement of these individual modal degrees is in accordance with symmetrical partitions: the A Z-cell, A-Bb-Eb-E, and permutations of its subsumed X-cell, B-C-C#-D.[30]

Ex. 11.24. Bartók, Music for Stringed Instruments, Percussion, and Celesta (1936), first movement, bars 1–4.

The extension of the fugue subject to a diatonic "entirely new melody" appears in the second movement (Ex. 11.25). The melodic contour of the first theme parallels the first half the fugue subject, and its pitch content likewise consists of juxtaposed Phrygian and Lydian partitions transposed to C as principal tone, C-Db-Eb-F-G/C-D-E-F#-G-A. The hidden relation between the fugue subject and the theme of the second movement is found in the cellular construction: the predecessor X-cells are extended in range to Y-cells (whole-tone tetrachords) that are interlocked as subsumed entities of the C Z-cell, C-Db-F#-G.[31]

The analysis of the fourth movement, as stated by the composer, "shows the main theme of Movement I, which is extended, however, by diatonic expansion of the original chromatic form"[32] (Ex. 11.26).

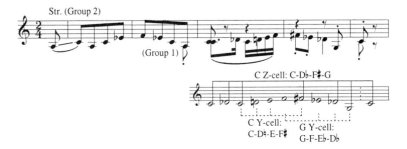

Ex. 11.25. Bartók, Ibid., second movement, bars 1–5.

Ex. 11.26 Bartók, Ibid., fourth movement, bars 203–209.

The extension results in a nondiatonic folk mode, C-D-E-F♯-G-A-B♭, which Bartók and Zoltán Kodály found among the folk songs in their Slovak collections (Ex. 11.27).[33]

Ex. 11.27. (a) *SV.*i, melody No. 318b, collected by Bartók in 1915, and (b) *SV.*ii, melody No. 870, collected by Zoltán Kodály in 1911. Both examples show the nondiatonic folk mode transposed to G as principal tone, G-A B-C♯-D-E-F♮.

The converse of diatonic extension is chromatic compression, a procedure that appears as a transitional device in the fourth movement. The diatonically extended theme "is gradually compressed into chromatic phrases associated with the original fugue subject."[34]

In Bartók's *Mikrokosmos* for piano, his comment refers to compression of a diatonic theme into chromatic form (Ex. 11.28).[35]

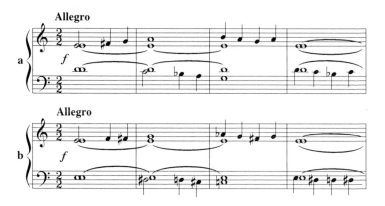

Ex. 11.28. Bartók, *Mikrokosmos* for piano (1926–1939), (a) diatonic melody No. 64a and (b) chromatically compressed variant, No. 64b.

TONE COLOR

Other innovations in Bartók's system of composition address specific methods for performance of percussion instruments, strings, and the piano.

Percussion instruments. The following directions are given in the score of the Sonata for Two Pianos and Percussion (1937):[36]

> The Bass Drum is to be played with a double-headed stick.
> The Triangle is to be played (a) with the usual metal beater; (b) with a thin wooden stick; (c) with a short, but rather heavy, metal beater.
> The Cymbal is to be played (a) with an ordinary timpani stick; (b) with the heavy end of a side drum stick; (c) with a thin wooden stick; (d) with the blade of a pocketknife or some similar instrument.
> The Side Drums, either with or without snares, are to be played with the usual sticks. If however, the Side Drum with snares should sound too loud, thinner sticks may be used.

String instruments. Perhaps the most telling description of Bartók's special sound effects in his Fourth String Quartet (1928) is this extract:[37]

> The percussive pizzicato (rebounding to the fingerboard with a snap) is now known as the Bartók pizzicato, but was at that time one of his most recent innovations. Other elements of color also appear: the tremolo-like chords and arpeggio pizzicati, the non-vibrato tone, the muted, veiled sound characteristic of the whole second

movement, the familiar ghostly technique of playing above the bridge, or the wooden, rapping, con legno effect; and again as a new means, the fantastic nightmare effect of extraordinarily accelerated and tremendous leggiero glissandi.

The Piano. Bartók's conception of the piano was in terms of its being an instrument capable of producing sounds, ranging from the most to the least percussive in quality, and he specified key-striking, the so-called percussive touch, as the basic way the piano is to be played. In fact, it is only in terms of percussive finger stroke as the fundamental approach to key depression that Bartók uses special symbols in his piano works, beginning with the first Bagatelle (Ex. 11.29).

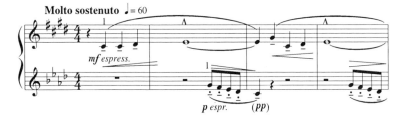

Ex. 11.29. Bartók, Fourteen Bagatelles op. 6, for Piano (1908), No. 1, bars 1–4.

The slurred tenuto signs in the upper staff indicate nonpercussive touch, that is, by pressing the key instead of striking it. The dotted tenuto signs in the lower staff are similarly nonpercussive, and the notes are never less than one-half their value.[38]

COUNTERPOINT

In 1928, Bartók responded to the query of a German musician who was preparing a study of the composer's piano works:[39]

> Why do I make so little use of counterpoint? I was inclined to answer you: because my beak grew that way. But since that is no answer, I shall attempt to clarify the situation:
> 1. In any case this is its character in performance;
> 2. In my youth my ideal of beauty was not so much the art of Bach or of Mozart as that of Beethoven. Recently it has changed somewhat: in recent years I have considerably occupied myself with music before Bach, and I believe that traces of this are to be noticed in the [First] Piano Concerto and the Nine Little Piano Pieces.

During Bartók's concert tours in Italy during March 1925 (Milan, Rome, Naples, and Palermo) and March 1926 (Bergamo, Cremona, and Florence) he became acquainted with the keyboard works of seventeenth- and eighteenth-century Italian composers, such as Azzolino Bernardino della Ciaia and Girolamo Frescobaldi. He transcribed their pieces for piano and introduced them for the first time during his 1926 concerts on Budapest Radio. Bartók's study of these works revealed a contrapuntal style significantly different from that of Bach, which led to a distinctive polyphonic dimension in his own works.[40]

The many examples of this dimension incorporate such devices as augmentation, canon, diminution, inversion, ostinato, pedal point, retrograde, and stretto.[41] Perhaps Bartók's most ingenious use of stretto is in the Concerto for Orchestra, where the development of the fifth movement is based on the exposition's closing theme as the subject of a monumental fugue.[42]

Notes

1. *BBE*, 432. The publisher, E. B. Marks Music, printed the Seven Sketches and Bartók's related comments in 1950, five years after the composer's death.

2. *BBE*, 432–33.

3. Ibid., 365.

4. Ibid., 433.

5. Ibid., 367.

6. Ibid., 363. In his comment to *Mikrokosmos* No. 32 (Vol. 1), he refers to them as "the so-called ecclesiastical modes." See also *BMP*, 44.

7. Ibid., 370.

8. *BBSE*, viii–ix.

9. Designated as such by Arthur Berger in his essay "Problems of Pitch Organization," *Perspectives of New Music* 2 (1963), 27.

10. *HFS*, 55. See melodies No. 153 and 196.

11. He was aware of Liszt's octatonic figurations in the latter's Prelude (on an ostinato bass after J. S. Bach). See *BBLW*, 44.

12. *BBSE*, scale No. 29. See also the smaller octatonic partitions in melodies No. 34 and 35.

13. In the second Dirge op. 9a for Piano (1909), bars 22–29, Bartók chromatically alters the pentatonic theme into an octatonic hexachord (see the illustration in *BBLW*, 71).

14. *BBCO*, 28–29, 31.

15. Ibid., 24.

16. The whole-tone scale and its partitions are important configurations in Bartók's musical language. See *BBMP*, 96.

17. Referred to as "cell Z" by Leo Treitler in "Harmonic Procedures in the Fourth

Quartet of Béla Bartók," *Journal of Theory* 3 (1959): 291–98.

18. *BC*, 121. See also *MBB*, 78–85.

19. *BC*, 117–20. See also *MBB*, 70.

20. *BBE*, 382–83.

21. Sándor Veress, "Bluebeard's Castle," in *Béla Bartók: A Memorial Review* (New York: Boosey & Hawkes, 1950), 45–49.

22. *MBB*, 89–93.

23. *BBE*, 383–84.

24. *BBE*, 44–47. The Bulgarian rhythm of 5/16 (subdivided into 3 + 2 or 2 + 3) is the rhythm of the *pajdushko horo*. See *BP*, 198.

25. Such as Vasil Stoin, *Chants populaires de la partie centrale de Timok à la Vita* (Sofia: Ministry of Public Education, 1928) (about 4,000 melodies). See Victor Bator, *The Béla Bartók Archives: History and Catalogue* (New York: Bartók Archives Publication, 1963), 32.

26. *BBE*, 128.

27. *HFS*, 18.

28. See *BBLW*, 154–55, and *BBCO*, 126, 148–49.

29. *BBE*, 381.

30. *BBCO*, 99. Transposition of the subject to E (bars 5–8) completes the A-Phrygian/Lydian twelve-tone polymode.

31. Ibid., 100.

32. *BBE*, 416.

33. *BBCO*, 101.

34. *MBB*, 135–36.

35. *BMP*, 60.

36. Hawkes Pocket Scores No. 51 (B & H 8675) (London: Boosey & Hawkes, 1942), 4.

37. György Kroó, *A Guide to Bartók*, trans. Ruth Pataki and Maria Steiner (Budapest: Corvina, 1974), 152.

38. *BMP*, 32.

39. Letter to Edwin von der Nüll in Berlin. In *Béla Bartók—Ein Beitrag zur Morphologie der neuen Musik.* (Halle: Mitteldeutsche Verlags A.G., 1930), 108. English translation in *LMBB*, 231–32.

40. *BMP*, 122.

41. See the index in *BBCO*, 260, for the specific pagination.

42. Ibid., 178–84.

12

Preface to *The Hungarian Folk Song*[1]

According to linguistic clues the Hungarian people apparently stem from a pre-historic community of Finno-Ugrian tribes who lived along the banks of the Karma River—about midway between the upper half of the Volga River and the Ural Mountains. Eventually the community split into Finnish and Ugrian branches; about 500 B.C. the latter further divided into Ostyaks, Voguls, and ancestral Magyars and moved westward to the middle Volga region. Here they added horse breeding to their main occupations of hunting and fishing.

During the following centuries the ancestral Magyars separated from their Ugrian kinsmen and came under the dominating influence of the Bulgars, a race of Turki horsemen, who provided the Magyars with new techniques in martial arts and social and political organization. Thus, through conquest, clans were organized into tribes, each unit and subunit headed by a chieftain, and then into a tribal confederation or empire headed by an overlord—the "king of kings."

Beginning about A.D. 830 the Bulgar-Magyar confederation was attacked by hostile tribes and moved further west to take up residence on the banks of the Don River. Here they came under the political control of another Turki nation, the Khazars, but less than seventy years later rebelled against this suzerainty. The Khazars then enlisted the aid of the Petchenegs, another newly arrived Turki nation, and the Hungarians (Magyars, Bulgars, and the Avars, a former Khazar tribal unit) were driven ever westward, across the Dnieper River and into territory held by eastern Slavic tribes. This area, "Great Moravia," also included the former Roman province of Pannonia (Western Hungary); both territories were quickly conquered by the Hungarians who, in 896, established themselves as masters of the Middle Danube Basin.

The Arpád Dynasty

Arpád (d. 907) became the first overlord of the Hungarian tribal federation, which was really a loose organization of clans and tribes headed by about forty to fifty family chiefs. Unilateral rather than joint forays quickly established the tradition of rivalry for power between the successor Magyar kings and their ennobled subjects.[2] When (St.) Stephen I was crowned as the first Christian king of Hungary in 1000, he consolidated his central authority by implementing a county system of administrative organization. Clan chiefs were awarded large grants of land as well as the resident mixed society of basically Magyar and Slavic freemen, together with serfs and slaves acquired from conquered peoples. Stephen also established bishoprics and monasteries with crown lands; other land grants were made to officers in his army. The resultant feudal society, castle centered and agriculturally based, lasted for two centuries.

During that time a class of craftsmen and traders grew, attracting immigrants from western and central Europe. This influx of workers, along with the conquest of South Slav territories in 1198 and the expansion north and east into regions inhabited by Slovaks, Ruthenians, and Romanians, resulted in a greater Hungary containing a population of about two millions in the thirteenth century.

But in 1241 Mongol hordes invaded the country, devastating the eastern half of Hungary to the Danube River line, withdrawing only after they had inflicted very heavy losses in human life and property. The defeated king, Béla IV, had no alternative but to share his land and his power with the Hungarian barons, in order to reorganize the country's defenses. The old castle-centered way of life, however, was replaced by urban developments in the form of chartered towns free from feudal obligations: thus a class of burghers emerged, separated from the peasantry. In addition to this middle social stratum another class was created, the so-called gentry or lesser nobility, small landowners who had achieved minor nobility through military service as officers in the king's army.[3]

In 1301 Andrew III, the last king of the Arpád Dynasty, died. The powerful clergy, whose properties and high offices were being expropriated by the barons, then succeeded in their attempt to place a non-Magyar ruler on the Hungarian throne: Charles I of Anjou was brought from Naples and crowned in 1308. By the end of the century—long after Charles had forcefully retrieved crown lands from the more powerful barons (c. 1321)—slavery had ended and serfdom was disappearing.[4]

THE HABSBURG MONARCHY

In 1437 Albert of Habsburg—Holy Roman Emperor and King of Bohemia— became the first Habsburg to wear the Hungarian crown.[5] This achievement, however, required baronial support with its attendant cost in terms of special rights. On the other hand, political conditions were thus created which enabled Hungary to resist the Turkish armies that invaded Transylvania in 1442 and the Serbian territory during the next decade.

The high cost of maintaining mercenary armies provided their officers with the opportunity to acquire lands in payment for their services, thus substantially increasing the class of feudal lords. Some of the peasants were able to purchase sizable acreage; others held smaller parcels, and a few were landless. But these gains were swept away in the war between the peasants and the nobles in 1514, an outcome of the aborted crusade against the Turks, in which the peasants were recruited by the clergy and given arms for the battle. The victorious nobles passed a law perpetually and universally binding peasants to the land and depriving them of the right to own land. Dissensions had also risen between the nobles and the gentry and, as always, between the nobles and their kings.

Finally in 1526 the resurgent Turkish armies destroyed the weakened Hungarian forces at the battle of Mohács, overran the Great Central Plain (the Alföld), and occupied Budapest. Transylvania became a principality under Turkish control, and the western (Transdanubia) and northwestern portion of the country was made part of the Habsburg Empire as the "Kingdom of Hungary."

NATIONALISM AND THE MINORITIES

After Mohács the barons took up residence in Vienna, adopted the language and customs of their Austrian royal hosts, and became a half-Germanized class of aristocrats to whom the Habsburgs entrusted the various high offices in the Hungarian army and governmental circles.

Protestantism in Calvinist, Lutheran, and Unitarian forms replaced the Catholic Church as the dominant religious influence in Hungary. The reformers preached in the Hungarian language and called for a national collaboration to defend Christianity against the pagan Turks. This awakening of national consciousness, despite the influx of non-Magyar, German-speaking peoples in the towns of western Hungary, had as an outcome the development of Hungarian patriotic verse and lyrical poetry.

In the essentially depopulated area of Central Hungary large numbers of Serbs took up residence as Turkish allies or as previous refugees from earlier Turkish invasions of the Balkans. The Transylvanian Principality, tributary to the Sultan, consisted of Magyars, Saxons, Székely,[6] and an ever-increasing population of Vlachs (that is, Romanians).

Fifty years later the great retreat of the Turks began, and in 1698 the Habsburg Emperor, Leopold I, recovered the central and eastern Hungarian territories. A plan was devised to recolonize depopulated or ungovernable Magyar districts with tractable foreign immigrants: South Germans (Swabians) flooded the western counties, thus reinforcing the German character of urban centers; a large group of Serbs was given national autonomy under the Emperor, in the south of Hungary; Slovak colonists settled in central and south Hungary; new Slavonian, Székely, and Romanian districts were also established along the southern tier; Ruthenians entered Hungary from the northeast, while Slovak expansion in the north enlarged the non-Magyar character of those areas; and the increase of more than a half million Romanians in Transylvania effectively completed the encirclement of Hungary with a ring of national minorities.[7] In fact, the total Magyar population in 1720 was 45 percent and sixty years later, 39 percent.

The Magyar barons, now thoroughly assimilated, sided with the Austrian emperors in attempting to Germanize the entire Hungarian nation. Records dating from 1784 indicate that Bartók's family on his mother's side came from such Germanized burgher stock which was later "diluted" by Hungarian-Slovak heritage.[8]

Musical Developments[9]

Old documents show that Gregorian chant appeared in Hungarian church schools and monasteries as early as the eleventh century. Latin texts were soon followed by Hungarian translations, and the most popular melodies eventually were transformed into a musical base for rural folk song.

In the sixteenth century, the first national musical style emerged: its most effective disseminator was the great Hungarian minstrel Sebestyén Tinódi (1505?–1556), who played a major role in establishing a people's music based on Hungarian epic song and lyric poetry.[10] Foreign influences returned during the Reformation, however, in the form of imported psalm-tunes underlaid with Hungarian texts. A further assault on the integrity of indigenous folk song followed the Turkish invasion and subsequent tripartition of Hungary.

Western Hungary, under the Habsburg Monarchy, was pervaded by Germanic culture in castle and town.[11] The ravaged, Turkish-occupied central Hungary was, as previously mentioned, severely depopulated; in fact, the southern portion was essentially devoid of the Magyar element. The Principality of Transylvania, however, which now included Magyar refugees[12] in addition to the resident Székely people, became the preserve for traditional Hungarian musical life.[13] At the end of the seventeenth century, following the Turkish withdrawal, Hussar officers of the Austro-Hungarian monarchy established the practice of recruiting young men by means of dance music performed on the bagpipe or by Gypsy bands. Designated *verbunkos*, the melodies are strikingly similar to the swineherd, heyduck, and Ukrainian *kolomyjka* dance tunes.[14]

The *verbunkos*, with its slow and fast forms, when removed from a military setting grew into the national Hungarian musical idiom of the nineteenth century. Indeed, professional Hungarian musicians[15] applied the instrumental *verbunkos* style to dance suites and other forms of chamber music. Later on the *verbunkos* influenced the vocal repertory of lyric songs.

During the transformation period of the *verbunkos* music, another musical idiom penetrated Hungary, through the intermediation of the German *Singspiel*: the *Volkstümlichlied*.[16] The immense popularity of this new type of urban folk song quickly led to the production of thousands of Hungarian imitations, for the most part by amateur (so-called dilettante) members of the educated Hungarian classes.

In 1812, in what is apparently the first Hungarian *Singspiel*, *Cserni Gyurka*, Gábor Mátray (1797–1875) merged Hungarian urban folk song, *verbunkos* music, and Viennese elements, all in an attempt to create a specifically Hungarian operatic style. During the midpart of that century, the younger generation of Hungarian peasants adopted and transformed those urban folk songs which strongly resembled traditional rural products.[17] This assimilation was part of the revolution in Hungarian musical life that Bartók designated as the new style of Hungarian peasant music.

The *verbunkos* and the related *csárdás*, in which slow (*lassú*) and fast (*friss*) sections alternate, received national emphasis and international attention during and following the Hungarian insurgency of 1848 under Lajos (Louis) Kossuth. This music and the urban folk-song genre—published in large numbers, with stereotyped piano accompaniments, in small and large collections—were propagated by urban Gypsy bands at home and by such composers as Brahms, Liszt, and Sarasate abroad.

Ferenc Erkel (1810–1893), preeminent Hungarian opera composer, and Franz Liszt (1811–1886) were the first and most illustrious faculty members of the Hungarian Academy of Music in 1875.[18] Liszt accepted the post of director; while German-born or German-trained musicians were appointed to the faculty, Hungarian-born virtuoso instrumentalists were also quickly developed,[19] and Béla Bartók, destined to become the nation's greatest composer and ethnomusicologist, attended the institution as a student in piano and composition from 1899 to 1903.

THE BARTÓK AND KODÁLY DICHOTOMY[20]

When Bartók was five years old, his mother, an accomplished pianist, began teaching him the piano. His father, also a gifted musician and amateur composer, further enhanced the musical atmosphere surrounding the child.[21] Bartók's pre–Academy of Music years were exclusively urban in terms of social and cultural environment. He was indeed fortunate to have had several years of piano and music-theory training with Erkel's son, László (1844–1896) in Pozsony (now Bratislava, Slovakia). This training was based on German classic and romantic piano repertories.

Toward the end of the century Bartók came in contact with nationalistic events by serving as piano accompanist or soloist during city celebrations of the Hungarian Millennium and the fiftieth anniversary of the 1848 revolution. At this time, however, he was composing songs with German texts and, as late as 1900, signing his manuscripts "Béla von Bartók." His student years in Budapest coincided with growing public clamor for a Hungarian national anthem to replace the Austrian *Gott erhalte* and for the Hungarian language to replace German in every aspect of national life. Bartók quickly became an ardent nationalist, began the study of Liszt's works, and in 1901 received the coveted Liszt Prize and glowing press reviews of his piano recitals.

In 1902 Bartók composed his first "Hungarian-style" settings of poetic texts by Lajos Pósa. (The four songs, Bartók's first published work, were produced by Ferenc Bárd, Budapest, in 1904.) Early the same year Bartók attended the first Budapest performance of a Richard Strauss work, the tone poem *Also sprach Zarathustra* (op. 30, 1896). The effect on young Bartók was like "a bolt of lightning," and he immediately plunged into an intensive study of Strauss's works.[22] Approximately one year later, a few months prior to his graduation from the Academy of Music, he began writing his first major work, *Kossuth*, a symphonic poem in ten sections.

Kossuth, because of its sensational content in the form of parodies of the Austrian national anthem, propelled its composer into the national limelight after the first performance in Budapest on 13 January 1904. International recognition came in February in England at the next performance of the work, by the Manchester Hallé Concert Society Orchestra. Now a recognized Hungarian composer as well as piano virtuoso, Bartók devoted himself to composition, from May until November, at a villa in Gerlicepuszta (now Grlica, Slovakia). He put the finishing touches on the Piano Quintet (October 1903–July 1904); composed the Scherzo for Piano and Orchestra in July and August, orchestrating it beginning in September; and then commenced work on the Rhapsody for Piano, op. 1, in October. The Rhapsody is particularly Liszt-oriented, Gypsy-styled, and an obvious attempt to create a genuine Hungarian musical idiom by means of original thematic material instead of popular urban folk songs.

Sometime during that summer another "bolt of lightning" struck Bartók, this time in simple, unaccompanied vocal form: the singing of Lidi Dósa, an eighteen-year-old Székely girl.[23] Dosá, nursemaid to the child of a Budapest family on summer holiday in the same villa, was overheard singing a number of tunes, among them "Piros alma leesett a sárba" (The Red Apple Fell into the Dirt).[24] At an interview in 1970 the eighty-five-year-old woman recalled that Bartók "liked the tune . . . [and] he wanted to note it down: After he noted it down, he went to the piano and played it, then he asked me whether he played it correctly. Well, it was exactly as I sang it . . . I had to sing continually, however, he only wanted to hear the ancient village tunes! He only liked those I had learned from my grandmother."

The immediate outcome of this fortuitous meeting was Bartók's transcription of "Piros alma" for voice and piano, and its publication in the musical supplement of the journal *Magyar lant* on 15 February 1905. Another song Dósa sang to him is published in *HFS*, melody No. 234a; both melodies originate from Hungarian art song (see Bartók's remarks in *HFS*, 63, 77).[25]

The other result was Bartók's decision to collect, transcribe, and publish similar melodies, for he realized that "Piros alma" contained significant differences from its art-song source: truncated ABC content structure instead of da capo quaternary form and, more importantly perhaps, modal alternation—in place of the original harmonic minor scale—in which the first two melody sections are Dorian and the third one is Aeolian. It seems reasonable to conjecture that Bartók may have suddenly concluded that popular art song (that is, urban folk song) thus "Székely metamorphosed"—rather than its Gypsy "contamination"—might be the autochthonous Magyar folk song and therefore the more appropriate thematic basis in his search for an innovative Hungarian style of composition. In fact in 1905 he applied for and received a grant-in-aid of 1600 crowns to study Székely folk music in Csík County. Because of other circumstances, however, he postponed the project till the summer of 1907.

Bartók, seeking to add international recognition to his recent achievements, entered the Rubinstein Prize competitions in piano and composition, which were held in Paris in August 1905. It was surely fortunate that his efforts failed, for Wilhelm Backhaus, who won the prize in piano, went on to a brilliant career as soloist and piano teacher (at the Royal College of Music in Manchester, England) immediately thereafter. Writing from Paris in mid-August, Bartók delineated his future musical posture:

> In reply to your letter, I must say that Bach, Beethoven, Schubert, and Wagner have written such quantities of distinctive and characteristic music that all the music of France, Italy and the Slavs combined, is as nothing by comparison! Of all other composers, Liszt comes closest to the Big Four, but he seldom wrote Hungarian music. Even if, say, my Funeral March [from the *Kossuth* symphonic poem] could hold its own in one respect or another, no nation could possibly appear in the arena with a single 4-page piece, however magnificent it might be! In short: we are still far from being ready to start. Work and study, work and study, and again, work and study. Then we may achieve something. For we're in a surprisingly favorable position, compared with other nations, in regard to our folk-music. From what I know of the folk-music of other nations, ours is vastly superior to theirs as regards force of expression and variety. If a peasant with the ability to compose tunes like the one enclosed [the music examples have since been lost] had but emerged from his class during childhood and acquired an education, he would assuredly have created some outstanding works of great value. Unfortunately, it is rare for a Hungarian peasant to go in for a scholarly profession. . . . A real Hungarian music can originate only if there is a real Hungarian gentry.[26]

While the foregoing lines were being written, Zoltán Kodály was in the village of his childhood, Galánta (now part of Slovakia) collecting songs from peasant informants as source material for his doctoral thesis, *A magyar népdal strófa-szerkezete* (The Stanzaic Structure of Hungarian Folk Song). Later that year, thirteen of those songs were published in the Budapest journal *Ethnographia*.[27] In a typically unassuming way Kodály later recalls 1905 as the year in which Bartók "made a thorough study of my first collection which appeared in the periodical Ethnographia and then my 1906 study on the verse structure of the Hungarian folk song, and made penetrating enquiries concerning contact with the people and the collecting methods. He became acquainted with the phonograph."[28] And so it was that Bartók, already a famous national personality, initiated the connection with the younger Kodály (b. 16 December 1882, d. 6 March 1967), who was to prove so decisive a force in shaping Bartók's multifaceted musical career. Let us therefore digress momentarily and explore Kodály's background.

The boyhood of Zoltán Kodály was spent in the village of Galánta and the town of Nagyszombat (both now part of Slovakia), then the northwest frontier territory of Greater Hungary. His father was station master for the Hungarian

State Railways, and the son enjoyed listening to the songs of the migrant peasant laborers as they waited for their trains. Indeed, it was at this time that the boy became a "collector" of folk music, for he knew that his parents—both amateur musicians—would reward him appropriately when he brought home a newly learned, interesting folk song he had picked up at the railway station. With very little formal instruction he learned to play the piano and stringed instruments, and he began to compose at a very early age: "playing instruments was never the thing for me. I composed more than I played music right from the start." Among the early pieces were an Ave Maria for solo voice and organ and a Mass for mixed voices and organ, both composed a few years prior to his matriculation at the Budapest Academy of Music in 1900.

Kodály's original plan was to study law at the University in Budapest: he therefore enrolled in the Department of Philosophy there. Although, like Bartók, he studied composition with Hans Koessler (1853–1926) at the Academy, the two students—attending class at different times during the week—did not meet until after they had graduated.[29] During his university years, however, Kodály decided to study music rather than law and to combine music teaching and composition. Seeking a suitable combinative topic for a Ph.D. thesis, following his graduation from the Academy of Music, Kodály decided to build on an earlier-acquired interest in Hungarian literature—particularly folk-song poetic texts. This decision was an outcome of his comparative study of existing folk-song publications and collections with the phonographic recordings of Béla Vikár (1859–1945).[30]

As described above, Kodály visited his "native" village[31] to undertake his first collection of rural folk song, returning with 150 specimens collected in that area. Although the extant sources indicate a close contact already developed between Bartók and Kodály beginning in the last month or two of 1905, it is not clear what role, if any, Bartók played in shaping Kodály's thesis.[32] As a comparison of the dissertation and various sections of the present publication reveals, Kodály's research made an indelible impression of a formative nature with respect to Bartók's methodology and conclusions. Yet it is equally apparent that Bartók's approach, which began as a codification of the pathfinding premises expounded by Kodály in 1906, became uniquely his own.

Kodály's first classification of Hungarian folk song, as presented in his thesis, is based on the rhythmical properties of the treated materials.[33] Two major classes are established, in terms of equal or unequal division of the strophe; two subclasses in each major category are formed on the basis of isometric or heterometric line structure; then groups and subgroups are derived in which the latter, for the most part, represent syllabic structures proceeding from lesser to greater numbers of text-line syllables. In the discussion of the eleven-syllable line is to be found the concept of "a régibb és újabb magyar ritmopoeia" (the older and newer Hungarian rhythmopoeia), which may have provided Bartók with the terminological basis for his later classification of Hungarian folk song in terms of "old"-, "new"-, and "mixed"-style major categories.

Returning to the Bartók-Kodály story, the two men decided to join forces in gathering and publishing Hungarian folk songs of a type "unknown till then," to publish them in separate booklets and with piano accompaniments, and to underwrite the costs of publication in order to maximize sales income as a funding base for their future field trips. Circulars were mailed to friends and ostensibly interested colleagues to subscribe to the future publication and thus enable "The final end, a complete collection of folk songs gathered with scholarly exactitude. . . ."[34]

During that summer Kodály traveled north to Nyitra County (Nitra, Slovakia) and Bartók headed east to stay with his sister Elza in Békés County. During his recording sessions in July Bartók may have encountered Slovak itinerant peasant workers: "Hardly had I begun this work when I concluded that the knowledge of the Hungarian material alone is insufficient for scientific consideration and that the most thorough knowledge of at least the neighboring peoples' material is absolutely needed to this end."[35] In the fall, therefore, while he was in Pozsony preparing for a recital, he visited Gerlicepuszta and collected Slovak folk songs.

In December, Magyar népdalok was published at a cost of 750 crowns (under the imprint of Károly Rozsnyai, Budapest, and in one booklet: Nos. 1–10 by Bartók, 11–20 by Kodály). This publication marked Kodály's first appearance in print as a composer. An indifferent public, now attracted by Viennese operetta hits and similar popular urban songs, purchased few of the thousand copies the young idealists had printed. The rejection, together with the 1907 appointments at the Academy of Music for Bartók (professor of piano, to succeed his own teacher) and Kodály (professor of theory, to teach ear training and music dictation), had great impact on their individual and collaborative aspirations during the next decade.

Kodály, a born teacher who was to achieve international renown for his theories and related works in music education, devoted himself almost exclusively to his pedagogical duties. He wrote little music: in point of fact it was not until 1910 that his First String Quartet (op. 2, 1908–09) was published; Sixteen Songs (op. 1, 1909) and the few other vocal and chamber works that were composed between 1907 and 1920 were not accepted for publication until 1921 or thereafter. Other than his transcription of the ballad *Szép Ilona*, which is printed following Bartók's "Transdanubian Ballads" in *Ethnographia*, 1909,[36] and a lengthy essay on the folk customs in the Zobor region (ibid., 1909), his published writings were extra ethnomusicological in content.

Bartók, on the other hand, because of his prestigious position on the piano faculty, was offered new publication opportunities. He began editing collections of works from the standard piano repertory (Bach, Haydn, Mozart, Beethoven, etc.) and, shortly after he returned from the previously postponed collecting trip to Székely villages in Csik County (summer 1907), he began composing folk-song-based piano pieces (Three Folk Songs from Csik County).[37] His folk-song settings were for the most part published without undue delay or during his lifetime, contrary to Kodály's experience. So far as scholarly writing is concerned, Bartók lost no opportunity to publish the results of his research and its related transcriptions from his collections of vocal and instrumental folk music in various Budapest journals.

"Székely Ballads" (*Ethnographia*, 1908) represents Bartók's first scholarly effort, in which he postulates that these old melodies are not closely bound to their texts and that epic and lyric melodies and texts are interchangeable within a rhythmic context. Another first effort, this time in the form of teaching pieces for the piano, was of more telling impact in penetrating the apathy of Hungarian educated circles toward their indigenous rural folk music. Between 1908 and 1909 he published Ten Easy Pieces and *For Children* (based on Hungarian and Slovak folk tunes).

In the fall of 1908, Bartók was in Maros-Torda County (now Mureş≲Romania) in the village of Torockó, where he met some Romanian girls from the nearby village of Székelyhidas (now Podeni). Their songs, which he noted down by ear (he was traveling without his phonograph at the time), were a decisive factor in his resolve to add Romanian material to his collections: the richly ornamented melodies seemed to relate to Székely performance style. On the other hand, he observed that certain structural features—three-section strophe and *tonus finalis* on the second degree of the scale—were quite unlike his Hungarian material.

He then made contact with a Romanian school teacher, Ion Buşiţia (1875–1953), who was also an amateur musician, and the two explorers set out in July 1909 to collect vocal and instrumental specimens in Bihor County villages. He returned the next summer to continue his work (which, in 1910, totaled 371 melodies), and, as he later confessed with regret:

> I did not heed all the requirements of folklore research in the first two years. At that time I attacked the problem purely as a musician, not minding extra-musical circumstances very much. The method of research changes according to the nature of the people whose folk music is in question; thus it took one or two years to familiarize myself with the new situation presented by Romanian folk music.[38]

Put in another way, while Bartók transcribed his growing collections of Hungarian, Slovak, and Romanian materials as a source for future compositions, he began to notice individual differences and reciprocal relationships among those materials. In the Slovak melodies, for example, he observed that certain tunes were similar to the "new"-style Hungarian ones. This similarity prompted second thoughts about his procedure of 1909, in which he had organized the four hundred Slovak folk songs in his manuscript collection according to village (the method followed in the Slovak publication *Slovenské Spevy*[39]). On the other hand, as mentioned above, the Romanian melodies from Bihor County appeared to have little if any relationship to Hungarian tunes. From this need to determine which musical characteristics are indigenous and which ones borrowed emerged what was ultimately to become Bartók's outstanding contribution to comparative music folklore: the determination of morphological elements by means of statistical treatment in the form of frequency of occurrence.

Between 1909 and 1910, however, he struggled to find a way to sort the mentioned materials. Apparently at Kodály's suggestion Bartók turned to the classification system devised by Ilmari Krohn (1867–1960), Finnish composer and musicologist, for *Soumen Kansan sävelmiä* (a collection of Finnish folk songs),[40] in which end tone and syllabic structure of each melody section constitute the major aspects of the sorting procedure. In order to compare his materials quickly and easily, Bartók modified the Krohn system somewhat: each melody would be transposed to end on g^1, a procedure which also minimized ledger-line notation. And he began to compile diacritical signs and special symbols to supplement the notation of text and melody.

Then, during the spring of 1910, he approached the Romanian composer, D. G. Kiriac (1866–1928) in regard to his new approach to the transcription of Romanian musical folklore and the possibilities for publication of the Bihor melodies in Bucharest. In a matter of months the Romanian Academy voted to include Bartók's transcriptions in their publication series of Romanian folklore studies and to provide him with funds in connection with his recording activities.

In these years prior to the outbreak of World War I Bartók's musical and scholarly involvement was so diverse in scope and significant in output as to border on incredibility. He extended his collecting to include Arab, Ruthenian, and Serbian materials, and he concentrated on recording the instrumental and vocal music of Romanian peasants in the various Transylvanian counties. The primitive instruments of village peoples fascinated him. He made careful measurements of bagpipes, flutes, and so on, and along with the first transcriptions ever made of the music involved, he published a series of essays on his findings in Budapest journals.

The tedious but indispensable task of transcription of his Slovak and Romanian collections continued at a feverish pace: by February 1911 he had compiled enough material for a second volume of Slovak folk songs. Of primary concern, of course, was the commissioned volume of Bihor folk music, which was completed in December.[41] In 1912, he published his essay "Comparative Music Folklore," and he wrote to the Berlin Phonogramme Archives about the possibilities of exchanging phonograph recordings—including "nearly 1000" of his own. He gave piano recitals which in 1911 featured pieces by Couperin, Rameau, and Scarlatti (later edited for publication in Budapest), and he composed large orchestral works in addition to piano pieces. Because of public antagonism to his compositions, in 1911 he and Kodály organized the New Hungarian Musical Society, whose purpose was to establish an orchestra that would adequately perform the new music. A series of chamber-music concerts, including vocal and piano solos by Bartók, were presented to raise funds. The financial failure of this short-lived enterprise affected Bartók deeply, according to a letter written in 1913:

> A year ago sentence of death was officially pronounced on me as a composer. . . . It therefore follows that since the official world of music has put me to death, you can no longer speak of my "prestige.". . . Therefore I have resigned myself to write for my writing-desk only. . . .
>
> My public appearances are confined to one sole field: I will do anything to further my research work in musical folklore! I have to be personally active in this field, for nothing can be achieved in any other way; while neither recognition nor public appearances are required for composing.[42]

Bartók's "I will do anything . . ." included a request to the Kisfaludy Society—put in final form and co-signed by Kodály—for support in the publication of "a monumental Hungarian 'Corpus Musicae Popularis.'" The request, published in letter form during the latter part of 1913,[43] opens with a survey of previously published folk-music collections (prepared by Kodály), then details the classification procedures to be followed (apparently drafted by Bartók), and concludes with a list of recommended scholarly appendixes for the publication (probably a joint contribution).[44] In December Bartók was gratified to learned that:

> The task of making a Complete Edition of Hungarian Folk Songs (containing approximately 5,000 songs) has been given to me and my colleague Zoltán Kodály (a first-rate musician), and in classifying them we have used Ilmari Krohn's system, with some slight modifications of our own. In order to be able to compare them with the songs of our neighbors, the Slovaks, I have classified about 3,000 Slovakian songs by the same method. And it is remarkable, I can tell you, to what a degree, through mere mechanical classification, the relation between the variants becomes clear. By this system of classification one can pick out any tune from a large collection with the greatest ease.
>
> When it comes to the popular songs of Romania the situation is a bit different. With the Slovaks, and even more with ourselves, the distinction between the categories is a little blurred, while the Romanians have kept the categories intact.[45]

Other than in 1915, when Bartók was concentrating on the composition of his first ballet, *The Wooden Prince*, and piano works based on Romanian folk music, the war years did not interrupt his fieldwork in Slovakia and Transylvania. Kodály, now professor of composition at the Academy of Music, decided to follow Bartók's footsteps in Csík County in 1910 and 1912 (collecting Székely melodies); then, in 1914, he recorded folk songs in Székely-Csángó villages further north in Bukovina.

Among the collected melodies were a number of ballads—particularly *Árgirus nótája* (Song of Argirus)—which, beginning in 1915, turned Kodály toward historiography in terms of the bearing of folk-music-derived data on Hungary's position in music history.[46] This turning point was emphasized in 1920, when his essay on Argirus appeared in *Ethnographia* (Budapest): here Kodály demonstrates that a proper understanding of ancient Hungarian prosody—for example, that of Tinódi (see p. 167)—can only be achieved by study of related folk song.

It is most interesting to observe that while Kodály was exploring Romanian territory for Hungarian material in 1914, Bartók had embarked on a fresh approach to ethnomusicology: the scientific treatment of data (that is, statistical evidence) in his 1913 collection of Romanian folk music from Máramaros County (Maramureş, Romania).[47] And while Kodály's tangential investigation of the Hungarian musical folklore was under way the next year, Bartók transcribed and studied the collected Hungarian material—now comprising more than 5,000 songs—with a determination that conceivably was an outcome of his reaction to Kodály's research.[48]

Then, in 1918, Bartók's essay on the melodies of Hungarian (folk) soldiers' songs (*BBE*, No. 10) introduced the concept of a dual classification system in terms of "old"-style and "new"-style melodies. Two years later he had augmented the classification with a third category: "melodies of heterogeneous kind" (*BBE*, No. 39, "Hungarian Peasant Music"); and in 1921, the same year that he completed the first version of *The Hungarian Folk Song* (*A magyar népdal* [Budapest: Rózsavölgyi és Társa, 1924]), he iterated the tripartite classification of Hungarian musical folklore (*BBE*, No. 11).

Economic and other conditions during and after World War I and the negative attitude of the Kisfaludy Society toward publishing folk-music poetic texts with their respective melodies was the major factor in the endless postponement of the "Corpus Musicae Popularis" project. Another, more subtle contributing factor was the ever-widening divergency of approach to Hungarian ethnomusicology between Bartók and Kodály. Bartók's philosophy, which he followed consistently to the end of his life, was to record "as rich a collection as possible" of rural folk tunes of "neighboring peasant classes that are in close contact with one another," transcribe and then scientifically classify the derived data, and by means of comparative methodology determine the musical styles and, "so far as possible," trace the origin of the derived styles (see *HFS*, 4). His ultimate goal, which is inherent in his monumental studies of east European and other musical folklore, was to construct a kind of "unified field" theory on the international level of comparative musicology that, with appropriate modifications, would be operative inside or outside Hungarian borders.

NOTES

1. This study, a revised extract from *HFS*, ix–xxix, is based on a number of historical sources, among them *An Encyclopedia of World History*, ed. W. A. Langer (Boston: Houghton Mifflin, 1948); *A History of Hungary*, ed. Ervin Pamlényi (London: Collet's, 1975); and C. A. Macartney, *Hungary* (London: Ernest Benn, 1934).

2. This adversary relationship endured for more than a millennium!

3. The barons, gentry, burghers, and clergy are collectively referred to as the educated classes in Bartók's later essays.

4. In fact, Charles was actively supported by poorer members of the provincial over-lord families, who had been exploited by their wealthier relatives.

5. Albert died of the plague two years later; he was followed by Polish and Hungarian appointees until the restoration of the Habsburg dynasty in the sixteenth century.

6. An enclave of Hungarian-speaking people of Bulgar-Turki origin.

7. This Austrian policy ultimately led to the dismemberment of Greater Hungary in 1920.

8. Paula Voit (1857–1939): her grandmother was Elisabeth Scherz (d. 1867); her mother, Teréz Polerentzky (d. 1874). The Voits lived in Pozsony (now Bratislava, Slovakia), where Paula became a primary school teacher. Her marriage to Bartók's father took place on 5 April 1880 in Nagyszentmiklos (Torontal County, now part of Romania), a small town that in 1910 consisted of Hungarians, Serbians, Germans, and Romanians. Bartók was born there on 25 March 1881.

9. Readers interested in a scholarly, audiovisual account of this subject should refer to *Musica Hungarica*, ed. B. Szabolcsi and M. Forrai (Budapest: Qualiton, 1970). See also Zoltán Kodály, *Folk Music of Hungary* (New York: Praeger Publishers, 1971), 5–9, 14–22.

10. He published a collection of pieces in Kolozsvár (now Cluj-Napoca, Romania) in 1554, titled *Cronica*.

11. Codices assembled between 1660 and 1689 (Markfelder, Vientórisz; also the virginal book of J. Stark) contain—in addition to material of German provenance—Hungarian, Slovak, and Polish tunes.

12. The heyducks (*hajdú*), who were peasant mercenaries but originally herdsmen, brought their recruiting dances into the territory.

13. The Kájoni Codex, named after János Kájoni, a Franciscan monk and church musician (d. 1687 in the Transylvanian county of Csík), was assembled between 1634 and 1671. It contains Hungarian folk dance tunes, sacred and secular songs, and foreign instrumental and vocal pieces (sacred and secular), all notated in organ tablature.

14. As well as the Romanian *Ardeleana* (the designation means "Transylvanian") melody type. See Bartók's discussion in his study, *RFM*.i, 48–50. See also his essay "Hungarian Folk Music and the Folk Music of Neighboring Peoples," in *BBSE*, 187–88, 196.

15. Violinist-composers and Gypsy band leaders like, for example, Márk Rózsavölgyi (1789–1848) and János Bihari (1764–1827).

16. A folk-like art song in the German vernacular, usually strophic in form and with architectonic (that is, rounded) structure. These simple songs, fitted with keyboard accompaniment, ultimately degenerated into squarely symmetrical, hackneyed tunes with slobbery texts. The *Singspiel*, which began as a comic play with musical interpolations,

became the national form of German opera after 1750; arias, choruses, folk-type songs, and other musical elements were connected by dialogue.

17. As a case in point, Bartók inadvertently included an urban folk song by Elemér Szentirmay (1836–1908) in Twenty Hungarian Folk Songs for Voice and Piano (No. 5, "Ucca, ucca"), which he and Kodály published in 1906. The song was omitted when the second edition was brought out in 1938.

18. Like his contemporary Liszt, however, Erkel composed musical Hungarianisms by way of Gypsy-styled, would-be popular Hungarian songs.

19. For example, the violinist Jenő Hubay (1858–1937) and the pianist Arpád Szendy (1863–1922), who became outstanding teachers at the Academy.

20. Four basic sources are recommended to the English reader: *BBE*; *Béla Bartók: His Life in Pictures and Documents,* ed. Ferenc Bónis (Budapest: Corvina Press, 1972); *The Selected Writings of Zoltán Kodály,* ed. Ferenc Bónis, trans. L. Halápy and F. Macnicol (Budapest: Corvina Press, 1974); and *Zoltán Kodály His Life in Pictures,* ed. László Eősze (New York: Belwin-Mills, 1971).

21. Béla Bartók Sr., 1855–1888, was principal of the Nagyszentmiklós Agricultural School and first president of the town's musical society. He died when Bartók was eight years old, and his widow—moving her family from town to town as she gradually improved her teaching assignments—supplemented her income by giving private piano lessons.

22. Bartók no doubt immediately recognized the relationship between Strauss and Liszt in terms of genre (program music) and structure (for example, thematic transformation). More important, however, was Strauss's innovative use of unresolved dissonance.

23. The story of Lidi Dósa's contact with Bartók is told by Péter Cseke in "Aki Bartóknak énekelt" (Who sang to Bartók), as published in *Bartók-könyv 1970–1971,* ed. Ferenc László (Bucharest: Kriterion, 1971), 89–92.

24. *HFS*, No. 313. The second verse of this melody, not given in the song texts (ibid., 188), is "Én felveszem [felvettem?] a sárbol, / Elbúcsuzom a régi babámtol" (I pick it up from the dirt, /I take leave of my old sweetheart).

25. See also D. Dille, "Gerlice Puszta: Mai bis November 1904," *Documenta Bartókiana* 4 (Budapest, 1970), 15–40. A facsimile of the *Magyar lant* musical supplement appears on pp. 25–26.

26. Irmy Jurkovics, Nagyszentmiklós, 15 August 1905, as published in *BBL*, 50.

27. Under the title "Mátyusföldi gyűtes" (collection), 16 (December? 1905), 300–5, without explanatory marginalia.

28. "Bartók the Folklorist," *Selected Writings,* 104.

29. Bartók and Kodály attended the Academy of Music from 1900 to 1903. Their first meeting, in 1905, occurred in the home of Emma Gruber (née Sándor), who was Bartók's piano student beginning in 1902. She also studied with Kodály (marrying him in 1910) and has been credited with bringing the two men together. She died in 1958.

30. Vikár had collected folk-song material in peasant villages by means of recording techniques in 1896. He was the first Hungarian folklorist to collect rural folk songs systematically in the manner.

31. In point of fact he was born in Kecskemét, but his parents moved from there when the infant Zoltán was a few months old.

32. Titled *A magyar népdal strófa-szerkezete* (The Stanzaic Structure of Hungarian Folk Song), the work was published in *Nyelvtudományi Közlemények* (Budapest 36 (1906), 95–136; also in offprint form. A reprint is in *Kodály Zoltán Visszatekintés*, ed. Ferenc Bónis (Budapest: Zeneműkiadó Vállalat, 1964): II, 14–46; and a detailed English summary appears in Stephen Erdely's study, *Methods and Pnnciples of Hungarian Ethnomusicology* (Bloomington: Indiana University Publications, 1965), 242.

33. Kodály's findings are based on data derived from the published collections of Bartalus, Színi, A. Kiss, J. Sepródi, and his Mátyusföldi publication of the previous year, and on recordings made by V. Seemayer as well as Vikár. Most of the phonograms were noted down by Bartók and a few by Kodály.

34. The circumstances connected with this ill-fated publication are told in Denijs Dille, *Béla Bartók-Zoltán Kodály: Hungarian Folksongs* (Budapest: Editio Musica, 1970), 49–52.

35. Béla Bartók, *Slowakische Volkslieder*, ed. Oskár Elschek (Bratislava: Academia Scientiarum Slovaca, 1959) 1: 51. He also collected Hungarian material in adjacent Bihar County (now Bihor, Romania) at that time; it therefore seems quite likely that he heard Romanian folk music too.

36. The transcribed ballads are published without explanatory remarks.

37. In a letter to Etelka Freund (a former pupil), dated 17 August 1907, Bartók writes: "I have made a rather strange discovery while collecting folk songs. I have found examples of Székely tunes which I had believed were now lost." This discovery in musical terms was pentatonic scale structure and a richly ornamented singing style.

38. *RFM*.i., 3.

39. He offered this publication his manuscript in June 1910.

40. This system is described in Erdely, *Methods and Principles of Hungarian Ethnomusicology*, 44–46, and in his unpublished paper, "A Preliminary Survey of the Basic Principles of Tune Classification" (read at the Washington, D.C., meeting of the American Musicological Society, n.d., 2). See also *HFS*, 6.

41. *Cântece poporale românesti din comitatul Bihor (Ungaria)—Chansons populaires roumaines du département Bihar (Hongrie)*. The book appeared in 1913.

42. Letter to G. V. Zágon, dated 22 August 1913, as published in *BBL*, 123–24.

43. Béla Bartók and Zoltán Kodály, "Az új egyetemes népdalgyűtemény tervezetet" (Plan of the New Universal Folk Song Collection), *Ethnographia* 24, no. 5: 313–16.

44. In view of the importance and the technical nature of this document it is given in outline form in *HFS*, xxxiv.

45. Letter to D. G. Kiriac, dated 18 December 1913, in *BBL*, 128–29.

46. Indispensable sources for this period of Kodály's life and work are L. Vargyas, "Kodály's Role in Folk-Music Research," *The New Hungarian Quarterly* 3, no. 8 (1962): 39–49; and L. Eösze, *Zoltán Kodály His Life and Work* (London: Collet's, 1962), 47–65. It should be noted that Kodály's new direction was implemented in 1915, when he published "Három koldusének forrása" (Source of Three Beggar's Songs) in *Ethnographia* 26. His essay relates folk song, popular church songs, and old psalm book material.

47. Intended for publication at that time, the work finally appeared in 1923 in a German edition (Drel Masken Verlag, München). See *RFM*.v, xv–xx, for a detailed history of the publication; see also there (pp. 264–67) the translation of Kodály's book review in the Budapest journal *Napkelet* 7 (1923).

48. Perhaps this circumstance underlies Bartók's opening discussion in *HFS*, 1–4, in which he defines "Peasant music"—a definition which appeared earlier in the Paris journal *La Revue Musicale* in November 1921 (English translation: *BBE*, No. 11).

13

Bartók and Hungarian Folk Music[1]

About two hundred years ago, when the Age of Enlightenment had reached Austria, the educated classes began to look toward rural arts, particularly folk poetry and music, as a means to elevate the peasantry which was still laboring under feudal conditions. At that time there was also a great interest in music performance, concurrent with the development of keyboard and other instruments. The educated classes, whether nobles or affluent commoners, formed orchestras and various kinds of ensembles. The result of all this activity was an insatiable demand for music, particularly vocal material with keyboard accompaniment.

The public interest in the rural arts and the demand for vocal material brought about the development of the *Volkstümliche Lied* in the German-language areas. This repertory was composed in imitation of simple rural folk-song style, that is, with tuneful or memorable melody, fitted with an amusing or otherwise interesting German text, and given a commonplace harmonic accompaniment easy to perform. Outstanding melodies, usually written by professional musicians, became part of the national repertory of so-called folk songs of the cities and large towns. Some of the tunes were even taken up by the peasantry and fitted with local poetic texts; in this case, too, the transformed melodies became a part of the village folk-song repertory.[2]

The continuing demand for this type of musical product and the shortage of trained musicians to create it had a negative outcome in the next century. Amateurs from the educated classes began to mass-produce pseudo folk songs of the most hackneyed musical content and with slobbery texts. These popular art songs or, as Bartók designates them, urban folk songs were propagated by Gypsy bands in Vienna, Budapest, and Hungarian towns. Sometimes a genuine peasant song, that is, a rural folk song, attracted the public fancy and was also added to the Gypsy repertory. The Gypsies, however, played only those urban or rural folk songs that were in current fashion. Furthermore, the Gypsy musicians rarely invented *Volkslieder*; they preferred to improvise on or embellish those melodies the public favored.[3] In the 1850s, perhaps as a result of international interest in the ill-fated revolution of the Hungarians under Lajos (Louis) Kossuth against the Habsburg Monarchy, the fame of the spectacular Gypsy performance style became so widespread that the songs they propagated were everywhere but mistakenly identified as the genuine Hungarian folk song.

There are three major categories of urban, Gypsy-disseminated pseudo folk songs that pervaded musical life in Hungary prior to the twentieth century. The first category is the old style of song construction, almost invariably a quaternary, in which the melodic structure overlying each text line usually has a different contour but with similar rhythm in each line to provide unity (Ex. 13.1).[4]

Ex. 13.1. "The Hut Is Burning" ("Ég a kunyhó")

The second category, the new style of urban folk song, that apparently followed the Kossuth Insurgency of 1848, became widespread in then Greater Hungary among the young people in rural areas.[5] The new style, also consisting of quaternaries, has a different arrangement of the overlying melody sections. The most prevalent content structure is ABBA, a purely Hungarian product, where the B sections are higher than the first or fourth.[6] In other songs the first and last lines are identical in melodic contour. But in every instance each text line has the same number of syllables. An outstanding example of a new-style urban folk song is the one composed in 1874 by Elemér Szentirmay (Ex.13.2a).

Ex. 13.2a. "There Is Only One Pretty Little Girl" ("Csak egy szép kislány van a világon").

The tune not only became transformed into a rural folk song (Ex. 13.2b) but was borrowed by Pablo Sarasate for his world-famous composition, Ungarische Zigeunerweisen (Hungarian Gypsy-Tunes).[7]

The third category is represented by Hungarian folk songs with features of different national provenance. Thus the melody might be altered by means of Slovak rhythm contraction, where a quaternary with eight-syllable text lines, ♪♪♪♪ ♪♪♪ ♩, has the third section contracted to ♪♪♪♪ ♪♪♪♪. Another case is a mixed-style Hungarian folk song that migrated between Hungarian and Slovak territories (Ex. 13.3).

Ex. 13.2b. *HFS*, melody No. 80, "I Went to the Feather-Trimming Last Night" ("Tollfosztóban volyam az este").

The ultimate transformation produced Hungarian and Slovak variants so memorable that they were taken up by the educated classes and, of course, by city Gypsy bands. In fact, Johannes Brahms heard the following melody played by a Gypsy band in a Vienna cafe and made it part of his Hungarian Dance No. 10 (Ex. 13.3).

Ex. 13.3. Brahms, Hungarian Dances for Orchestra, No. 10.

This kind of urban popular music provided Brahms with as much international recognition as that accorded Sarasate. The source of his transcription is a Hungarian popular song (Ex. 13.4).[8]

Ex. 13.4. "I Should Love to Plough" ("Szeretnék szántani").

Variants were collected by Bartók in a Hungarian village in 1907 and a Slovak village in 1915.[9]

Franz Liszt, the greatest composer of Hungarian music in the Gypsy style—Hungarian born but culturally west European—was convinced that Gypsy music was the authentic Hungarian folk music. In fact, Bartók thought so too while he attended the Budapest Royal Academy of Music beginning in 1899, particularly the *lassú-friss* (slow-fast) formal style of Liszt's Hungarian Rhapsodies. In 1903, Bartók's last year as a piano and composition student, he composed a work based on events during the 1848 Revolution. Bartók, a dedicated nationalist, was carried along in the wave of national desire for independence that was sweeping across Hungary. He therefore decided to combine the new but dissonant harmonic novelties of Richard Strauss with the Hungarianisms of Franz Liszt, and he borrowed themes from Liszt's Hungarian Rhapsody No. 2 and transformed them for his *Kossuth* symphonic poem (Ex. 13.4).

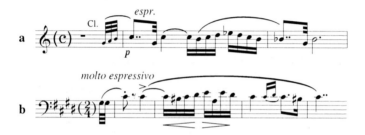

Ex. 13.4 (a) Bartók, *Kossuth*, section IX, bars 449–51, and (b) Liszt, Hungarian Rhapsody No. 2, bars 10–14.

In the summer of 1904, while Bartók was composing more music in the Liszt style, he overheard a girl singing a melody which had very unusual qualities. The incident took place in a villa in northern Hungary, now Slovakia, and the girl was a nursemaid who had been born and raised in a small village in the southeast corner of Transylvania. Bartók was so struck by the sound that he persuaded her to sing other songs from her limited repertory while he notated them in his sketch book. His analysis convinced him that he had fortuitously chanced upon an ancient type of melody unknown till then and totally different from the so-called Hungarian folk songs that pervaded Budapest musical life.

Ex. 13.5. *HFS*, melody No. 313, "The Red Apple Fell into the Dirt" (Piros alma leesett a sárba"). Note the three-section form instead of the traditional Hungarian quaternary.

On his return to Budapest in the fall he noticed that a collection of folk songs, newly published by a younger Academy student named Zoltán Kodály, had been gathered in villages not far from where Bartók spent the summer. And these songs, too, were refreshingly simple, unpretentious, and with special musical features unlike the urban folk-melody style. Bartók, genius that he was, immediately realized that those special musical features could provide him with a new sound for the development of a unique, truly Hungarian style of composition. He therefore applied for and received a travel grant to visit Transylvania to collect rural musical folklore, and he met with Kodály for advice on how to accomplish that mission.

The two similarly motivated young composers decided to pool their resources as folk-song collectors and collaborators: they would select the best specimens, clothe them with piano accompaniments in accordance with the prevailing fashion, underwrite the costs of publication, and use the royalties to support their future field trips throughout Greater Hungary.

In the fall of 1906, after they had returned from a summer of folk-music collecting, the publication appeared under the title Twenty Hungarian Folk Songs for Voice and Piano (Magyar népdalok). Bartók transcribed the first ten, and No. 6, " Through My Window Falls the Moonlight" ("Ablakomba, ablakomba") is an ABBA "new"-style folk song, where the first and fourth melody sections are double lines with 8+7 syllables (Ex. 13.6).

Ex. 13.6. Bartók, Twenty Hungarian Folk Songs (1906), No. 6.

Unfortunately the venture was a financial disaster. The Hungarian public was enraptured with the music from Franz Lehár's new operetta *The Merry Widow* and, moreover, neither the folk melodies nor Bartók's "radical" harmonies in the piano accompaniments were appreciated. Nevertheless Bartók and Kodály used their salaries as newly appointed teachers at the Academy of Music to support their research in this exciting new area of musical treasure hunting. Bartók, for instance, collected melodies in 1907 from villages in Tolna County, not far from Lake Balaton, where he found a folk song with a pentatonic structure (that is, where the principal tones are G-Bb-C-D-F or similar intervallic constructions). Ex. 13.7a shows the first half of the quaternary monophonic melody, "When I Was a Cowherd" ("Mikor guláslegény voltam"). Note that Eb functions only as a passing tone.

Ex. 13.7. (a) *HFS*, melody No. 7a, bars 1–4, and (b) Bartók, fourth Bagatelle, bars 1–4.

That same year Bartók began to study the innovative Impressionist compositions of Claude Debussy, and he was astonished to find that Debussy, too, had discovered pentatonicism and was using it in new harmonic ways. In 1908, Bartók composed fourteen experimental piano pieces, called Bagatelles, and arranged the fourth Bagatelle as a piano piece by harmonizing the pentatonic folk-song melody with chains of chords and perfect fifths as innovated by Debussy (Ex. 13.7b).

This sound was quite shocking to the Hungarian public, and the Budapest music critics were negative in their reception of the Bagatelles. Bartók, now professor of piano at the Academy of Music, turned to writing easy music for children and older piano students. Between 1908 and 1909, he transcribed Hungarian and Slovak folk songs as easy pieces for young pianists, and he selected examples from his collections that were representative of the three major categories—"old," "new," and mixed styles—that he had discovered in Greater Hungary. An interesting mixed-style folk song is also used as a swineherd's dance tune (Ex. 13.8).[10]

Ex. 13.8. Bartók, *For Children*, Volume I (Hungarian folk tunes), No. 39.

This type of dance tune is in close relationship to its Ruthenian ancestor, the *kolomyjka* (round dance) melody. Because of its characteristic, infectious rhythm, ♫♫♩|♫♩♩|♫♫♩|♩ ♩, the swineherd's dance (*kanásztánc*) was used by Hussar officers of the Hungarian army during village recruiting activities, beginning in the eighteenth century. The alternation of slow and fast dance music became known as *verbunkos* (recruiting) and, in the nineteenth century, the related *csárdás*.

Bartók's immense success as a composer—which, like Mozart, came into full fruition after his death—was due to his uncanny ability to dig deep into the characteristic features of east European musical folklore and make them an integral part of his unique musical language. But this language did not emerge full-blown like Botticelli's portrait of Venus; it was built in five stages that were not perfected until twenty years had elapsed and scholarly studies had been written about the folk music of Hungary and its neighboring peoples.

The first stage of Bartók's musical language is embodied in his folk-song transcriptions in which the folk tune is considered to be the jewel, and the accompaniment is supportive, as if it were the mounting. The second stage is where the melody and its accompaniment are equally important, and the third one uses the folk melody as a kind of motto, to the extent that the composition can be categorized as an original work. A remarkable example is Bartók's Eight Improvisations on Hungarian Peasant Songs op. 20, for Piano (1920). The fourth stage is reached when the melody is invented by the composer in imitation of a genuine rural folk song, avoiding commonplace musical elements (Ex. 13.9).

Ex. 13.9. Bartók, Ten Easy Pieces for Piano, No. 5: (a) first theme, bars 1–4, (b) second theme, bars 10–15.

The two rhythmically contrasting themes reflect old- and new-style Hungarian folk melodies, respectively: a slow old-style folk song which alternates with a new-style instrumental dance piece. Note, however, that Bartók's inventions are based on the same anhemitone-pentatonic scale, E-G-A-B-D, the ancient pentatonic structure the Magyars brought with them from central Asia more than a millennium ago.

The highest level is reached when the work is pervaded with the atmosphere of folk music: the creation of abstract compositions in which folkloric characteristics of rhythm, melody, and other elements are embedded.

It is perhaps appropriate to close this chapter with a quotation from the 1936 Yearbook of the Budapest Academy of Sciences. Bartók, awarded a chair in that prestigious institution four years prior to his emigration to the United States, and in view of his stature as one of the founding fathers of modern ethnomusicology, was commended in the following statement: "He, the first man to reach back to the source of our ancient folk songs, is nevertheless dissatisfied with research of a segregated, autochthonous Magyar folklore and therefore places on an equal plane the study of the neighboring peoples' material and of the distant, more primitive musics, and points also to their ancient pentatonic roots."

NOTES

1. The previous version of this revised study was published in *The Folk Arts of Hungary*, ed. Walter W. Kolar and Ágnes. H. Várdy (Pittsburgh: Duquesne University Tamburitzans Institute of Folk Arts, 1981), 149–59.

2. *BBLW*, 9–10.

3. *HFS*, 99.

4. György Kerényi, *Népies dalok* (Popular Songs), 19. The first publication of the melody was in 1833 (ibid., 209).

5. *BBLW*, 7–8.

6. *HFS*, 43.

7. Ibid., 202. See also Bartók's remarks in *BBE*, 100.

8. Kerényi, *Népies dalok*, 25. The first publication of the melody was in 1834 (ibid., 210).

9. *HFS*, melody No. 39, and *BBSE*, 269, melody No. 84a (a reprint from *SV*.i, 255). See also Bartók's transcription in *Mikrokosmos* for piano, vol. 4, No. 112.

10. The folk song source and its description will be found in the introduction to *Piano Music of Béla Bartók*, The Archive Edition, ed. Benjamin Suchoff (New York: Dover Publications, Inc., 1981), Series I: xiv.

14

Slovak Folk Songs: Music and Politics

When in 1867 the dual Austro-Hungarian monarchy was established, the Hungarian magnates and lesser nobility owned most of the land in Slovakia. Their mistreatment of the basically peasant population served as a stimulus for the nationalist movement then under way by the clergy and other intellectuals from the small middle class.[1] The first attempts to revive national consciousness among the people included plans to publish simple transcriptions of village folk songs, together with legends, proverbs, witticisms, and other material. The first publication appeared in Vienna, as *Sborník slovenských národných piesni* (Collection of Slovak Folk Songs, sixty-six melodies), in 1870, published by the Matica Slovenská, a literary society in Turčansky Sv. Martin, and the second volume followed in 1874 (65 melodies).[2]

Beginning in 1875, periodical booklets titled *Slovenské Spevy* (Slovak Songs) were printed; most of the collectors were village teachers, and many of the melodies were edited by Karol Ruppeldt, a Slovak musician. These publications were intended as a guide to "show the kind of songs to be sung at social gatherings and offering instruction as to the manner in which they were to be performed."[3]

In 1906, when the third volume of *Slovenské Spevy* was under way, Bartók and his colleague, Zoltán Kodály, "set out to collect Hungarian peasant music unknown until then."[4] Among Bartók's first specimens was a Slovak folk song collected during August in Gemerská County (Ex. 14.1).

Ex. 14.1. *SV.*i, melody No. 16x. The six-syllable proper text line is not given here. *Ej* is a complementary syllable that is not part of the proper text and therefore not counted in determining syllabic number. All Slovak melodies are transposed to G as final tone, and each enclosed numeral 1 (1 = G) indicates the location of a melody-section end tone.

This variant, a *valaská* (shepherd's song), is one of the few melodies that were not recorded during Bartók's fieldwork and is published here to show the simple music notation. The numeric symbols, on the other hand, represent the innovative, systematic approach to classification of musical folklore used by Bartók.[5]

Four years after Bartók had collected, transcribed, and prepared a fair copy of 400 Slovak folk songs, on 25 February 1911 he wrote to Matica Slovenská and offered the collection for publication as part of their *Slovenské Spevy* series.[6]

> The negotiations between Bartók and Matica Slovenská dragged on and on and ended dismally in 1913. It is, of course, probable that a certain mistrust against the "professor of the Royal Hungarian Academy of Music" played some part in the negotiations; the principal cause of the failure to come to an agreement was, however, the fact that the editors of *Slovenské Spevy* (after the death of Karol Ruppeldt) were absolutely at a loss to comprehend the system of Bartók's notations. The contributors of the *Slovenské Spevy* made no real efforts to record songs in any systematic and accurate manner: they were, on the contrary, quite proud if they succeeded in ridding the melodies of all vulgarities of popular representation (glissando, fluctuating intonation, rhythmic irregularities), and satisfied if they managed to present in their collections the urban variants of folk songs. Even Karol Ruppeldt, a comparatively erudite musician (he had studied in Prague), was in the habit of modifying notations, and justified these arbitrary corrections in his Notes by affirming that "changes were unavoidable, for no writing of music can be published with such arbitrary songs that defy all rules."[7]

When the Slovak folk-song manuscript was returned to Bartók without explanation, his disappointment was tempered by the successful outcome of his fieldwork in Romanian villages of northern Transylvania during March. His collection included variants of the previously undiscovered *hora lungă*, a "very ancient, endless series of variations, of uncertain form and richly ornamented, of a single unmodulated melody of a manifestly instrumental character."[8] Bartók prepared the fair copy of the collection and mailed it to the Academia Română (Bucharest) in December.[9] Publication was delayed until the music notations were engraved and translation of Bartók's preface into French was completed.

Undeterred by his unfortunate negotiations with Matica Slovenská, Bartók continued his fieldwork among the Slovak minority villages. During April 1914 and August 1915, in the county of Zvolenská, he discovered the existence of one of the oldest strata of Slovak folk song, the so-called *valaská* melodies (Ex. 14.2). Although there are some exceptions, most of the melodies show double first melody lines (that is, 6 + 6 text-line syllables), parlando rhythm, and the melodic contour has the "specific, quite frequent, and very striking descending interval of a perfect fourth, that is extremely characteristic. . . . It seems that the *valaská* melody is a specialty not only of Slovakia but of a more delimited area: Zvolenská County and the western portion of Gemerská County."[10]

Ex. 14.2. *SV.*i, melody No. 16a. "The *valaská* variants under No. 16 (16a to 16z) are actually one and the same melody, performed in an improvisatory manner."[11]

The other category of autochthonous Slovak structures in Bartók's collection are certain lullabies, hay-making, harvesting, wedding, and midsummer night songs. The complete material not only includes 2,500 melodies he recorded and transcribed, but also about 8,000 melodies published by other collectors. The latter melodies were classified by Bartók and listed as variants in his manuscript. "A striking feature is the frequency of occurrence of the Lydian mode which is completely missing from the Hungarian material [Ex.14.3]."[12]

Ex. 14.3. *SV.*i, melody No. 164. The song was recorded by Béla Vikár in 1905 and later transcribed by Bartók. The performers, two women, sang in Western-influenced parallel thirds and the characteristic Slovak Lydian folk mode.

The nonautochthonous material includes a substantial number of melodies of Hungarian origin, such as the architectonic structures AA^5A^5A, AAA^5A, the characteristically Hungarian ABBA, and AABA with dotted rhythm. In addition, there is frequent borrowing of Hungarian refrains as part of the Slovak text (Ex. 14.4).[13]

In his introduction to *SV.*i, Bartók describes the general and regional peculiarities in the folk texts:

> I tried to notate the texts as far as possible in dialect. Here I encountered several difficulties which impeded the possibility of a consistent procedure. First of all,

one does not find among somewhat cultured peasants an absolute consistency in
the pronunciation, which is especially apparent during the recitation of the texts
(reading and schooling influence the dialectal pronunciation). Secondly, in some
places I had assistants from the educated class (teachers, priests) who for the most
part did not write down the texts in dialect. Nevertheless, there are certain dialectal peculiarities that will become quite obvious in this publication, to which I
would like to draw the reader's special attention.[14]

Ex. 14.4. *BBSE*, 212, melody No. 22a. The borrowed Hungarian refrain is "ragyogo
csillagom, galambom" (my bright star, my dove).[15]

Bartók's own "peculiarity" is his use of beamed values in vocal music notation, to the consternation of "old-school" music editors:

> I always use beams instead of old-style flags for a succession of notes sung to
> different syllables; to melismatic groups (that is, to different notes sung to the
> same syllable) I apply a slur. The usage of flags (or hooks) in vocal music, still
> prevalent in our day, may have historical and logical foundations. However, stick-
> ing to this usage in folk music purely because of tradition is, in my opinion, rather
> senseless. A profusion of these hooked notes, especially when they have mixed
> values, are decidedly confusing to the eye. Moreover, if hooks are used, articula-
> tion remains unexpressed; ♩♩ ♩♩ and ♩♩♩♩, although they have different mean-
> ings, become indistinguishable if hooks (♪♪♪♪) are used. I cannot afford to dis-
> card the valuable advantage in articulation by the other method.[16]

POLITICAL EVENTS AND EDITORIAL PROBLEMS

Bartók's fieldwork in Slovakia abruptly ended in August 1918, before he had
the opportunity to investigate the rest of the northern villages and add to his
collection—for the most part vocal pieces—of 3,223 melodies.

> In January 1918, the Vienna munitions workers' strike spilled over into Hungary,
> and the mutiny of Hungarian army units in May was followed by a general strike
> in June. The Republic of Austria was proclaimed on 12 November, the Republic
> of Hungary proclamation on the 16th. Although the national minorities had previ-

ously supported the Dual Monarchy, beginning in November their councils took over the civil administration of Transylvania, northern Hungary, and the territories along the southern tier of the country. New borders were drawn in the territories surrounding dismembered Hungary, which effectively prevented Bartók from traveling in those areas.[17]

Beginning in September 1919, Bartók was granted a leave of absence from his teaching duties, and he began the transcription and classification of thousands of folk songs in his Hungarian collection. He divided the material into four Hungarian-speaking regions, each characterized by a different musical dialect; II, the northern region (north of the Danube and of the upper Tisza rivers) included villages in which he had collected indigenous Slovak folk songs.[18] In order to determine the reciprocal relationships between Hungarian and Slovak folk songs, Bartók included the transcription and study of his Slovak material and discovered that to a certain extent it could be classified according to the same principles he had developed for the Hungarian fund.

Antal Á. Baník (b. 1900), a Slovak folklorist who had been providing Bartók with published Moravian folk-music collections, apparently discussed Bartók's Slovak folk music research—including the determination of reciprocal relationships among the Czech, Moravian, and Slovak folk songs—with Miloš Ruppeldt (1881–1943), a professor at the Bratislava Academy of Music and Performing Arts, who served as a representative of Matica Slovenská. The latter asked Bartók to bring his Slovak collection and several field recordings to Bratislava for evaluation with regard to prospective publication by the society. On 20 August, Bartók received his visa from the Czechoslovak consulate, and two days later mailed a letter to Ruppeldt, to the effect that it was quite unlikely that the required export license would be granted for a phonograph and recordings.

> From the beginning of September, I will no longer be free; after a yearlong vacation I must again start my activity as a professor. But my wife has the intention to travel to Pressburg [that is, Bratislava] in September, in the event she receives the Czech visa. At this opportunity she would bring the first part (about 1/7th of the entirety) of my Slovak collection in a fair copy, so that it could be seen what it is all about. She would then also negotiate orally what must be done further—because in view of my critical situation, I cannot say anything in writing. So I ask you to make it possible that my wife receives the Czech visa without difficulties.[19]

In 1921, Matica Slovenská notified Bartók that they would publish the complete collection, provided that his manuscript would be delivered in September 1922. In that event, they stipulated that the work would be published within four years at the latest. In October 1922, he informed the publisher that he had completed the fair copy of the music examples in the first volume, but it was not until the next year that fair copy of the first two volumes was completed. He asked for sample proofs of the text and music examples, to avoid future delay when the third volume would be ready for press. The publisher had no intention of beginning work on the project until the complete material was at hand, nor did they inform Bartók of that decision. It was not until 1926 that Bartók was contacted for information concerning the third volume, and he responded that he was still waiting for the requested proofs while continuing work on the volume from time to time.[20]

Perhaps the publication of Bartók's seminal Hungarian treatise on Hungarian folk song, *A magyar népdal* (The Hungarian Folk Song), in 1924 or its German edition a year later was brought to the attention of Matica Slovenská. Bartók's introduction has many references to Slovak folk song, particularly the following statements:

> Not so the *tempo giusto* tunes in sub-Class I. Most of these were probably taken over from Slovakia, or cropped up under the influence of tunes taken over; for there is no essential difference between them and the tunes which must have served as models.
>
> This question cannot be considered at greater length here. It would be necessary to go deep into the study of the Slovakian peasant music fund. Therefore the whole matter will find place in a book on Slovakian folk music. Let it be pointed out, meanwhile, that most of the invariable *tempo giusto* forms (many represented by the Slovakian variant of the corresponding purely Hungarian tune) are in use in Slovakia.
>
> The so-called Slovakian rhythm-contraction occurs in seven or eight Hungarian tunes only, but in many Slovakian tunes. So that tunes in which it occurs may safely be considered as of Slovakian origin.[21]

Bartók's growing international recognition as an outstanding composer brought with it an increasing demand for his appearance as pianist, to the point where, in 1926, he felt the need to add a concerto and small piano works to his repertory. Thus he composed the First Piano Concerto, Piano Sonata, Nine Little Piano Pieces, and recital pieces. The next year he composed the Third String Quartet and embarked on a concert tour of the United States. And he conscientiously attended to his teaching duties at the Academy of Music, the earlier commitments with regard to the publication of his Romanian and Hungarian folk-music studies, and the editorial requirements during the printing of his composed works by his Vienna publisher, Universal Edition.[22] Notwithstanding these achievements, however, was the lingering bitterness concerning the enforced cessation of his fieldwork:

> And I am hopelessly cut off from the one thing that is necessary to me as fresh air is to other people—the possibility of going on with my studies of folk music in the countryside. There's no time or money for it! It now seems that nowhere in the world is there any interest in this work.[23]

Bartók completed the third volume of his Slovak collection and delivered it on 22 June 1928. Matica Slovenská paid the author's royalty, and the four-year publication agreement was thereby invoked. A year later, the chauvinist reaction to the content of the third volume was disclosed by Ruppeldt's letter in which he requested the elimination of all melodies showing Hungarian influence. Bartók responded by quoting the clause in his contract which stipulated that the Slovak collection would be ordered according to classification system, and he added that it would be an unscholarly procedure to exclude Hungarian-influenced Slovak folk songs (see Ex. 14.4).[24]

A second unfortunate incident began in 1930, when Matica Slovenská's house editor informed Bartók that preparation for publication had started and requested the name and specific location of the Slovak villages where the melodies had been collected. He was unaware that the publisher decided to change his dialectal peasant texts into literary equivalents by consulting the village priests and schoolteachers and thereafter entering the changes directly in the manuscripts.[25]

In 1931, Bartók received a specimen proof, returned it with his corrections, and asked for a second proof as well first proofs of additional pages. When they were returned with several typescript pages of the texts that had been prepared by the editor with a proposal for publishing them in a separate volume, Bartók responded that:

> I am pleased to hear your plan to publish the texts separately from their melodies. In that way, the texts also could be grouped according to their content; the separation is justified scientifically only by such a presentation . . . but every text must be provided with the number to which it belongs. . . . The texts marked with the exact numbers of melodies should be sent to me, I will group them according to their content and send them back (ballads, soldiers' songs, humorous, etc. and unclassifiable songs).[26]

The publisher had no intention of adding a fourth volume of texts and replaced the editor with Ivan Ballo, a Slovak music critic. Although Bartók had already included detailed instructions for the printer with the manuscript, Ballo decided to prepare a new list along with his proposed fee. Since the amount was four times the royalty paid to Bartók, the publisher demanded return of the manuscript. Ballo refused to comply unless he was compensated for the editorial work he had already done, resulting in litigation to force the recovery.

Bartók had not been informed of the publisher's editorial and legal problems and was disturbed by the continuing lack of communication. Thus on 15 June 1932, a week before the contractual obligation to publish his Slovak manuscript was due, Bartók realized that more forceful steps had to be taken in order to determine whether or not Matica Slovenská intended to fulfill the contract.

> Many years ago I sold the manuscript of my Slovakian collection to Matica Slovenská. They are obliged to publish it by June 22 this year, otherwise I have the right to buy back the manuscript from them, that is, they are obliged to return the manuscript to me if I return to them the original price, almost 10,000 č.k. I need

someone whom I could authorize to execute this transaction and I would ask you for this task. The procedure would be like this:

The Sl. M. sends you (or its representative living in Pozsony) the manuscript; you make sure that it is complete (I would send you detailed information concerning this later) and you inform me about it. Then I would write to one of my friends to send you the money. If you get the money, the transaction could take place.—If you could undertake this task, I should know when you are not in Pozsony, lest the manuscript would arrive there at that time. Of course, I have to be prepared for the SL M. raising difficulties or simply ignoring completely my demand. In that case, I would need a lawyer. Could you recommend somone?[28]

During the ensuing weeks Bartók mailed several letters to the publisher, none of them answered except the one dated 22 July, in which he stated that: "Should I not receive an answer to this letter by 22 August, I will be forced to take the necessary legal steps to obtain what is due me."[29] The threat of a lawsuit prompted the 4 August reply that the first part of the work was in press, the other parts would also go to the printer, and they apologized for not responding sooner because of the serious illness of a colleague. Bartók therefore granted a temporary postponement.[30]

Later on Bartók's attention to the Slovak publication problem was diverted by his transfer from the Academy of Music to the Academy of Sciences in 1934, where he was commissioned to classify the multiple thousands of Hungarian folk songs he, Kodály, and other collectors had gathered. It was not until January 1935 that Ballo returned the Slovak manuscript to Matica Slovenská, and, in February, a Slovak philologist was appointed as production supervisor. These events were followed by a letter to Bartók from Miloš Ruppeldt—the first editor!—stating that he had asked the publisher for permission to revise the manuscript. The combination of Ruppeldt, who wanted to eliminate the Hungarian-influenced Slovak material, and a Slovak philologist to supervise the transformation of dialectal texts into literary equivalents, apparently convinced Bartók that Matica Slovenská intended to abrogate the contract and modify the manuscript more or less in accordance with the format of the defunct *Slovenské Spevy* publications.

While Bartók was working on the classification of Hungarian folk songs, he was preparing his Romanian collection for publication and discovered that his transcriptions of the field recordings were not sufficiently exact: "This meant the revision of all the old notations and even making of entirely new transcriptions of some of the recorded melodies."[31] Although most of his Slovak recordings had been transferred to Matica Slovenská, part of them remained in Budapest as property of the ethnographical section of the National Museum. He decided to review these recordings and determine whether revisions should be made. One outcome of this activity can be seen by comparing the published version of melody No. 2 (Ex. 14.5) with its revision (Ex. 14.6).[32]

2.
(Svadobná)

5, 1–5   B.F. 1070a; Hrušové, Nitrianska; III. 1907; Anna Krajčovičová.

Ex. 14.5. *SV.*i, melody No. 2. The notation and classification symbols are a close approximation of Bartók's corrected printer's proof.[33]

F. 22 a)
M. F. 1070 a)   Anna Krančevič

Ex. 14.6. *SV.*i, revised melody No. 2. Among the many differences are transcription of the other two stanzas and the use of arrows to indicate instability of pitch.[34]

Beginning in the mid-1930s, the main objective of Hungarian foreign policy was revision of the Versailles Peace Treaty and, later, to support Nazi Germany in its plan to dismember Czechoslovakia. When, on 2 November 1938, the Axis Powers decided to give the largely Hungarian-inhabited southern strip of Slovakia to Hungary, the opportunity to restore "Greater Hungary" was welcomed enthusiastically by the population, including the peasantry.[35] The effect of the political situation on Bartók's career as artist and folklorist is evident in his letter to Sándor Albrecht, a Slovak citizen living in Bratislava:

> Don't be surprised that I haven't written to you in such a long time; I have so much to do and to arrange whenever I am in Budapest that it defies description; it's almost unbearable, really. I am very sorry that the Pozsony [Bratislava] people didn't get a permit for me: it was just as well that I didn't accept the invitation for the chamber-music festival to be held in August! They would have me as guest of honor, of course, but do not grant permission for a concert; what a gang! I didn't

even have time to do anything in that Sl. Mat. affair.—It has occurred to me meanwhile that I could, perhaps, have my entire Slovak collection copied in Budapest
from the rough draft, and that could hardly cost more than buying back the whole
manuscript. But at first I would have to take a good look at that rough draft at
home and see if it wasn't too rough![36]

On 28 January 1939, Bartók's letter to Matica Slovenská states that the
publisher's delay and silence has forfeited their right of publication and demands return of his manuscript. Furthermore, he accuses the company of mis-
handling his field recordings to the point that they have become useless: "I
shall not miss a single opportunity to make this shameful fact public. Had I but
had the faintest idea of your utter incompetence in the handling of musical articles, I would have certainly refused to have any dealings with you." And he
ends the letter with a demand for their response not later than 28 February 1939;
otherwise he will consider their silence as an agreement with its contents.[37] Matica
Slovenská's immediate response was that they were no longer interested in publishing the work nor any copyright claims to it, and that the manuscript would
be returned when Bartók reimbursed them for the royalty previously paid. And
they justified their termination of the contract on the following points: (a) the
opinion of their experts is that the work gives a one-sided picture of the actual
character of the true Slovak folk music; (b) the work presents difficulties in the
reconstruction of the texts; and (c) there are unsolvable problems in restoring
the uniformly transposed melodies to their original tonality.[38]

Put in another way, the editors of Matica Slovenská had originally informed
Bartók that the dialectal peasant texts had to be replaced by the literary forms,
and that a third volume of Hungarian-influenced Slovak folk songs had to be
withdrawn. The latest objection, regarding transposition of the melodies to a
common final tone (G), apparently pointed to a politically unacceptable adop-
tion of a Hungarian classification system for ordering Slovak folk songs.

When Bartók's mother died in December, he made plans to emigrate to
America where he was scheduled for a concert tour. Thereafter, in October 1940,
he arrived in New York, accepted a research appointment at Columbia University, and began work on the investigation of Yugoslav folk songs that had been
recorded but not transcribed. He completed preparation of the fair copy of that
material as well as of his Romanian and Turkish folk-music collections. In 1945,
shortly before his death, Bartók wrote to his younger son, Peter, that he should
return to his Slovak "rough draft" collection and prepare it for publication. But
he questioned whether it would be worthwhile to spend thousands of hours on
such painstaking work, only for it to be destroyed twenty years later.

In 1959, the posthumous edition of the first volume of *Slowakische Volkslieder*
was published in Bratislava by the Academia Scientiarum Slovaca, and the second volume appeared in 1970. But where is the maligned, Hungarian-oriented
third volume?[40]

NOTES

1. The Magyars conquered Slovakia in the tenth century A.D. The region was considered to be the northernmost Hungarian province until 1918.

2. Jozef Kresánek, "Bartók's Collection of Slovak Folk Songs." In *Studia Memoriae Belae Bartók Sacra*, ed. B. Rajeczky and L. Vargyas (London: Boosey & Hawkes, 1959), 56.

3. Ibid., 57.

4. *BBE*, 409. At that time Hungarian peasant music included the vocal and instrumental material collected from the minority villages inhabited by Slovaks, Romanians, Serbo-Croatians, and other peoples.

5. See *HFS*, xxxiv, 6–8. Bartók's classification methodology for his Slovak material is given in *BBSE*, 242–49. The *valaská* was Bartók's own designation for the category of Slovak shepherd's songs.

6. *BBL*, 108–9.

7. Kresánek, "Bartók's Collection of Slovak Folk Songs," 57.

8. *RFM*.v, x.

9. Ibid., xvii. Bartók's book, *Rumanian Folk Songs from Bihor County (Hungary)* was published by the Academia Română in 1913.

10. *BBSE*, 256–57.

11. Ibid.

12. *BBE*, 128, 132.

13. Ibid., 131.

14. *BBSE*, 253.

15. Ibid., 183.

16. *YFM*.i, 12–13.

17. *BBLW*, 88.

18. *HFS*, 4, 92–93.

19. János Demény, ed., *Bartók Béla levelei* (letters) (Budapest: Zeneműkiadó, 1976), 259–60.

20. There are a number of publications in which Bartók's correspondence about his Slovak collection appears. See Demény 1976 and Vlado Čižik, *Bartóks Briefe in die Slowakei* (Bratislava: Slovenské Narodné Múzeum, 1971).

21. *HFS*, 61–62.

22. See my essay "Bartók's Odyssey in Slovak Folk Music" in *BC*, 20.

23. *BBL*, 153–54.

24. Bartók's scientific study and findings are given in *BBSE*, 178–87.

25. János Demény, ed., *Bartók Béla levelei* (Budapest: Zeneműkiadó, 1955), 250–52.

26. Ibid., 258.

27. Ibid., 263.

28. *BBLW*, 121–22, letter to Sándor Albrecht. It is interesting that Bartók uses the prewar Hungarian Pozsony designation instead of the current Bratislava.

29. Demény, ed., *Bartók Béla levelei* (1955), 265.

30. See *BP*, 23, for further details.

31. *RFM*.i, 1. Bartók's Romanian folk-music transcriptions reached a new height of notational accuracy. See *RFM*.ii, 46, and its appendix II.

32. *SV*.i is a posthumous edition, published in 1959. Only the first seventy-five pages of music examples had been proofread by Bartók. See *BBL*, 427.

33. The music example is my computer-processed copy of the published version, slightly modified according to a facsimile page from Bartók's manuscript in Demény, ed., *Bartók Béla levelei* (1955), 239.

34. The music example is my computer-processed equivalent of Bartók's holograph in Envelope 76a (pp. 1–150) of his Slovak collection in the *PBA*. See the description in Victor Bator, *The Béla Bartók Archives: History and Catalogue* (New York: Bartók Archives Publication, 1963), 32–33.

35. Ervin Pamlényi, ed., *A History of Hungary* (London: Collet's, 1975), 493–97.

36. *BBL*, 264, letter dated 31 January 1938. Albrecht (1885–1958) was a friend and former pupil of Bartók at the Budapest Academy of Music.

37. Ibid., 275.

38. *BP*, 26.

39. Ibid.

40. During my tenure as successor-trustee of the New York Bartók estate, I visited Bratislava and discussed this question with Professor Oskár Elschek, one of the coeditors of the first two volumes. It was his recollection that the third volume had been sent to Prague for printing. For details concerning my editorial work on the draft, see *BP*, 27, nn. 26–28.

15

Bartók's Romanian Folk Music Publication[1]

As the morphological aspects of the Romanian folk music material collected by Béla Bartók have been ably examined by him in his great, five volume study *Rumanian Folk Music* (1967–1975), this essay is devoted to a discussion of certain highlights in and about the work, such as a brief history of Bartók's odyssey in quest of publication, the editorial problems involved in guiding his study toward publication, and some of the unique contributions to Romanian and general ethnomusicology contained in the work.

BACKGROUND

Rumanian Folk Music properly speaking, consists of three manuscripts in the form of transparent master sheets in Bartók's holograph, deposited by him in the Special Collections section of Butler Library, Columbia University (New York). Volume I, an essay on instrumental melodies, and volume II, on vocal melodies, were completed in New York in 1942. The third volume, the complete folk texts, was finished in March 1945, not quite six months prior to Bartók's death. The fourth volume is a revised version of Bartók's 1935 *Colinde* publication. The fifth volume is a similar treatment of the 1923 publication about the folk music of the Maramureş Romanians. These last two volumes contain English translation of the prefatory matter and the poetic texts.[2] Bartók's first book on Romanian folk music, the 1913 Bihor County study,[3] was revised by him in 1932 and incorporated in the first three volumes of *RFM*. The five volumes contain more than 3,400 melodies and 2,400 poetic texts.

With rare exception, Bartók's attempts to publish his Romanian ethnomusicological studies were frustrated either by lack of interest on the part of publishers or by their reluctance or unwillingness to fulfill Bartók's high editorial standards. The evidence for this assertion can be found in two pages of manuscript that Bartók wrote and subsequently withheld when he drafted the final copy of his preface to *RFM*.i.

> *Habent sua fata libelli. . . .* I can't help thinking of this melancholic proverb when following the fate of my folklore publications. I would not recall here these sometimes only too personal troubles would this not serve a special purpose in connection with the present publication. I have to point to some disturbing but inevitable

circumstances which always arose and followed the preparatory work with unwavering consistency. Due to this are mostly the many deficiencies in text and print
of the musical part.

My first publication of greater significance was the *Hungarian Folk Music* published by Oxford University Press, London, in 1931. Trouble started right there. I
obtained the proofs, containing mistakes mostly due to misunderstanding. These I
corrected and asked for a second proof. This didn't seem to suit the publisher who
published the book without sending me any more proofs. The result: a great many
inaccuracies due to incorrect translation in the publication. In order to save face I
prepared a list of corrections, requesting the publisher to have it printed and attached to each copy. As for printing, the list was sent to me in print, but I have
never seen a copy of the book including it.

The second publication by the same publisher was to include my collection of
Rumanian Colinde or Winter-solstice songs. Their extremely interesting texts were
supposed to appear in original as well as in English. After several years of delay
the translation into English prose was completed, one part in adequate archaic
English, the rest (by someone else) in most unsuitable Kitchen-English. The publisher didn't wish to change this though. Result: I published the book at my own
expense, however, only the musical part, because of lack of sufficient funds. The
texts are still in manuscript, even today.

My third publication was to be my collection of about 2,500 Slovak folk songs.
I transferred the rights to publish this collection, as well as the phonogram-records
of the songs to the "Matica Slovenská" (a literary Society in Slovakia) in 1922. I
submitted the manuscript between 1925 and 1928. According to the contract they
were to publish the complete work within four years. Years passed but nothing
happened except for a series of empty excuses. Finally, in 1939 I dissolved the
contract: the rights of publishing became mine, but I couldn't regain the completed manuscript from the Matica Slovenská.[4]

Bartók omits mention of the difficulties involved in producing his book on
the folk music of the Maramureş County Romanians, which was ready for press
years before its publication in 1923 in Munich. It was necessary for Bartók to
underwrite the costs for the engraving of the music examples, costs he was
never to regain.[5]

His study of Serbo-Croatian folk music, published after his death, would not
have been written if friends had not provided the funds for his reappointment as
research fellow at Columbia University. Indirectly, therefore, Bartók partially
subsidized this publication.

And in 1940, Bartók, out of income derived from concert fees, paid for the
printing of the music examples in the first two volumes of *RFM*. In this way he
hoped to provide some publisher with an incentive to publish the work. But the
money was completely wasted. Not only were publishers disinterested in such a
project, but most of the printed and unfolded large sheets of music examples of
both volumes, that had been stored by Bartók in a warehouse, were destroyed in
a fire nine years after Bartók's death.

Editorial Problems

The editorial problems involved in the publication of *RFM* were considerable, indeed. The reason why is perhaps best answered in these paragraphs from Bartók's preface to the first volume:

> When preparing these folk melodies for publication, I discovered in 1932 that my transcriptions of the records were not sufficiently exact. This meant the revision of all the old notations and even the making of entirely new transcriptions of some of the recorded melodies. In addition, the systematic grouping of the whole material had to be done and, finally, master sheets of the complete musical part had to be prepared. . . . My intention was to place this material before the public as carefully prepared and in as perfect a form as is called for by its unparalleled value. The deplorable circumstances of the last six or seven years, however, prevented the fulfillment of this plan by producing tensions over tensions which caused the work to be accomplished, at least partially, in an unfavorable haste and anxiety.[6]

Bartók wrote these words in 1942. The next year he tried to convince the New York Public Library to sponsor the publication, but they rejected the work as beyond their budgetary means. Bartók's music publisher, Boosey & Hawkes, also was approached by the author. Ralph Hawkes, president of the company, was interested. Because of wartime paper shortages and lack of competent editorial help, however, the publisher was unable to accept the work. In one case, a friend of Bartók's contacted a private foundation, but with no result. During this time Bartók was concertizing to a considerable extent in order to support himself and his family, and he was engaged in preparing the drafts and fair copy of his book on Serbo-Croatian folk songs for Columbia University Press. These disappointments and difficulties, together with the intermittent periods of poor health that were to lead to his death from leukemia in 1945, were the causes underlying his decision to deposit the manuscript fair copy of the first two volumes of *RFM* in the Columbia University Library in 1943.

In 1944, however, convalescing in Asheville, North Carolina, and with little to occupy his fertile mind, Bartók began work in a new field, the scientific study of Romanian folk-text material: a study that had its origin in his earlier, unpublished second part of the 1935 *Colinde* book. Naturally, such a study involved reexamination of the vocal melodies in *RFM*.ii and the "dance-word" and other melodies with text contained in *RFM*.i. While reviewing the material, Bartók discovered many errata; he therefore made a number of corrections and additions in another copy, sometimes in several copies, of the final manuscript or printed form of the music examples in both volumes.

It is noteworthy, too, that he had carefully saved the field transcriptions (that is, the manuscripts notated on the spot in Transylvania) and batches of papers having to do with peripheral matters, such as calculations of percentages, indices, texts and translations, discarded melodies, and the like.

In summary, then, the editorial situation from 1959 to 1960 was this: the so-called final copy of *RFM*.i–iii, consisting of holographic transparent master sheets, was in the Columbia University Music Library. The corrigenda and addenda to these drafts were in the New York Bartók Archive (*NYBA*), as well as the published copies of the projected reprints of *RFM*.iv–v.[7] Constantin Brăiloiu, the eminent Romanian ethnomusicologist, had been designated editor of *RFM* in 1953 by Victor Bator, then trustee of the New York Bartók Estate. Brăiloiu decided to commence the project with a reprint of the *Colinde* material, including the complete texts. Five years later, shortly before his death in 1958, Brăiloiu had prepared preliminary and revised drafts of his brief foreword, in French, to Bartók's study. In addition, he had studied and corrected Bartók's draft of the texts that the latter had deposited in the library of the University of Basel (Switzerland).[8] His death in December 1958 occurred during our correspondence in connection with translation problems and other editorial matters, and I accepted the trustee's request that I take over as editor of the project.[9]

Turning to the editorial processes commenced in 1959, the first and most important step was the determination and location of all the extant primary and secondary source materials. Because the bulk of related documents was already on hand, the determination of the remainder was comparatively simple, its location more difficult, and its acquisition sometimes impossible to achieve. At the same time the sources were being assembled, part of my time (for a period of about a year and a half) was devoted to the preparation of the music examples for facsimile reproduction. This experience, published in my editorial preface to *RFM*.ii (p. xxx), is perhaps worthy of mention here.

In her book titled *The Naked Face of Genius,* published in Boston in 1958, Agatha Fassett relates how Bartók would work with unfailing patience, bending over bits of white paper that made up his Romanian folk-song collection. This narrative brings to mind my own tasks, prior to the editorial process, of repairing and restoring the music master sheets so that they could be made suitable for photographic reproduction. The bulk of the 1,274 leaves comprising the music notations consisted of pages of two or more sections which were linked together by snippets of transparent adhesive tape. Indeed, a number of the melodies had been cut up, staff by staff, and reassembled—quasi mosaically!—into page length. Alas, tape, too, knows old age! On the one hand, the adhesive bled through the film backing so that many of the leaves stuck together and had to be painstakingly pried apart. On the other hand, the tape dried and flaked away, carrying with it portions of the autograph beneath. Thus the old tape had to be secured with fresh strips and missing characters reconstructed by calligraphic approximation of Bartók's autography on the related pages of his previously printed music signatures.

The various drafts of each of the three volumes of *RFM* and the results of the comparative study made of them are described in detail in the editorial prefaces to the respective volumes. In addition to historical backgrounds and manuscript surveys are tabulations whose titles give some idea of the scope of the editorial work, such as "Corrections of the Musical Part"; "Additions to the Musical Part"; "Missing Designations"; "Diacritical Additions to Data Sections"; "Errata in the Notes to the Melodies"; "Dance-Word Translations"; "Concordance of *Bihor-Rumanian Folk Music* Melody and Text Numbers"; "Additions to the Notes to the Melodies"; "Corrections of the Texts"; "Typographical Additions to the Texts" (of vols. I, II, and III); "Additions to the Refrains"; "Corrections of Index Material"; "Missing Text Lines"; "Romanian Orthography"; "Children's Songs"; and miscellaneous tables of editorial origin.

Another task was the editing of Bartók's English prefaces and introductions, notes and remarks, and similar explanatory matter. The guiding philosophy in this work is perhaps best expressed by this quotation from my editorial preface to *RFM*.i (p. xliii):

> During 1941 and 1942 Bartók worked alternately on the preparation for publication of his Serbo-Croatian and Romanian folk music collections, completing the former in November and Volumes I and II of the latter in December, 1942. In the subsequent years, probably using the same working procedure, he revised this material, submitting the final version of the Serbo-Croatian book to Columbia University Press in December, 1944, and bringing to a close the master sheet draft of the Romanian poetic texts in the Spring of 1945. The various correspondences on the subject, beginning in August, 1944, reveal the discontent of Bartók with certain phases of the editorial rewriting of his Serbo-Croatian book.
>
> I decided, therefore, to retain as far as possible the essential flavor of the author's expository style as expressed in the master sheet draft of *RFM*, even at the risk of including non-idiomatic English phraseology, so long as clarity of meaning was not voided. On the other hand, because of the identicalness of sentences and even paragraphs in the Romanian and Serbo-Croatian drafts, in a few cases adoptions or adaptations from the Serbo-Croatian book replaced portions of the Romanian study where the need for revision was indicated. In fact, it was further decided to follow the format of the Serbo-Croatian book in order to present to the public, ultimately, Béla Bartók's folk music publications in homogeneous form.

Concurrent with the drafting of editorial prefaces in explanation of my work, after completion of the basic tasks which I have just explained, was the frustrating necessity for finding a publisher for *RFM*. The story of this search would make up another essay. Let it suffice to say that after we had been rejected by a number of international commercial and university presses, Martinus Nijhoff of The Hague, the Netherlands, took up the torch in 1964 and accepted the five-volume project.

It is interesting to note the time factor involved in bringing *RFM* to publication since the time Bartók collected his first Romanian folk songs in the village of Podeni (formerly Székelyhidas, Turda County; now the region of Cluj) in November 1908.[10] Bartók himself lists the place of Torockó (now called Remetea, region of Alba). My visit to both villages in July 1968 provided a possible solution to the apparent contradiction in points of origin. Each locality is situated in a valley, separated by a rather large mountain; travel between them, therefore, is best accomplished by means of circuitous roads. In view of the function of Torockó, beginning about the twelfth century, as the regional center for fairs, it seems likely that Bartók met and recorded his informants in Torockó, and he indicates the month of November as the starting date. The termination of his labors in Romanian ethnomusicology, he further indicates, took place on 30 March 1945, in New York City. His odyssey spanned thirty-seven years. Our own involvement extended this time span another twenty-two years, as the first three volumes of *RFM* did not appear in the bookshops until 1967. And another eight years must be added for the publication of the revised versions of the *Colinde* and *Maramureş* books in 1975. Thus a total of sixty-seven years have elapsed until the publication of Bartók's lifework in Romanian folk music.

THE VOLUMES

Turning next to content in *RFM,* this aspect of the work may serve also as additional evidence why Bartók and, later, we encountered seemingly inordinate delays in the attempts to expedite completion of publication.

If we examine *RFM*.i, subtitled *Instrumental Melodies*, we find an extensive and diverse store of information, beginning with Bartók's classification of the material in terms of function. There are melodies of either determined or motivic (indeterminate) structure that serve as dance music, melodies with text played on instruments and without specific function, bridal and other wedding music, and alphorn music and its imitation on other instruments. Bartók then takes up the discussion and description of instruments: the peasant violin, guitar, and cello; various types of peasant flutes; Balkan and eastern central-European bagpipes; alphorns and the jew's-harp; and percussion instruments. Next follows a list of eighty classes of dance genres and their order in Sunday dancing. An innovative inclusion is Bartók's description of the choreography of certain dances, together with diagrams of the dance steps.

The remainder of the author's introduction is devoted to musical characteristics, such as rhythm—including so-called Bulgarian (or *aksak*) rhythm—structural characteristics which include a comparison of Transylvanian-Romanian dances (*Ardeleana*) with Hungarian *verbunkos* (recruiting music) and Ukrainian *kolomyjka* (round dance), and commentaries concerning the part played by the so-called dance-words (*strigături*) that Bartók amusingly likens to the role played by spices in enhancing food. Addenda include lists of variants, remarks on the performers, signs and symbols used in the notations, statistical data, and a bibliography.

The 607 pages of music examples, painstakingly transcribed from the field recordings, consist of the most intricate folk-music notations I have ever encountered, other than those in *RFM*.ii, that are further complicated by all kinds of special signs and symbols Bartók devised for classification and analytic purposes. The book closes with Bartók's notes to the individual melodies.

In *RFM*.ii, *Vocal Melodies*, Bartók explains the ways in which he approaches the transcription of the poetic texts in order to publish them according to the pronunciation of the singers. One innovation is the use of the inverted breve to indicate semivowels. Other diacritical features are the use of underlines to indicate complementary syllables that change catalectic lines (that is, five or seven-syllable lines) into acatalectic ones (those with six or eight syllables) and wavy underlines to indicate supernumerary syllables.

The proper text lines are not organized according to principles of stanza structure and, moreover, may include two- or three-line rhymes. There are refrains, pseudo refrains containing one or more words of indefinite meaning, and strings of loose syllables without any meaning.

Bartók then classifies the melodies: nonceremonial melodies divide into six classes, including parlando and *tempo giusto* types, dance melodies, dotted rhythm tunes, those with indeterminate structure, and the *Cântec lung* ("long-drawn" melody) and its variants. Other genres include mourning-song melodies, wedding songs, harvest songs, and rain-begging songs. Bartók also mentions that the *Colinde* (Winter-solstice songs, that is, carols and Christmas songs) is an additional category taken up in his preceding (1935) publication on that genre.

Next follows an innovation in the form of a table of Z symbols. The letter Z is used in two or three sizes to indicate the proportion of sectional lengths in terms of their syllabic number. That is, heterometric structures composed of alternating eight- and six-syllable lines would be symbolized by alternating large and small sizes of Z (*ZzZz* = *8,6,8,6,*).

The section devoted to musical characteristics of the vocal melodies begins with a description of features of certain areas called dialectal areas by the author. The dialects comprise those of Bihor, Hunedoara-Alba, Banat, and Campie. Bartók also mentions the Maramureş dialect and refers the reader to his 1923 publication (*RFM*.v).

Bartók summarizes his findings in a short section of conclusions. The usual lists of data follow: Romanian variants, foreign variants, remarks on the singers, explanation of signs and symbols, statistical data on villages and counties, and a bibliography. The 667 pages of musical transcriptions, including the fully recorded texts, are followed by the author's extensive "Notes to the Melodies."

RFM.iii, *Texts*, may prove to be Bartók's crowning achievement in systematic ethnomusicology. The 16,100 proper text lines and 690 refrain lines that make up the 1,335 individual texts appear in this volume in Bartók's calligraphic handwriting: in all, 332 pages of carefully prepared autography. This material is classified in minute detail and according to topic. For example, Class A, the Love Song genre, is subdivided into four subclasses, depending on whether the subject or object is male or female. These subclasses are again divided into as many as eighteen groups, with such titles as Longing, Jealousy, Ugly or Bad Wife, and Adversity in Love. Class *B*, Songs of Sorrow, includes an interesting category, Going to America. Other classes are Soldiers' Songs, Death, Nature (birds, plants, stars, and forests), Jeering and Jesting Songs, the so-called Dance-Words Gypsy texts, and the important subclasses of Mourning Songs.

The author examines the individual lines for rhyming techniques, lists seven groups of *Frunză* (leaf) lines, and then explains their function. This exposition is followed by a lengthy discussion of refrains that are, Bartók states, a special characteristic of Romanian rural folk texts from the Banat and adjacent Serbo-Croatian regions.

In his discussion of the relationship between rural and urban folk texts, Bartók offers three categories of musical and poetical products: Category 1 contains products by exceptionally gifted individuals, which are high-quality creations constituting higher urban art; Category 2 contains products by less gifted individuals with more or less urban education, which are mediocre creations constituting lower urban art; and Category 3 represents the products of a community consisting of individuals with insignificant or no urban education, which are high-quality creations constituting rural art.

Bartók closes the introduction with a section on poetic texts as expression of a rural community's sentiments and character. He points to Class *C*, the Soldiers' Songs, as evidencing a complete rejection of compulsory military service and all soldiering, and he states that the love songs indicate that girls are more jealous than boys—love relations are more momentous to them. The comparative lack of highwaymen texts, he adds, may indicate that Romanians were perhaps more peaceable, more law-abiding than certain of their neighbors. He makes special mention that he saw no expressions of hatred in Romanian peasant texts, that hate and persecution of other peoples just because of their nationality is an urban invention.

Following a list of variants published in other sources, Bartók presents his conclusions, a bibliography, and an interesting addenda chapter in which he points to the similarity of the *Frunză* lines to the three-line quinaries of the *Stornelli* and the eight- or six-line love poems or *Rispetti* of the Italians. Bartók points to other resemblances between Romanian and Italian versification, and he states that common features of the two peoples' folk-text materials may be considered as a sign of the great antiquity of those texts; indeed, that they may date back to the epoch when the ancestors of the Romanians left the soil of Italy.

After the texts and their translations appear some important appendices, including the classification of Romanian refrains.

NOTES

1. This study is a revised version of my lecture presented at the Institute of Ethnography and Folklore (Bucharest) and the University of Cluj-Napoca (Romania) in July

1968. The original version appears in *Tribuna* (Cluj-Napoca) 13, nos. 30–31 (1969); *Magyar Zene* (Budapest) 10, no. 2 (1969); and *Ethnomusicology* 15, no. 2 (May 1971): 220–35. With the exception of Bartók's designation of *Rumanian* in the title of his publications, the accepted English orthography "Romanian" is used.

2. Both volumes, then in press, were published by Martinus Nijhoff, The Hague, in 1975.

3. Béla Bartók, *Chansons populaires roumaines du département Bihar (Hongrie)* (Bucharest: Academia Română, 1913).

4. The MS is in the *PBA*.

5. *BBLW*, 79–80.

6. *RFM*.i. 1.

7. The fourth volume was *Melodien der rümanischen Colinde* (Weihnachtslieder), a paperback edition published in 1935 by Universal Edition, Vienna. The fifth volume was *Die Volksmusik der Rümanen von Maramureş*, published in 1923 by Drei Masken Verlag, Munich.

8. The corrections were made in ink on the typescript manuscript. As I later discovered, a carbon copy of the Basel draft had been deposited by Bartók at the university library in Amsterdam, and I found, moreover, a newer, fair-copy version that was among his papers at *NYBA*.

9. For further details, see Victor Bator, *The Béla Bartók Archives: History and Catalogue* (New York: Bartók Archives Publication, 1963), 15.

10. *RFM*.ii, 51.

16

Bartók and Yugoslav Folk Music[1]

When Hungary signed the Treaty of Trianon on 4 June 1920, almost three-quarters of its territory and two-thirds of its inhabitants were distributed among Austria on the west, Romania on the east, and the newly created national states of Czechoslovakia on the north and Yugoslavia on the south. This circumferential dismemberment allotted the Burgenland, with its German majority and basically Croatian-Magyar minority, to Austria; Slovakia and Ruthenia, each with a large Magyar minority, to Czechoslovakia; Transylvania[2] to Romania, from Maramureş in the north to and including parts of the Banat in the south; and Croatia, Slavonia, Bácska, and part of the Banat, with Croat or Serb majorities and essentially Magyar-German minority, to Yugoslavia.[3]

One of the far-reaching effects of the treaty was the curtailment of field trips in formerly Hungarian territories by Hungarian ethnomusicologists. As Bartók put it:

> But no one is allowed to take phonographs across the frontier, neither one way nor the other! They wouldn't even let me bring my own notebooks through! The most I could hope for would be to procure some special permits from heaven knows how many different authorities, and that only after I don't know how many weeks of running around for them! No, the curtain has been drawn over that work . . . [phonograph cylinders] would be confiscated at the border.[4]

The impact of this "drawn curtain" on Bartók, hardly measurable by the foregoing laconic lines, can be reliably assessed in terms of his ethnomusicological objectives. Fifteen years before, in 1905, he had set out to "collect and study Hungarian peasant music unknown until then," impelled by an earlier examination of Hungarian "folk music" which led to the discovery that "what we had known as Hungarian folk songs were more or less trivial songs by popular composers and did not contain much that was valuable."[5] At that time Bartók's interest in folk song concerned his own activity as a composer; he was seeking a basis on which to develop a compositional style with Hungarian roots. Significantly, and in order to determine the morphological aspects of autochthonous Hungarian folk music, Bartók decided to base his investigation on scientific method; on-the- spot phonograph recording and transcription by ear would make possible the subsequent extraction of accurate data for analysis. But Bartók soon realized that there are foreign elements in the

210

peasant music of Hungary; indeed, the next year he collected folk music in Slovak villages and, beginning in 1908, in Transylvanian-Romanian ones, in order to test his newly formed hypothesis that a kinship or reciprocal influence existed between the folk music of linguistically differentiated peoples living within the borders of old Hungary.

> Such adopting of [Hungarian] melodies cannot be avoided among neighboring countries. Of course it is only a person very familiar with the musical folklore of both countries who is able to see his way through this chaos. For this reason my opinion is only temporary and can be settled only after I have collected in many more regions.[6]

During these first years of folk-music exploration Bartók was able to "rejuvenate" his compositions by means of the pentatonic and modal configurations in the music he encountered in the peasant village. But his compositions were so negatively received by Budapest audiences, in comparison to the welcome given his first book-length essay on folk music[7] by Bucharest scholars, that in 1912 he decided to withdraw from the artistic scene and devote himself primarily to ethnomusicological activities, for he was by now well aware that a vast treasure of musical folklore was at hand or awaited unearthing in the field, that this material had a value far beyond compositional utilitarianism, and that he himself already was one of a small band of pioneers in the newly established discipline of comparative musicology. Bartók the artist thus turned to Bartók the scholar. The new objective, one which he followed with untiring energy and unwavering integrity until the end of his life, was that:

> Systematically scientific examination of the morphological aspects of folk music material (consisting first of grouping the material according to certain methods, and then, of describing the typical forms and structures which will appear in a material thus grouped) will enable us to determine clearly the types and to draw various conclusions concerning the transformation, migration of the melodies, their connection with foreign materials, etc.[8]

Although the greater part of Bartók's avocational time and attention was addressed to the collection and study of Slovak and Romanian folk music (he had been appointed professor of piano at the Budapest Academy of Music beginning in 1907), he nevertheless found it necessary to consider the folk music of Yugoslavia. It seems reasonable to conclude that Bartók's turn toward south Hungary stemmed from his brief collecting trip in Nagyszentmiklós (now Sânnicolaul Mare, Torontal County, Romania), the place of his birth, in January 1910. Among the instrumental pieces recorded there was a peasant flute (*fluer*) melody which the performer said was a Serbian dance melody.[9] In addition, Bartók collected forty-eight vocal melodies, of which more than a third contained refrain lines of a type to be found outside of the Banat (that is, southwestern Hungary which contains Romanian villages near Serbian and Slavonic territories).[10] One of the songs had a peculiar heterogeneous character, as if it were "a foreign body in the bulk of the Romanian material."[11] Then Bartók apparently compared its melody with the Yugoslav folk songs collected by Fr. Š. Kuhač and there found three variants;[12] in fact, he was at first pleased with Kuhač's transcriptions, commenting in 1912 that the melodies "are correctly notated as well as ordered according to the text. It is regrettable that the work has been expanded by the addition of wholly unnecessary piano accompaniments. . . . we need to supplement Kuhač's collection which lacks extent."[13]

During March and November 1912, therefore, while collecting in the Banat counties of Temes (now Timiş, Romania) and Torontal, Bartók sought, found, and recorded several Serbian folk musicians in the villages of Temesmonostor (now Mănăştiur) and Sarafalva (now Saravale, formerly Sarafola), respectively. He collected and subsequently transcribed twenty-one instrumental and vocal pieces (see *YFM*.i, 451–71), for additional information concerning this Serbian material). Probably on the basis of this small number of transcriptions, apparently the only Serbian folk-music recorded by phonograph up to that time, Bartók revised his opinion of Kuhač's contribution. Thus, in 1919, Bartók complained in print that the folk music collections published by Yugoslavs were jotted down by amateurs and that systematic classification of the material, like that of western Europe, was carried out almost exclusively according to the texts.[14] Later, in a lecture given in the United States in 1940, Bartók elaborated on the problem:

> Eight or ten years ago, if we wanted to examine the Serbo-Croatian material, we found ourselves up against a few obstacles. The available material consisted of about 4,000 tunes, for the most part in prewar [First World War] transcriptions made by ear, without the aid of an Edison phonograph or gramophone. Subtleties of execution and ornamentation can scarcely be studied at all in this material, since they [the subtleties] are lacking in these rather amateurish transcriptions; but at least types and classes could be established. The Serbo-Croatian scholars never used recording instruments, for reasons unknown to me.[15]

Bartók managed to continue his accumulation of the incredibly rich Slovak and Romanian materials well into 1917. As if in anticipation of the forthcoming political and economic conditions that were to terminate his field trips, beginning in 1914 he produced a number of small piano and vocal compositions based on folk music and, more importantly, composed theater music in the form of the ballets *The Wooden Prince* (1914–1916) and *The Miraculous Mandarin* (1917–1918). The earlier ballet was produced in Budapest in 1917; its success marked a change in attitude towards Bartók's compositions. The next year his Second String Quartet (1915–1917) and his opera *Bluebeard's Castle* (1911) were performed; a contract with the publishing house of Universal Edition, Vienna, followed on 4 July 1918.

After these promising beginnings there followed, alas! the complete political and economic breakdown of 1918.

The sad and troubled times that followed for about a year and a half were not conducive to serious work.

And even today [1921] conditions are not such as would allow us to think of continuing our studies in musical folklore. They are a "luxury" we cannot afford on our own resources. Political conditions are another great impediment. The great hatred that has been worked up makes it almost impossible to carry out research in parts of countries that once belonged to Hungary.[16]

The "drawn curtain" previously referred to prevented Bartók from personal contact with south Slavic folk music, and he therefore turned to the collections made without the aid of the phonograph, published by Kuhač, Kuba, Bosiljevac, Kačerovski, Djordjević, and Žganec.[17] He needed source material in the 1920s, for comparative purposes, during the preparation of three major studies for publication: *A magyar népdal*, that is, *The Hungarian Folk Song* (1924, also published in German in 1925 and in English in 1931), *Melodien der rumänischen Colinde* (completed in 1926, revised and published in 1935), and *Slowakische Volkslieder* (completed in 1928 and published posthumously).

There is only brief mention of Yugoslav material in Bartók's monumental book on Hungarian folk song: genuine Romanian melodies are nearer to Yugoslav tune types than they are to Hungarian ones, and south Slav peasant music shows no similarity to the old Hungarian parlando-rubato pentatonic melodies of eight or twelve syllables.[18] Later, in 1926, Bartók was able to say that Romanian Christmas carols ending with a half cadence can most plausibly be traced back to south Slavic influence, since the terminal half cadence, as well as certain scale patterns diffused in Romanian areas, plays a predominant role in Yugoslav music.[19] Expressed in another way, the same year, Bartók wrote:

> As to the *main* musical dialect of the Romanians [of Alba, Hunedioara, Bihor, the Banat], I think it must have come into existence under Yugoslav influence. Unfortunately I do not know Serbian folk music well enough to support my opinion, but I do know this much: in Serbian folk music the most characteristic structure is the F major hexachord in which g^1 serves as final tone and half-cadence, and in which the first, third and fifth tones are the main degrees of the scale. Exactly the same scale is widespread among the Banat Romanians. In Alba and Hunedioara, as the result of the tonal shift upward one step, the fourth and sixth degrees replace the third and fifth as the main ones. Out of the latter structure arose the Lydian hexachord in Bihor, with first, fourth (natural), and sixth main degrees.[20]

In his book on Slovak folk song, Bartók mentions that the construction of the Slovak bagpipe is almost identical with that found in Hungarian, Romanian, and Serbian regions and moreover, that the Serbian bagpipe has small bellows.[21]

In addition to his ethnomusicological writings, including smaller pieces published in various international journals, Bartók undertook concert tours as a pianist, and he began composing piano works for the purpose. In 1926, for example, he produced four important works: the First Piano Concerto, the Piano Sonata, *Out of Doors*, and the Nine Little Piano Pieces. Serious difficulties with the publishers of his folk-music studies—circumstances that were to plague him throughout his life—interfered to a certain extent with other creative and scholarly activities well into the 1930s. Nevertheless, in 1932 he decided to rework his entire Romanian material, revising old notations and making entirely new transcriptions of some of the recorded melodies. The ultimate purpose of this task was to produce a series of volumes that would supplement his 1923 publication, *Volksmusik der Rumänen von Maramureş*, revise the melodies of the 1913 Bihor study (*Chansons populaires du département de Bihar*) and those of the *Colinde* (whose unpublished manuscript was still in the hands of Oxford University Press in London), and add thousands of other Romanian vocal and instrumental melodies that he had gathered between 1908 and 1917.[22]

Bartók's reexamination of his Romanian material, coupled with a statistical survey he had made of aspects of Žganec's 1924 publication of Medjumurje[23] melodies, may have prompted him to consider writing a documented comparative survey of all the east European musical folklore that he had investigated up to that time. Taking advantage of newly opened opportunities in radio broadcasting, on 21 November 1933, Bartók gave a lecture on the Budapest Radio entitled "The Influence of Hungarian Folk Song on Neighboring Folk Music," which he illustrated with piano and recorded examples and which in 1934 appeared, "appropriately enlarged," in printed form—including 127 music examples in Bartók's autograph—under a somewhat different title. In the closing chapter, entitled "The Folk Music of the Serbo-Croatians and the Hungarian Folk Music," Bartók states that he had reviewed and classified about 2,500 melodies collected in Croatia, Slavonia, Dalmatia, and in Bosnia and other regions inhabited by the Serbs, for the most part from the collections of Kuhač and Kuba. He goes on to aver that there is hardly any connection between these melodies and the Hungarian material. But in Žganec's Medjumurje collection of 636 melodies, Bartók found that a total of 66 percent of them were either old Hungarian (190), new Hungarian (158), or other Hungarian "dotted" rhythm types (41). The most remarkable fact is that so many borrowings were made from the old Hungarian tune types. Bartók notes that there is a greater proportion of old Hungarian pentatonic melodies in Žganec's Yugoslav collection (33 percent) than in Bartók's Hungarian material (9 percent).

> There can be no doubt of the Hungarian origin of the pentatonic tunes of Muraköz [Medjumurje]; on the one hand they are completely identical with the old Hungarian melodies propagated throughout Transdanubia, on the other hand no similarity between these tunes and the others of the Serbs and Croats can be found. It would truly be an exaggeration to concede that melodies of this type had been propagated from the region of these two districts, throughout the Hungarian linguistic territory, and as far as the Székely-inhabited region of Transylvania.[24]

Bartók concludes the chapter with the plea that, since the Croat collection constituted one of the most important sources for study of old Hungarian melodies, one of the most urgent tasks ahead should be the publication of the "universal anthology" of the more than ten thousand Hungarian folk songs collected thus far, so as to provide "convincing testimony of the ancestral origin of the most important part of the Hungarian folk songs."

Whether the lecture, the resulting publication, or a combination of various factors was responsible for Bartók at long last achieving his cherished desire to devote himself to ethnomusicology as his principal vocation is uncertain. In September 1934 he moved from his piano studio at the Budapest Academy of Music to a small room on the first floor of the Academy of Sciences: his commission from the ministry was to work on folk music.[25] Bartók immediately set out, by means of correspondence, to remedy two deficiencies in his quest to circumnavigate the varied seas of foreign stylistic character that surround the Hungarian island of musical folklore. One of them, the influence of Bulgarian rhythmic patterns, will only be lightly touched, since this aspect of musical style is perhaps best examined within another context. The other, the matter of Serbo-Croatian autochthonous material, seems to have been approached through contact with Vinko Žganec and Ludvik Kuba.[26]

In what appears to be the first[27] in a series of letters between Bartók and Žganec, the former asks,

How is the collecting activity proceeding in Yugoslavia at present? Could I study phonograph recordings somewhere? Is the phonograph used at all? Are there anywhere any major (unpublished) collections, noted down and in a state suitable for study in Zagreb or Belgrade for instance? Is any major publication planned? I would be very interested to see such material, not from the Hungarian point of view, for, as one can see from Kuhač's and Kuba's great (Bosnian and Hercegovinian) collection (published in Sarajevo), with the exception of the items from Muraköz, there are hardly any points of contact. But it is with Romanian folk music that I would like to compare it as thoroughly as possible; for I suspect, especially in the music of the Romanians in the Banat, a strong Southern Slav influence; what is more, I even think that the music of the Romanians in the Bihor region came into existence as the result of the crossing of pentatonic and Southern Slav melodies.

After discussing certain performance peculiarities he has noted in the Kuhač and Kuba materials, Bartók mentions that he would like to determine whether the so-called Bulgarian type of rhythm occurs in the Serbo-Croatian linguistic territory. The letter concludes with a postscript indicating that Bartók can "only understand the [Croatian] folk texts, but the literary language, hardly."[28]

On the same day Bartók mailed the recently published "booklet containing my radio talks" to Žganec; a few weeks later it was "returned from the Yugoslav frontier, stamped 'ZABRANJENO, INTERDITE'! I don't suppose the frontier guard read the booklet; it rather seems he has imposed an intellectual blockade."[29] Another copy, with a dedication, probably sent out at the same time, was received in Prague by Ludvik Kuba. Bartók also sent a letter to Kuba, probably containing the same or similar lines as those in his letter to Žganec, since Kuba responded that "It will be a great pleasure to meet you in Prague and to cooperate with you in scholarly matters."[30] When the two met in Prague, during the last week in November—Bartók performed his Second Piano Concerto with the Czech Philharmonic Orchestra on 28 November—it was decided that Kuba would correct his published material from Bosnia and Hercegovina and send an edited copy, together with unpublished songs, for Bartók's use.[31] Not until May 1938 was Kuba able to complete the work: "It was no easy task to extricate these 160 vanished songs from my fifty-year-old notes, and I would not have undertaken this if you, dear Master, had not shown such keen interest in them. No wonder that it took such a long time."[32]

Other than information concerning source materials, Bartók's contact with Žganec was hardly fruitful. The correspondence between them, during 1934–1936, which included shipments of Bartók folk-music publications, seems to focus on Bartók's candid references to the lack of melodies from Serbo-Croatia collected on phonograph records.

> I am surprised to read in your letter that Kuhač has still 4,000 unpublished melodies. These are surely in some library where they can be studied, aren't they? In my opinion it would be better not to publish these, Kuhač's notations being very defective, but rather to use the money thus earmarked for new collecting activity, namely, collecting organized scientifically with all kinds of equipment (phonograph!).[33]

Toward the latter part of 1935 Bartók revised his earlier notations of Serbian melodies collected in the Banat in 1912 and sent a copy to Žganec.[34] The latter's response, dated 22 April 1936, may have been their last communication.

> The extremely interesting music material of the book [*Musique paysanne serbe et bulgare du Banat*], that you collected with so much affection, gratified me exceedingly. I showed it to my friends, and all of them were amazed by the precision of your notation. Such accuracy as revealed by you is something new in the realm of folk music collecting.
>
> As soon as I shall have the leisure I intend to write a detailed and long review of this book and will mail it to you.[35]

Any lingering thoughts Bartók may have had about the possibility of still visiting Yugoslavia to collect folk music were diverted by negotiations leading to an official invitation, during the same month, to lecture in Turkey on "les méthodes d'étude sur la musique populaire en général, et les éléments principaux de votre École tout particulièrement."[36] At long last, at age fifty-five, Bartók achieved international recognition of his twin attainments. Since he was asked also to compare Hungarian and Turkish folk music, and since he managed to widen the purpose of his visit to include the collecting of Turkish peasant music, he plunged into the study of Turkish folk music in general and the language in particular. Following a busy concert schedule that spring, moreover, was the June invitation from the Basel Chamber Orchestra to write a composition to commemorate its tenth anniversary. The work, Music for String Instruments, Percussion, and Celesta, was completed in September, the Turkish lectures were drafted and mailed to Ankara in October, and on 2 November Bartók left Budapest for Istanbul.

Bartók broadcast the results of his activities in Turkey in a lecture given on the Budapest Radio on 11 January 1937 that was later published in booklet form.[37] Comparing Turkish and Serbo-Croatian materials, he found that "rainbegging" songs are generally known by the Turks, and that the songs correspond in text and melody to Yugoslav songs used for the same purpose: their melodies are similar to the nursery rhymes and children's play songs of the Hungarian, Slovak, or other western European nations. Although he collected only ninety tunes, he found that 20 percent of them were similar to the old Hungarian music, a statistic that takes on great significance when it is considered that the old Hungarian tune type, other than in its borrowed form, cannot be found among the Yugoslavs. In September, Bartók prepared a report of the work done at the Academy of Sciences in connection with the publication of the comprehensive collection of Hungarian folk songs.

> We have been engaged in preparing these for the press since September, 1934. During this time I have revised the transcriptions of all the phonograph cylinders, 1,026 in number. Meanwhile, Kodály has selected all relevant material from what is already in print. We have copied, and partly systematized, the song material—necessary for purposes of comparison—of the neighboring peoples of Hungary (Bulgarians, Serbo-Croatians, Slovaks, Poles, Ukrainians).[38]

The report goes on to estimate that the material will be ready for the printer by the end of 1940. But the political events beginning in 1938 interrupted this plan as well as dashing whatever hope may have remained of a collecting expedition to Yugoslavia or elsewhere. The nazification of Europe, including his Vienna publisher, hardened his resolve to leave Hungary.

> I would like best to turn my back on the whole of Europe. But where am I to go? And should I go at all before the situation becomes unsupportable, or had I better wait until the chaos is complete?[39]

Bartók found the answer to his dilemma—by means of Yugoslav musical folklore—during his concert and lecture tour in the United States in April and May 1940. A few days after his lecture at Harvard University on 22 April, on problems of east European folk-music research (see page 212, above, for his

original remarks on Yugoslav material, which he later revised), a letter arrived
from Albert B. Lord, who had attended the lecture, advising Bartók that, contrary to the latter's assumption that there were no recorded collections of Yugoslav folk music, a fairly large collection of recordings (made in Yugoslavia by
the late Professor Milman Parry of Harvard, from June 1934 to September, 1935)
was on hand; that a description of the collection would be mailed to Bartók; and
that Bartók, while in New York, should meet George Herzog and Samuel Bayard,
the two other scholars interested in the musicological aspects of the Parry collection.[40]

Bartók's concert at Columbia University on 1 May provided him with the
opportunity to discuss the possibility of a future position there with Herzog,
Douglas Moore, and Paul Henry Lang, all professors at Columbia.[41] Moore,
newly appointed as chairman of the music department, offered to investigate
the chances of obtaining a grant from the university's recently established Alice
M. Ditson Fund (set up for "the aid and encouragement of American musicians"); Herzog and Lang were to look into the possibilities of Bartók transcribing the heroic songs from the Parry Collection at Harvard (working, however,
under Columbia's auspices), which had not been previously examined and whose
transcription was needed as illustrative music material for Lord's planned book
on the textual aspects of those songs.[42] Also at this time Bartók's new publisher,
Boosey and Hawkes Inc. (the New York office of the London company), serving in a managerial capacity as well, was arranging for another, more extensive
concert tour of the United States by Bartók in the 1940–1941 season.[43] Bartók
therefore returned home that summer to make his preparations for the possibility of permanently leaving Hungary. Although his economic future—in a foreign land —surely must have then seemed precarious, the opportunity of at long
last coming into contact with recorded autochthonous Serbo-Croatian musical
folklore provided Bartók, now fifty-nine years old, with the strength to take this
bold step.

> The reason for inviting me here (apart from the fact that it would help me person-
> ally) was so that I could accomplish certain research work, that is, to study and
> transcribe this incomparable material on Yugoslav folk music. It is, in fact, this
> work which brought me here (as far as work is concerned, without taking into
> consideration my own feelings); material such as this can be found nowhere else
> in the world, and (apart from some Bulgarian material) is what was badly lacking
> to me over in Europe.[44]

Hardly had Bartók and his wife, Ditta Pásztory Bartók, disembarked in New
York on 30 October 1940, when they set out on a recital and lecture tour of the
United States. The following year, in February, came the good news of his ap-
pointment, until June, as visiting associate in music at Columbia University.
And on 27 March he began work on the transcription of the folk epics on the
Parry Collection recordings that had been sent down from Harvard for the pur-

pose.[45] Certain recordings also contained lyric songs, and when Bartók heard them he realized that the songs could serve as the basis for undertaking a definitive study of Serbo-Croatian musical folklore.

> This unique collection of over 2,600 phonograph records—to my knowledge the only collection of Yugoslav folk music on acoustical recordings—contains a very large mass of epic song accompanied by the gusle, a primitive one-string instrument. The style and musical treatment of these heroic songs is probably as close to that of the Homeric poem as any folk music style found today may be. While from the historical, literary, and musicological point of view this material is invaluable, from the musical-esthetic point of view the lyric songs or "women's songs" and the instrumental pieces in the collection are more rewarding. The epic songs are carried by a mode of chanting which, while on the whole simple, varies somewhat from region to region and singer to singer. The chant itself is undoubtedly part of old European folk heritage, but the gusle accompaniment occasionally shows parallels with Arabic melodic treatment—probably due to an influence during the long Turkish occupation.
>
> There are two ends in view according to which the collection ought to be studied. One is the transcription into musical notation of the most important samples of the epic material, to be incorporated into its literary and textual study at Harvard University. The other is the transcription of the other materials in the collection, for an inclusive picture of Yugoslav folk music. This latter could well result, as you once suggested, in a book on Yugoslav folk music. I estimate that transcribing those parts of the collection which are the most important in these two respects would take a year's time, not including my work during the current semester.[46]

On 27 October, Bartók's examination of the Parry material had progressed to the stage where he felt capable of writing "a short paper on the result of my research-work at Col. Univ. for publication somewhere."[47] The paper, entitled "The Parry Collection of Yugoslav Folk Music," which appeared in the *New York Times* on 28 June 1942,[48] apparently was prepared originally for use by Douglas Moore, who, in January, obtained a grant from Columbia's Ditson Fund to underwrite the expense of a book on Yugoslav folk music to be written by Bartók and Albert B. Lord.

Although Bartók completed the first draft of his portion of the work, *Serbo-Croatian Folk Songs*, early in 1943, a combination of frustrating circumstances continuously delayed the attempt to arrive at the final form of the book, the editorial assistance of Paul Henry Lang and George Herzog notwithstanding. Wartime shortages; collaboration with Lord by means of correspondence; multilingual text matter, including many special symbols devised by Bartók, that presented special problems for solution by the printer; and, above all, Bartók's struggle with the English language as well as the difficulties he had with the autographer of the exceedingly complex music examples—all contributed to one postponement after another. It was not until 1951, six years after Bartók's death, that *Serbo-Croatian Folk Songs*—the first full-length scholarly study of that subject in the English language—finally appeared in published form.

NOTES

1. The first version of this essay was published in the *Musical Quarterly* 57, no. 4 (October, 1972): 557–71. The second, enlarged version will be found in *YFM*.i, ix–liv.

2. An enclave of more than a half million Székely, Hungarian-speaking people who lived in the eastern part of then Hungarian Transylvania.

3. The port of Fiume, on the northeast Adriatic coast, was given to Italy.

4. *BBL*, letter to Ion Buşiţia dated 8 May 1921, 153–55.

5. *BBE*, 409.

6. *Bartók Béla levelei*, ed. János Demény (Budapest: Zeneműkiadó Vállalat, 1955), 22–23. Letter to Ion Buşiţia dated 14 August 1909.

7. *Cântece poporale românesti din Cormitatul Bihor (Ungaria)* [Romanian Folk Songs from Bihor County (Hungary)] (Bucharest: Academia Română, 1913. The collection, inadequately titled, contains instrumental pieces (Nos. 292–362) among the 371 melodies.

8. *BBE*, 37.

9. See melody No. 252 and its note in *RFM*.i.

10. Unlike the Romanian double refrains, which alternate in melody-stanza pairs, the Serbo-Croatian type occur always in the same melody stanza. In addition the Serbo-Croatian refrains may contain Turkish words (invariably unintelligible to the singer); the Romanian do not. See *RFM*.iii (lxxix–lxxx).

11. Melody No. 394c in *RFM*.ii, 494. See also p. 22 for Bartók's discussion of Class B (*tempo giusto*) melodies.

12. Nos. 601–3 in the second volume of Kuhač's anthology, *Južno-slovenske narodne popievke* (Zagreb, 1878–1881).

13. *BBE*, 155–58.

14. Ibid., 159–63.

15. Ibid., 173–92.

16. *BBE*, 409.

17. See Bartók's description of published and unpublished source materials in *YFM*.i, 22–27.

18. *HFS*, xxii–xxxiii. By means of comparative studies, after he had collected Turkish folk music in Anatolia in 1936, Bartók determined that the so-called old Hungarian folk-music style can be traced back to the sixth or seventh century A.D. (see Bartók's preface in *TFM*, 39). The so-called new Hungarian style, which arose in the nineteenth or eighteenth century, differs from the old in terms of form (rounded or architectonic)

and scale (modal and modern major and minor).

19. *RFM*.iv, 30.

20. *Bartók Béla levelei,* ed. János Demény, 1955, 164, letter to Emil Riegler-Dinu, 4 June 1926. The description of the scale appears as music notation in Bartók's original letter.

21. *SV*.i, 64.,

22. *BBE,* 37. Vol. IV of *Rumanian Folk Music* is the revised edition of *Colinde,* entitled *Rumanian Carols and Christmas Songs,* and Vol. V, also a revised version, is entitled *Maramureş County.* Both volumes, edited by the present writer, were published in 1975 by Martinus Nijhoff, The Hague.

23. Or Mur Island (Muraköz in Hungary), a triangle of land, about 795 sq. km. in area, between the Mur River, the Drave River, and the old Austrian frontier. The reader interested in a description of and studies about former Hungarian territories should consult C. A. Macartney's excellent book, *Hungary and Her Successors: 1919–1937* (London, 1937).

24. *BBSE,* 198–99.

25. *BBL,* 238. Letter to Imre Deák, 5 March 1935.

26. See note 17, above.

27. Bartók may have previously requested Žganec to send the second volume of Medjumurje material (published in 1925?), which contains 264 religious folk songs.

28. *BBL,* 229–33, letter of 27 October 1934.

29. Ibid., 236, letter of 7 November 1934.

30. *Documenta Bartókiana* 3, ed. Denijs Dille (Budapest, 1968), 171. Letter of 8 November 1934, Prague. According to Dille (p. 172) a facsimile of the first and last pages of Bartók's letter to Kuba, unavailable at the time of this writing, appears in Stanislaw's biography *Ludvik Kuba, Kniznise Hubednich Rozhtedi* (Prague, 1963), 192–93.

31. *Documenta Bartókiana* 3, ed. Denijs Dille, 178–79, letter from Kuba, 16 November 1935.

32. Ibid., 222, letter of 24 May 1938. Kuba was then more than seventy-five years old. Bartók's regard for this material is evident by the fact that he brought it with him when he emigrated to the United States in 1940.

33. *BBL,* 239–40, letter from Bartók, 3 July 1935. It seems reasonable to conjecture that Bartók was subtly attempting to suggest that Žganec —a lawyer in the city of Zombor (formerly Hungarian territory)—might be able to arrange for a subsidy or at least official permission for him to undertake a collecting trip in Yugoslavia.

34. See p. 212, above.

35. *Documenta Bartókiana* 3, ed. Denijs Dille, 191-92.

36. Ibid., 190, letter from the president of the Ankara Halkevi, 14 April 1936. It is not

clear whether the word *école* refers to Bartók as ethnomusicologist or as composer.

37. *BBE*, 137–47.

38. *BBL*, 262–63, letter to the secretary-general of the Hungarian Academy of Sciences, 14 September 1937.

39. Ibid., 275-76, letter to Dorothy Parrish [Domonkos], 8 February 1939.

40. *PBA*, letter dated 23 April 1940. Dr. Lord, also a Harvard professor, accompanied Parry on the expedition (see Lord's editorial preface to *Serbocroatian Heroic Songs* 1 [Cambridge: Harvard University Press, 1954], xiii–xvi, 3–6).

41. On 17 May, Bartók wrote to Dorothy Parrish that "There are plans (excepting concertising) to make it possible to me (and to my wife too, of course) to stay here longer, perhaps for several years. I am not authorised to give details, but I hope these plans can be turned in reality." See *BBL*, 282–83.

42. Douglas Moore, "Bartók at Columbia," *The Long Player* (New York), October 1953, 16. A letter from Bartók to Moore (copy in the *PBA*), dated 2 May, states: "I certainly was glad to have the opportunity to meet you personally and to have a quiet talk with you, which was extremely interesting for me. Unfortunately, I cannot change my plans, which I explained in my letter to Dr. Nicholas Murray Butler [then President of Columbia University]." The letter to Butler (copy in the *PBA*), dated the same day, states that Bartók must return to Hungary "to save my life work: the collection of many records of Hungarian folk music . . . I intend to return to the United States at the end of October 1940 and then will stay several months."

43. In a letter from Ralph Hawkes, head of the company, to Bartók, dated 22 August 1940 (copy in the *PBA*), a postscript reassures him that an attempt will be made, during September and October, "to find a spot for you as Professor for a season or so," in accordance with Bartók's wishes.

44. *BBL*, 306, letter to his elder son, Béla Jr., 20 June 1941.

45. Ibid., 299, letter to Béla Bartók Jr., 2 April 1941.

46. *PBA*, letter to Douglas Moore, 18 April 1941.

47. *PBA*, letter to Douglas Moore.

48. Bartók subsequently corrected the published article; see *BBE*, 148–51.

17

Preface to *Turkish Folk Music from Asia Minor*

The sequence of events which ultimately were to lead Béla Bartók to the collection and investigation of his Turkish folk-music material apparently began in December 1935. It was on the first day of that month that László Rásonyi, a Hungarian-born philologist and professor at the newly founded University of Ankara, wrote the first of a series of letters to Bartók in which he extended a preliminary invitation to travel to Ankara for the purposes of lecturing and collecting local musical folklore.[1]

Bartók's exhilaration over the possibility of widening the range of his ethnomusicological studies is hardly concealed in his affirmative and lengthy reply. Indeed, Bartók was also willing to perform in concert without fee, providing that the voyage would not be made at his own expense. With characteristic integrity he questioned the propriety of his lecturing on the relation between Hungarian and Turkish folk music, since knowledge of Turkish material—other than previous editions that were essentially Arabic in character—was lacking in Hungary. On the other hand, he was aware of the assertion made by the Turkish ethnomusicologist Mahmud Raghib Gazimihâl that "the genuine Turkish folk music includes many pentatonic melodies."[2]

Bartók, however, found that Gazimihâl's assertion was "based on scanty material which does not permit one to draw broad inferences," and he asked Rásonyi to send the Turkish folk-song publications edited by Gazimihâl and to arrange for his visit to the music folklore center in Istanbul, prior to his lecture in Ankara, "because I shall only be able to give useful hints after having been informed what was done till now and what was neglected."[3]

The next year, in April, Bartók received an official invitation from the Ankara Halkevi[4] to visit there in May and lecture on "methods for the study of folk music in general, and the principal elements of your School in particular."[5] Bartók, committed to a series of concert performances in April and May, suggested a postponement until October and offered a five-point program for Ankara which would include three lectures, a concert with orchestra, the collecting of Turkish folk music, and "conversations with the competent people on future tasks."[6]

Bartók availed himself of Rásonyi's presence in Hungary that summer for help in learning Turkish. He found the undertaking more difficult than he had presumed, particularly "the twisted sentences, contracting in one sentence what is expressed in other languages by ten. Fortunately, this rarely occurs in the texts of the folk songs; now I shall be busy with the pertinent part of the Kúnos collection."[7]

In October, Bartók completed and mailed to Ankara the promised three lectures,[8] and in a humorous letter to a former pupil residing in Ankara, added this postscript: "I learned a little Turkish and can already make very interesting statements in this language, for example, 'At deveden çabuk gider' or 'Kedi köpekden küçüktür,' etc.! But I am not as yet on friendly terms with the literary language! They use terribly long expressions and an appalling number of participles!"[9]

Following his stay in Istanbul during the first week in November, Bartók had the opportunity to listen to a number of the sixty-five double-faced records (produced by Columbia and His Master's Voice, since 1930, on commission from the city) of performers—mostly peasants—who had been brought there for recording purposes. He voiced a number of objections to the collection of almost 130 melodies: (1) since the material was not collected on the spot, it was not possible to determine systematically what should be collected and, subsequently, which pieces should be recorded; (2) the performers were itinerant musicians and, therefore, could not be very authentic sources of village music linked to the site; (3) the recorded melodies had not been notated nor were the texts written down. And, in the latter case, since the performers were no longer available, deficiencies in the recordings could not be corrected. In fact, even the Turks themselves were unable to understand the texts on some of the recordings that were played for Bartók during his Istanbul visit.

During the following week, Bartók presented his lectures and a concert in Ankara. A short collecting trip had been planned for him, following these appearances and prior to a repetition of the concert program on 17 November, but illness prevented its realization. After a full recovery and with his obligations met, Bartók had approximately ten days remaining for fieldwork. His companions were the composer A. Adnan Saygun, whose task was the collecting of data from the performers as well as the jotting down of the texts, and two composition teachers from the Ankara Conservatory of Music, who were to witness how musical folklore is collected on the spot.

Having been warned by his Turkish escorts that it would be necessary to fraternize with the peasants for weeks before they finally would be induced to sing, Bartók set out with mixed feelings. As the result of their conversation concerning words common to the Hungarian and Turkish languages, Saygun suggested to Bartók that they construct a sentence that would be almost the same in both tongues. Then, whenever they met peasants who were intimidated by the presence of a stranger, Saygun would say that the Hungarians were only Turks who had settled somewhere else, that they had always spoken Turkish, but that evidently in the course of centuries their accent had become more or less different. Then Bartók was to repeat the sentence that had been concocted. The amusing sentence (in English translation: *In the cotton field are much barley and many apples, camels, tents, axes, boots, and young goats*) was understood by all and provided the researchers with the means to facilitate the collection.[10] In a summary of the results of his trip, Bartók indicated that what had been achieved did not come up to his standards of perfection. One great shortcoming, for example, was his inability to obtain all the relevant information about the collected material: designation of the songs, how they had been handed down, and so forth. And, in a number of cases, the obtained data were either incorrect or contradictory; there was not enough time to thoroughly check these data and simultaneously pursue the recording of the available performers. He was also considerably handicapped by linguistic problems: he could not talk to the peasants directly. Communicating through an interpreter, he was unable to discover whether two or more performers ever sang together and, if they did, on what occasions. The fact is that he could never get people to sing together, not even those who lived together in the same village: "All my trials resulted in a complete failure, which would indicate that singing in chorus was unknown in this part of the world. But even that statement should be accepted with caution. It is almost unthinkable that Turkish people should never sing together, never form a chorus (if only in one part)." The greatest shortcoming of all, however, was his inability to record songs performed by women: Muslim women did not sing in public, especially not in the presence of a stranger. And, lastly, it was not always possible to write down the complete texts on the spot, with the result that they were for the most part preserved only on the phonograph records.[11]

Saygun's memoirs present yet another circumstance that hampered the research. The old Edison recording machine that Bartók brought with him from Budapest could not clearly record both voice and accompanying instruments at the same time.[12]

No sooner had Bartók returned to Budapest when he set to work transcribing the sixty-four cylinders he had recorded. In fact, he reported that a quarter of them had been completed by the first week in January. In this report, the first in a brief series of exchanges with Saygun, Bartók wrote that he was anxiously expecting the promised French translation of the Turkish song texts and that with one exception—a recording in which "the singer has performed changes that were not written down (and, it goes without saying, I cannot understand)—the words of the original Turkish texts were written down very exactly."[13]

By the following week Bartók had researched his material to the extent that he was able to list these conclusions: (1) the peasant music in the Adana region of Turkey has little in common with the music (possibly Arabic influenced) in the Turkish cities; (2) rhymed prose hardly can be found in rural music; (3) Aeolian, Dorian, and, sporadically, Mixolydian modes occur; (4) deviations from the pure intonation of the diatonic scale do not exceed Hungarian ones in particular and those of east Europeans in general; (5) augmented seconds are rarely encountered.[14]

In May, Bartók had completed the major part of his transcriptions and, looking ahead to an edition of the work, had initiated steps to obtain a joint Turkish-Hungarian publication.[15] Later that month he received his first reply from Saygun who reported that difficulties had been encountered in transcribing the texts and the *taksim* (improvisations) that precede the dance. Saygun was doubtful that these improvisations were folk products, especially when performed throughout the record, and in cases where the *taksim* preceded the dance, it would no longer be an improvisation if the same *taksim* were to be played alike by all performers.[16]

On 20 June, Bartók responded to Saygun's letter with the announcement that the latter's text translations had arrived, along with Turkish folk-music material collected by Saygun in the northeastern (Black Sea area) part of the country. The greater part of Bartók's letter was devoted to a critique of Saygun's transcriptions, of which the following remarks are worthy of quotation here:

> There were practical reasons that prompted us to select g^1 as the final tone. Because this tone is—up to the present time—applicable to melodies *of all peoples*. A lower tone (for example, f^1 or d^1) would be impossible for many Western European melodies, since they often descend as much as an octave below the final tone. A higher tone, on the other hand, would present inconveniences, since many Turkish and Hungarian melodies go higher than the final tone by as much as thirteen steps! With g^1 as the final tone we have at our disposal the compass of g through c^3 or d^3. . . .
>
> You asked me whether or not the "improvisations" should be notated. You are right if it is a matter of a genuine improvisation, then one cannot consider it to be a "folk melody." However, if improvisations of this kind are in vogue among the peasant musicians of the villages, one must collect them, from the folkloristic viewpoint. This is my opinion, and, as a matter of fact, I myself have collected pieces of this kind (by the way, they are quite rare here). In your country it is only necessary to check whether the improvisators are truly permanent village residents or are wandering troubadours. In the latter case one must consider their improvisations with suspicion, with distrust.[17]

The hiatus of more than nine months in Bartók's correspondence concerning his Turkish collection was probably due to a number of disparate factors. The principal one, perhaps, was composition: the Sonata for Two Pianos and Percussion was written during July and August, the Second Violin Concerto was commenced in August (and completed at the end of the next year), and *Contrasts* for violin, clarinet, and piano was sketched prior to the end of September. The second factor was the matter of preparation for concerts and recitals: he and his wife, Ditta, gave the world premiere of the Sonata for Two Pianos and Percussion on 16 January 1938 in Basel; Bartók then went on alone to play recitals in Luxembourg, Brussels, Amsterdam, The Hague, and London. The third and most significant factor was the German occupation of Austria in March: Bartók resolved to leave Hungary and began making preparations for his exile.[18]

A letter from Saygun in April, which informed Bartók that Saygun's book[19] on the music, instruments, and dances of towns in northeastern Anatolia had been forwarded to Budapest, may have prompted Bartók to return to his Turkish collection.[20] For his own reasons Bartók broke off contact with Saygün and turned to László Rásonyi for help with the Turkish texts:

> Alas! it did not come off by any means to have the Turkish texts checked: nor could I busy myself with them! . . . Under the impact of your letter I resumed with difficulty the task of making fair copies of the texts; we completed half of them, I enclose them herewith.
>
> One more request: in the Turkish texts kindly underline the words of Arabic origin in blue pencil, those of Persian origin in green pencil; in particular those which are in public use; underscoring once the fully acclimatized words, and twice, the words used only in more educated circles. That would have great importance for me, since I could then infer many things.[21]

In May, Bartók sent the remainder of the Turkish texts to Rásonyi, with additional instructions concerning orthographical matters: "The difficulty is with ğ and y, since even the Turks confound them (for example, değil, deyil, eğlemek, eylemek!); how could I, poor Hungarian, know which to use?!" And, after a remark that he ought to emigrate, he makes this statement concerning the fate of his Turkish collection: "It would be of great importance that the Halkevi enter into negotiations with Rózsavölgyi [Bartók's Hungarian music publisher]: I am afraid that otherwise, in view of the general slump, they would drop altogether the publishing project."[22]

In his response, dated 3 June, Rásonyi informed Bartók that examination of the texts disclosed very few Arabic and Persian words, and that those that occurred were in common usage. Rásonyi added that he noticed fluctuations of the phonetic notation but that he refrained from altering them, since the pronunciation of *j* and *u* might vary.[23]

The political and economic climate in 1938 and 1939 was hardly conducive to the publication of such esoteric works as Bartók's Turkish folk-music collection. Fully resolved to emigrate, and counting on his new publishers in England for assistance, Bartók prepared the fair copy of the Turkish music examples on master sheets and a typescript draft of the Turkish texts.[24] His prefatory study, originally planned as a French-language version and at that time apparently unwritten in any form, was temporarily deferred. His creative energies, on the other hand, continued unabated: composition of the Divertimento for String Orchestra and the Sixth String Quartet, and completion of the Second Violin Concerto and the *Mikrokosmos* for piano. He was also feverishly at work preparing the fair copies of his Romanian folk-music collection, an enormous undertaking which resulted in the production of almost 900 master sheets by the time Bartók made his first visit, in 1940, to the United States for concert and lecture purposes.

The second voyage, with Bartók as emigrant, was made in October. Taking up residence in New York, he commenced a busy schedule of public appearances as recitalist and lecturer (for the most part on tour of the United States); as research fellow at Columbia University, where he transcribed recordings of the Milman Parry Collection (owned by Harvard University) of Serbo-Croatian folk music; and as ethnomusicologist, simultaneously preparing prefatory studies for his vast collection of Romanian material and the newly acquired, less extensive Serbo-Croatian women's songs.

Although he was able to obtain a contract for the publication of the latter work, finding a publisher for *Rumanian Folk Music* (he had completed separate volumes of instrumental and vocal melodies in December 1942) proved to be an unrealizable venture.[25] Prior to this attempt, however, Bartók completed his Serbo-Croatian study (in February) and several of the series of lectures he planned as newly designated visiting lecturer at Harvard University, beginning in February 1943. These lectures exhausted him and led to his breakdown and subsequent hospitalization, beginning in mid-March, for a period of seven weeks. But the indefatigable Bartók, abhorring indolence, was "poring over some Turkish poems with the help of a handwritten Turkish-Hungarian dictionary that he himself had compiled. The poems, scattered about on his bedspread, were also in his handwriting, together with his attempts at translation. Dissatisfied with the efforts of some philologists on his behalf, he was now having a try at it single-handed."[26] In fact, between April and June, Bartók had "prepared for publication my Turkish material, again with a 100 pp. introduction, etc. All this was very interesting for me. The trouble is that extremely few people are interested in such things, although I arrived at highly original conclusions and demonstrations, all proved by very severe deductions. And, of course, nobody wants to publish them."[27]

During this period of time, Bartók was also undergoing frustrating negotiations with the New York Public Library for the publication of his two volumes of Romanian folk-music material. That institution's enthusiasm for the undertaking quickly waned when cost estimates were presented by their printer, and they withdrew their offer of publication.[28] It was perhaps then that the idea occurred to Bartók to offer the much smaller Turkish collection in place of the rejected Romanian project. He had taken with him the various drafts of the Turkish material when he left the city for a summer convalescence in Saranac Lake, New York, at the end of June. By the time he was to return to New York, in mid-October, he had completed the fair copy of the extra musical portion of the work (introduction, texts and translations, marginalia) and, moreover, the sketch of the Concerto for Orchestra.[29] On 3 October he wrote to the Library that:

> Nothing can be done with the Rumanian material for the time being. Fortunately, however, I have another work, to offer for publishing, about less than half the size of the Rumanian one. It is the "Turkish rural folk music from Asia Minor. . . ."
> This work contains the first collection of rural Turkish folk music ever made by

systematic research work, and ever published. The Introduction contains a description of how to determine the approximate age limit of rural folk song material, in certain specific cases. Such problems have never yet been described and published. Therefore, this feature of the book has an international significance. Besides this, many other highly interesting questions are treated in the Introduction.[30]

The Library's rejection of the Turkish book on 15 October, coupled with Ralph Hawkes's 8 September letter that a Boosey & Hawkes publication of the Romanian volumes must await the end of the war, prompted this reaction from Bartók:

> As for the bad ones [news]—I mention only a few. First: the impossibility of publishing my scientific works (Rumanian, Turkish folk music material). Of course my Essay on Serbo-Croatian folk songs is going to be published by the Columb. University Press, perhaps next fall it will be issued. But for the others, there is not much hope. What made me especially angry was the unfair way negotiation with the New York Public Library was conducted. It would take too much space and it is not worth while to describe the details of these unhappy dealings.[31]

On 14 December Bartók deposited the master-sheet draft of the first two volumes of *Rumanian Folk Music* (and, on 1 July 1944, *Turkish Folk Music from Asia Minor*) "at the Columbia University Music Library—there they are available to those few persons (very few indeed) who may be interested in them."[32]

NOTES

1. *Documenta Bartókiana* 3, ed. Denijs Dille (Budapest: Akadémiai Kiadó, 1968), 179–83. Rásonyi asked Bartók to lecture on three questions: (1) the connection between Hungarian and Turkish music, (2) the development of Hungarian music and its apparent state, and (3) how a Turkish national music could develop.

2. *Zenei Lexikon* 2 (Budapest, 1931): 621.

3. *Bartók Béla levelei*, ed. János Demény (Budapest: Zeneműkiadó, Vallalat, 1955), 406–8. Written from Budapest, the letter is dated 18 December 1935.

4. The designation of the social institutes set up throughout Turkey.

5. *Documenta Bartókiana* 3, ed. Denijs Dille, 190.

6. *Bartók Béla levelei*, ed. János Demény, 1955, 411–12.

7. Ibid., 413. Bartók brought with him to New York, in 1940, a Turkish primer for the second grade (*Okuma kítabi,* Istanbul, 1936), that contains his annotations in Hungarian and French. The Kúnos collection of Turkish folk-song texts, published in Budapest, was copied by Bartók in a small notebook, also with Hungarian and French annotations.

8. Published in Ankara (1936) under the title *Halk müziği Hakkinda*, and in Hungarian translation (by László Rásonyi) in *Új Zenei Szemle* (Budapest, 1954).

9. János Demény, ed., *Bartók Béla levelei*, vol. 2 (Budapest: Művelt nép könyvkiadó, 1951), 119–20. The translation of Bartók's Turkish phrases is: The horse is faster than the camel; the cat is smaller than the dog.

10. A. Adnan Saygun, "Bartók in Turkey," *Musical Quarterly* 37 (1951): 89. The sentence in Hungarian: *Pamuk tarlón sok árpa, alma, teve, sátor, balta, csizma, kicsi kecske van.* In Turkish: *Pamuk tarlasinda çok arpa, alma, deve, çadir, balta, çizme, küçük var.*

11. Béla Bartók, "Népdalgűjtés Törökországban" (Folk Song Collecting in Turkey), *Nyugat* (Budapest, 1937): 173–81. This article, an expanded version of the lecture given by Bartók on Budapest Radio (11 January 1937), appears in revised form in English in *BBE*, No. 20.

12. Saygun, "Bartók in Turkey," 7. Saygun also recalls that the tempo of each song was verified by means of a metronome, and the register of the voice by means of a pitch pipe.

13. Letter dated 2 January 1937. Written in French, a photocopy of this letter is in the *PBA*. In German translation in *Béla Bartók Ausgewählte Briefe*, ed. János Demény (Budapest: Corvina Press, 1960), 170–71.

14. *Bartók Béla levelei*, ed. János Demény, 1955, 419, letter to János Bán (Hungarian professor of Turkish linguistics and author of the article on Turkish art music in *Zenei Lexikon*), dated 8 January 1937.

15. Ibid., 423–24, letter to Rásonyi, dated 13 May 1937. Bartók's futile attempts to achieve publication of his Turkish material offer another example of the failures and frustrations that plagued him throughout his ethnomusicological career. The interested reader will find a detailed description of these setbacks in *RFM*.i, viii–xix.

16. *Documenta Bartókiana* 3, ed. Denijs Dille, 210, letter dated 27 May 1937.

17. *PBA* Correspondence File. See also *Béla Bartók Ausgewählte Briefe*, ed. János Demény, 176–77. The letter ends with Bartók's report that he was busy with the study of the Turkish texts, aided by Saygun's translations, and that he would like permission to use the latter's work in a French-language edition of the collection that was in preparation for publication in Hungary.

18. See Ralph Hawkes's recollections in *A Memorial Review* (New York: Boosey & Hawkes, 1950), 14-17. Hawkes flew to Budapest a few days after the German-Austrian *Anschluss* and obtained from Bartók an agreement for publication of his future works.

19. A. Adnan Saygun, *Rize, Artvin ve Kars Havâlisi, Türkü, Saz ve Oyunlari* (Istanbul: Nümune Matbaasi, 1937).

20. *Documenta Bartókiana* 3, ed. Denijs Dille, 219–20, letter dated 6 April 1938. According to Saygun's article in the *Musical Quarterly* ("Bartók in Turkey," p. 9), he received a typewritten letter from Bartók, shortly after the *Anschluss*, asking whether a position could be found in Turkey that would enable Bartók to establish permanent residence there.

21. *Bartók Béla levelei*, ed. János Demény, 1955, 429–30, letter dated 28 April 1938.

22. Ibid., 431, letter dated 12 May 1938.

23. According to the Hungarian passage quoted in László Somfai's letter to me, dated 8 June 1971. This and three other unpublished letters from Rásonyi to Bartók are in the *BBA* (dated 22 April 1936, 1 September 1936, and 24 January 1937); also contained there, and annotated by Somfai for me, are five unpublished letters from Saygun to Bartók dated 7 February 1937, 13 March 1937, 1 September 1937, 24 November 1938, and 19 March 1939).

24. He probably had the help of a former pupil, Jenő Deutsch, for the autography (see *RFM*.i, 2).

25. The contract for *Serbo-Croatian Folk Songs* (with Albert B. Lord as coauthor) was signed in July 1943; the posthumous publication, by Columbia University Press, was in 1951. The revised edition appears in *YFM*.i.

26. Joseph Szigeti, *With Strings Attached*, 2nd ed. (New York: Alfred A. Knopf, 1967), 271.

27. *PBA* Correspondence File, letter to Ralph Hawkes, dated 31 July 1943. The use of the word "them" refers also to the two volumes of *RFM* mentioned in a preceding paragraph in this letter which, as a matter of fact, probably was intended as an indirect approach to Boosey & Hawkes to publish both studies.

28. *PBA* Correspondence File, letter from the New York Public Library to Bartók dated 30 June 1943.

29. This draft appears in Bartók's Turkish field sketchbook, *PBA* 80FSS1.

30. *PBA* Correspondence File.

31. *PBA* Correspondence File, letter to Wilhelmine Creel Driver, dated 17 December 1943. See also *Bartók Béla levelei*, ed. János Demény, 1951, 181.

32. *PBA* Correspondence File, letter to Wilhelmine Creel Driver, dated 17 December 1943.

18

Bartók as Man of Letters[1]

Bartók's literary efforts range from books and shorter monographs to essays of various lengths. According to recent findings, there are more than 130 writings, for the most part on ethnomusicological subjects.[2] The composer's first essay, an analysis of his *Kossuth* symphonic poem, appeared in print in 1904.[3] It is interesting that except in 1907 and 1915, at least one of his writings was published each year of his life, in a considerable number of languages, and frequently in widely known journals. His essays may be divided, according to their topics, into eight basic categories (although there is some overlapping): I, The Investigation of Musical Folklore; II, National Folk Music; III, Comparative Musical Folklore, IV, Book Reviews and Polemics, V, Musical Instruments, VI, The Relation between Folk Music and Art Music, VII, The Life and Music of Béla Bartók, and VIII, Bartók on Music and Musicians.

I. The Investigation of Musical Folklore

The end of the First World War marked the end of the greater part of Bartók's fieldwork to collect musical folklore. During the first half of the 1920s, he devoted himself to the scientific study and preparation for publication of his Hungarian, Slovak, and part of his Romanian materials.[4] Then, in 1929, he embarked on a series of essays concerning his fieldwork and research experiences in the investigation of folk music.[5] These essays are in the form of big questions to which Bartók provides the answers. What is folk music? What is the best way to start collecting it? What is urban (popular) art music? Why should we collect folk music? How do we collect it? Some of the answers are light in tone: for example, the amusing narrative of the problems he encountered as a gentleman collector of rural songs. He notes that the peasants found it difficult to believe that he would sacrifice city comforts just to listen to them sing. In fact, they concluded that he was a tax collector, visiting them with a new purpose in mind: a tax on music![6]

In 1943, three years after his arrival in America, and in a somewhat unusual introspective mood, Bartók stated that the time he devoted to his work in musical folklore was the happiest part of his life, despite the tiresome aspects, the enormous physical effort, and the self-sacrifice involved.[7] From 1942 to 1945, the last year of his life, Bartók worked on the various drafts of his book on

Serbo-Croatian folk songs.[8] The introductory chapter of this study is in essence his final testament in the investigation of musical folklore. Here, in detail, he offers a superb essay on methods of transcription and systematic classification of folk melodies. The scholarly writing style, so markedly different from earlier essays on the same subject, is most fitting for what may be considered one of the finest of all expositions on the approach to ethnomusicological research.

II. NATIONAL FOLK MUSIC

What kind of folk music did Bartók collect? Relatively few readers, even among ethnomusicologists, may be aware that his interests were not basically directed toward autochthonous Hungarian material. The supporting evidence is quite apparent when Bartók's essays on musical folklore are examined. They are annotated here in alphabetical order of nationality.

Shortly after he arrived in New York in 1940 Bartók became interested in American music. In fact, he even began the morphological analysis of a number of West Virginian folk songs and ballads. Then, in 1942, he wrote a short essay calling for the application to American, British, and west European folk music of the systems developed for the scientific examination of that of eastern Europe.[9]

In 1917, which is to say, about five years after he had visited North Africa, Bartók wrote a monograph on Arab peasant music stemming from the Biskra district in Algeria.[10] In contrast to this study is his interesting sketch of the Arab music he heard in Cairo in 1932 that, to his surprise, consisted in part of genuine village music played by city musicians.[11]

Bartók wrote only one essay devoted to Bulgarian music—restricted to discussion of the rhythmic aspect—although he had examined and classified nearly 10,000 Bulgarian folk melodies.[12]

His numerous smaller essays on Hungarian folk music range from the non-descriptive transcription of Székely ballads that appeared in the Budapest journal *Ethnographia* in 1908, to the extended essay on the peasant music of Hungary, that was published in the *Musical Quarterly,* New York, in 1933. Although he wrote an abbreviated rehash of the subject for a Hungarian encyclopedia[13] two years later, he subsequently discussed Hungarian folk music only in the broader context of comparative studies.

Mention should also be made of his collaboration with Zoltán Kodály to produce their book on Transylvanian-Hungarian folk songs in 1923, and of the publication during the next year of his great treatise on Hungarian folk song that was later published in German and English editions.

The posthumously published three-volume study titled *Rumanian Folk Music*[14] is the culmination of almost thirty-seven years of intermittent collecting, transcription, and scientific examination by Bartók. In fact, the third volume was completed barely six months prior to his death in 1945. In this volume

Bartók advocates a new discipline: the philology of poetic folk-song texts. In the other two volumes, which are illustrated with the most complex transcriptions of folk music ever notated, he is found at the height of his powers of scholarly writing.

These contributions to the study of Romanian musical folklore were the culmination of various preliminary works. The first was a book-length treatment of the folk songs of the Transylvanian-Romanians in Bihor County, that was completely revised twenty years after its publication in 1913. It was followed by essays of varying length and by two books: one on the folk music of the Maramureş County Romanians, published in 1923, and the other on the Romanian carols and Christmas songs (1935). The latter, by the way, contains in its formerly unpublished second part[15] Bartók's first philological attempt in the area of textual folk-song material.

The first essay on Slovak folk music, an abbreviated description of Bartók's own findings, was written for *A Dictionary of Modern Music and Musicians* (ed. A. E. Hull, London, 1924). At about the same time Bartók had completed his huge, three-volume manuscript on Slovak folk music. In apparent contradiction to his custom of following completion of a major treatise with a considerable number of shorter essays on the same subject, there are only four, quite small articles—three of them in abbreviated form for use in encyclopedias, and the other one published in New York in the general music magazine, the *Musical Courier* in 1931.

A possible explanation of this unusual circumstance is that Bartók may have changed his original premises concerning morphological aspects of his Slovak material. Among the manuscripts of the Slovak treatise are a significant number of complex revisions of certain melodies. Their presence prompts the conjecture that perhaps he intended to reexamine his Slovak material before again committing himself in print on the subject.

In 1936, Bartók received an official invitation to collect folk music of nomad tribesmen in the south Anatolian area of Turkey. This last field trip resulted in an essay notable for its interesting narrative style. Seven years later, Bartók tried to interest the New York Public Library in publishing a smaller work than the Romanian folk-music study (which they had rejected as being too costly to produce) and to that end quickly drafted a new work entitled *Turkish Folk Music from Asia Minor.* This study, published by Princeton University Press in 1976, is of great importance in ethnomusicology: in it Bartók proves conclusively that part of his newly collected Turkish material is related to the old Hungarian folk music of the fifth or sixth centuries.

The last ethnic area explored by Bartók is the Yugoslav one. Before he emigrated to America he had collected a small number of Yugoslav melodies and, more significantly, had assembled and analyzed a vast number of published and unpublished ones that had been collected by ethnomusicologists of that area. All these materials provided him with the supporting data for the important book on Serbo-Croatian folk songs that he wrote during his research fellowship at Columbia University. He was destined never to see this work in print. Moreover, the form in which it was finally published in 1951 was not the one intended by its author; for Bartók planned to incorporate the above-mentioned sources as an appendix in the form of a lengthy tabulation of their morphological aspects. He did have the satisfaction, however, of seeing his report on the subject—his first, small essay on Serbo-Croatian folk music—published in the *New York Times* in 1942.

III. COMPARATIVE MUSICAL FOLKLORE

After Bartók had set out in 1905 to "study and collect the Hungarian peasant music unknown till then," he soon realized that a quantity of reliably transcribed melodies was needed in order to examine them scientifically. Moreover, the presence of seemingly foreign elements in the Hungarian material he began to accumulate prompted him to attempt the determination of prototypes and the comparison of the various melodies for reciprocal influences. Thus Bartók became master of a science which in 1912 was still in its infancy: comparative music folklore, or as it is known today, ethnomusicology. And it was in 1912 that Bartók published the first of his articles to be devoted to the comparative aspect of folk-music research.[16]

It is amusing to find that Bartók, in his second article on this subject, published in 1919,[17] adopts an accountant's approach to the practical problems involved in the interarchive preparation and exchange of folk-music recordings, including actual figures for freight charges! Ten years later he reported on his achievements in collecting and comparing thousands of Hungarian, Slovak, Romanian, Ruthenian, Serbian, Bulgarian, and Gypsy folk melodies.[18] And in 1934, he wrote his superb monograph on the folk music of Hungary and its neighbors, which was simultaneously published in Hungarian, German, and French editions.[19]

But this last-named work, seemingly in the form of a summary of his career in comparative musicology, was incomplete. His discovery of the previously-mentioned Milman Parry collection of recorded Yugoslav material, his analysis of Bulgarian rhythm, and his study of newly acquired Turkish material, were later (1941?) integrated with the findings from the 1934 monograph to produce a lecture titled "Some Problems of Folk Music Research in East Europe."

IV. BOOK REVIEWS AND POLEMICS

The existence of eleven essays in the form of reviews or polemical responses to criticisms of his work in ethnomusicology reveals a little-known side of the literary Bartók. The first of these writings occurred in 1914, in reply to an unfavorable and unjust criticism of his first book on Romanian folk music. Twenty-two years were to pass before another such criticism of Bartók's Romanian studies appeared in print. This one, too, provoked a sharp reply from the injured Bartók.

When an anthology of supposedly authentic Hungarian folk songs was published in 1929 in Germany, Bartók was impelled to draft a devastating review whose length, supporting data, and illustrative music notations give it the aspect of a monograph. This review, titled "Gypsy Music or Hungarian Music?" provoked a series of published charges and countercharges between Bartók and the editor of the compilation.[20]

Another scathing rebuke from Bartók was occasioned by the publication in 1934 of the first League of Nations volume on folk music and folk song. A similar tone is evident in his earlier (1921) article, "He Who Knows No Arabic," in which an anonymous Hungarian author is taken to task for misinterpreting a French review of a Paris concert in which Bartók and Kodály took part. Bartók, with characteristic preciseness, offers an alternative French translation in support of his contentions.

Finally there is the 1935 "Letter to the Kisfaludy Society," in which Bartók bitterly opposes that organization's award to him for the scarcely representative First Suite for Orchestra, op. 3, written thirty years earlier, at the age of twenty-four. Obviously deeply hurt by the society's tacit rejection of the more important works composed in his maturity, and particularly in the period between 1929 and 1934, Bartók rejects the honor by declaring that "I do not wish to accept the Greguss Medal in the present or in the future, neither alive nor dead."

V. MUSICAL INSTRUMENTS

A by-product of Bartók's research in musical folklore is a series of essays on musical instruments. In fact, he stands above other lexicographers with regard to eastern Europe, since his precise descriptions of the various instruments he encountered are also profusely illustrated by detailed transcriptions of the performed musical material. In addition to four independent articles on folk instruments, which were published in 1911, 1912, 1917, and 1931, there are sections or chapters from monographs or books devoted to the folk music of Romania, Slovakia, Turkey, Yugoslavia, and the Biskra Oasis Arabs of Algeria.

Bartók's exploration of the percussive nature of the piano, and his study of early keyboard music, led to short essays on those subjects in 1910, 1912, and 1927. With regard to Bartók's pithy comments concerning pedagogical aspects in piano technique and musicianship, see my book Bartók's Mikrokosmos (Scarecrow Press, 2002). In the previously mentioned Dictionary of Modern Music and Musicians (1924), Bartók briefly describes some Hungarian art music instruments. Perhaps the crowning achievement in this category is his discourse on mechanical music. Written in 1937, it contains prophetic as well as topical comments on gramophone and sound-film recording, radio broadcasting, and electronic music.

VI. The Relation between Folk Music and Art Music

The writings considered so far are representative of Bartók the folklorist, and this aspect of his career has been given pride of place here in order to emphasize the impact of his ethnomusicological research on his artistic output. Indeed, the importance of this work is quite apparent if the quantity of Bartók's literary output is used as a criterion: almost half of his essays are concerned with musical folklore. In addition there are ten essays that serve as links between his work as folklorist and his work as composer. They could therefore be brought under the heading, "The Relation between Folk Music and Art Music."

The scope of this essay does not permit more than a brief mention of two of these most important insights into Bartók's creative process. One of them, a rather extended essay published in 1921,[21] investigates the folk-music influence on composers of three musical eras: Haydn and Beethoven, Chopin and Liszt, and Stravinsky and Kodály. More importantly, however, it contains a tentative exploration of relationships between the arts, with specific mention of painting and poetry. This interest obviously received considerable attention during the ensuing years: in Bartók's lectures, given at Harvard University in 1943, he describes parallels between revolution and evolution in art and music, citing the painting of the Dutch artist Piet Mondrian as an example of revolutionary oversimplification of means, and Alois Hába's use of quarter tones and avoidance of repetition as revolutionary overcomplications. In the next section he discusses twentieth-century literary trends in similar terms, with emphasis on the use of words for sound rather than sense. Finally, he turns to the music of Schoenberg, Stravinsky, and the creators of the "new" Hungarian art music— that is, Kodály and himself—and maintains that it is evolutionary in concept.

VII. The Life and Music of Béla Bartók

And what did Bartók have to say about himself and his work? The autobiographical writings, which range from 1911 to 1945,[22] reflect the opinion of friends and colleagues, who describe him as a modest and unpretentious person. Characteristically devoid of verbiage are his commentaries and analyses of his compositions, which begin with the essay on the symphonic poem *Kossuth* in 1904 (mentioned above as perhaps his first literary publication) and conclude with a draft preface to an album of his early piano pieces that he compiled in America during the last year of his life.

VIII. Bartók on Music and Musicians

The final category of Bartók essays shows him as musicologist, as music critic, and as a kind of musical 'foreign correspondent' reporting to the world about concert life in Budapest. These essays cover a wide range and clearly indicate his deep interest in musical life at home and abroad. Among the composers he writes about are such well-known contemporary figures as Debussy, Delius, Dohnányi, Kodály, Ravel, Schoenberg, Richard Strauss, and Stravinsky. He even took on the role of "public defender" in his writings on Kodály and Toscanini, and his one attempt at biography honors the eminent Hungarian musicologist, Bence Szabolcsi.

Of special interest to the music educator is the essay Bartók prepared, originally in the form of a lecture, "On Music Education for the Turkish People," for presentation in Ankara in 1936. He recommends an "active" rather than a "passive" approach to music education for the masses, on the grounds that students who are able to produce sounds from musical notation are better equipped to deal with the intricacies of those sounds than are listeners. Bartók prefers the vocal to the instrumental approach; the latter requires many years of hard work before the technical difficulties are mastered and is therefore not feasible on a mass basis. He stresses the importance of note reading as opposed to rote learning, on the grounds that unless singers are musically literate the goal of bringing people nearer to the mysteries of music will not be reached. He therefore emphasizes the need for enthusiastic, well-trained musician-teachers, and for good materials from the sacred and secular repertoires of the fifteenth to sixteenth centuries. Beginner choirs should perform easy pieces specially composed for them by native composers, and foreign texts should be translated in such a way as to observe the rules of good prosody and reflect popular idiomatic speech as closely as possible.

From the literary point of view, no description of Bartók's prose could do justice to its quality or be an adequate substitute for the actual reading. The one general observation that seems valid concerns the integrity that underlies and unifies his entire written output. Bartók as man of letters can be characterized by his own motto, "exactitude above all!"[23]

NOTES

1. The first version of this lecture appeared in *International Musicological Conference in Commemoration of Béla Bartók 1971*, ed. József Ujfalussy and János Breuer (Budapest: Editio Musica, 1972), 89–96. A revised version appears in *Tempo* 102 (1972): 10–16.

2. See *BBE*, *BBSE*, and the entries in *BBGR*.

3. "*Kossuth*: Szinfónai költemény," *Zeneközlöny* 6 (Budapest, 10 January 1904): 82–87.

4. *A magyar népdal* (1924), *Slowakische Volkslieder* (1959, 1970), *Die Volksmusik der Rumänen von Maramureş* (1923), and *Die Melodien der rumänischen Colinde* (*Weihnachtslieder*, 1935).

5. *BBE*, 3.

6. Ibid., 4.

7. "Folk Song Research in Eastern Europe," *Musical America* 1 (January 1943), 27. This title appears on the MS. draft; the printed version is "Bartók Views Folk-Music Wealth of Hungary."

8. Published by Columbia University Press in 1951.

9. *BBE*, 37. This essay also appears on the dust cover of the three volumes comprising Bartók's *Rumanian Folk Music* study (see note 14 below).

10. Published in *Szimfónia* (Budapest) and, in an extended revision, in *Zeitschrift für Musikwissenschaft* (Berlin), 1933.

11. *BBE*, 38–39.

12. Published in *Enekszó* (Budapest) in 1938.

13. *Révai Nagy Lexikona* (Budapest), vol. 21.

14. Edited by Benjamin Suchoff and published by Martinus Nijhoff, The Hague, 1967.

15. This work, in revised form under the title (Rumanian) *Carols and Christmas Songs (Colinde)*, appeared in 1975 as vol. IV of *Rumanian Folk Music* (ibid.); the revised Maramureş County study as vol V.

16. Published in *Uj Elet* (Budapest).

17. *Musikblätter des Anbruch* (Vienna).

18. In three Budapest publications: *Zenei Szemle, Ethnographia,* and *Magyar Tudományos Akadémia Kiadása*.

19. And in English in *BBSE*.

20. In *Zeitschrift für Musikwissenschaft* (Leipzig, 1931) and *Ungarische Jahrbücher* (Berlin, 1932).

21. "The Relation of Folk Song to the Development of the Art Music of Our Time," *Sackbut* (London).

22. "Onéletrajz," published in the *Budapesti Ujságirók Egyesülete Almanachja,* and "My Activities During the War," which appeared in Belgium under the title "I Salute the Valiant Belgian People."

23. *BBL*, 209, letter from Bartók to Hubert Foss (Oxford University Press, London), dated 20 May 1931.

19

The Bartók–Kodály Connection[1]

At the turn of the century, following the celebration of the Hungarian millennium and the fiftieth anniversary of the ill-fated 1848 revolution against the oppressive Habsburg monarchy, a swelling tide of resurgent national feeling brought a great demand for a specifically Hungarian literature, art, and music. Béla Bartók and Zoltán Kodály, destined to be counted among the nation's most illustrious sons, were in the vanguard of politically oriented students at the Budapest Royal Academy of Music—yet they were not to meet until after their graduation in 1903.

"Everyone, on reaching maturity," Bartók wrote his mother, "has to set himself a goal and must direct all his work and actions toward this. For my own part, all my life, and in every sphere, always and in every way, I shall have one objective: the good of Hungary and the Hungarian nation."[2] Musical proof of Bartók's intention was realized in his *Kossuth* symphonic poem (1903), with its sensational parody of *Gott erhalte*, the Austrian national anthem. The first performance of *Kossuth* in January 1904 propelled Bartók into the national limelight as a composer, and he quickly followed this success with his Rhapsody op. 1 for Piano and Orchestra (1904) and, in 1905, the First Suite op. 3 for Large Orchestra.

The Budapest press hailed the twenty-two-year-old genius as "the Hungarian Tchaikovsky," thus adding to his previously won acclaim as a "piano virtuoso, the worthy successor to Liszt." Nevertheless, Bartók felt that his works were leading him to a dead end, since they were predominantly a combination of Liszt's Gypsy-styled Hungarianisms, Richard Strauss's overblown orchestral forces with a dissonant harmonic texture, and Hungarian popular art songs, that is, *magyar nóták* (national melodies), as thematic source material.

At that time Bartók and his predecessors—indeed, the rest of the musical world—erroneously assumed that the national melodies, that were mainly composed by amateurs from the educated classes and disseminated with typical distortions by city Gypsy bands, were the true Hungarian folk music. But during the summer of 1904, while he was composing the Rhapsody op. 1, Bartók overheard a girl singing a melody that had very unusual qualities. She was of peasant origin, born and raised in a Hungarian-speaking village in the southeast corner of Transylvania (now Romania). He notated her song repertory, convinced that he had chanced upon an ancient type of melody significantly different from the so-called Hungarian folk songs that pervaded Budapest's musical life. He decided to investigate further.

"I set out in 1905," Bartók recalled in his 1921 autobiography, "to collect and study Hungarian peasant music unknown till then. It was my great good luck to find a helpmate for this work in Zoltán Kodály who, owing to his deep insight and sound judgment in all spheres of music, could give me many a hint and much advice that proved of immense value."[3] Their meeting that year was brought about by Emma Gruber, a gifted composer and Bartók pupil, who married Kodály in 1910.

Kodály's "spheres" included an Academy of Music diploma in composition and, in 1905, a university degree as teacher of Hungarian and German languages. He then returned home to Galánta (formerly in northwestern Hungary, now part of Slovakia) to collect folk songs in neighboring villages. These specimens and other sources available to him were analyzed and the resultant findings published in his remarkable Ph.D. dissertation, "The Stanzaic Structure of Hungarian Folk Song," in 1906.

Bartók and Kodály initiated their lifelong friendship that same year, when they decided to collaborate on the self-publication of twenty rural Hungarian folk songs, fitted with easy piano accompaniments appropriate to their simple, unpretentious character. For many years they were unable to sell a single copy, in part due to the appearance in Budapest of song hits from Franz Lehár's operetta, *The Merry Widow*.

During Bartók's fieldwork in 1907, he discovered a previously unknown melody type in Transylvanian-Hungarian Székely villages, whose characteristic tonal organization is the central Asian pentatonic scale.[4] In addition to this ancient Magyar heritage, however, he found other examples of "pure" Hungarian peasant song that had been "contaminated" by certain elements the villagers had taken over from transient Slovak farm hands and peasant workers from other national minorities of pre–First World War Greater Hungary. He became fascinated with this "Mixed Class" of Hungarian material and, until 1917, collected thousands of vocal and instrumental melodies in Hungarian villages inhabited by Slovak, Romanian, Ukrainian, Bulgarian, and Yugoslav peasants. And in 1913 he visited Arab villages in North Africa and recorded their unique music.[5]

Kodály, on the other hand, concentrated on collecting Hungarian folk music, extending his field trips to Slovak and Romanian areas for Hungarian material. Among the melodies he collected in 1914 was a folk song related to a seventeenth-century ballad, the Song of Argirus (*Árgirus nótája*). Kodály's remarkable achievement in reconstructing the long-lost music notation—on the basis of the peasant melody!—turned him toward historical musicology, in terms of the bearing of folk-music-derived data on Hungarian art music. His next, related step was the investigation of Hungarian folk song with regard to its connection with popular art song and church music.

Bartók, meanwhile, inspired by the tonal and rhythmic diversity of the huge corpus of musical folklore he had collected, composed pieces incorporating the ancient Magyar pentatonic scale and the more recent "dotted" rhythm (e.g., "Evening in Transylvania," No. 5 from Ten Easy Pieces for Piano, 1908), Romanian bagpipe motifs strung together in indefinite form (first Romanian Dance, op. 8a, 1908), and, in *Allegro Barbaro* (1910), the so-called Slovak rhythm contraction and the Lydian folk mode (a major scale with an augmented fourth degree).

Eventually Bartók arrived at a fusion of national music styles, to the point where their characteristics and performance peculiarities became his "musical mother tongue." The outcome of this attainment was a unique compositional style which reflects the atmosphere or "spirit" of folk music. A dynamic example of the newly won means is found in Bartók's Dance Suite for Orchestra, commissioned in 1923 to commemorate the fiftieth anniversary of the merging of Pest, Buda, and Obuda. The first movement of the Dance Suite is based on a chromatic melody within the interval of a tritone. This kind of narrow-range chromaticism is characteristic of the Arab peasant music that Bartók collected in North Africa in 1913. The rhythm schema, however, is that of the Ruthenian (i.e., Ukrainian) *kolomyjka*, a dance rhythm which is commonplace in Slovak folk music, the Hungarian *kanásztánc* (swineherd's dance), and the Romanian *Ardeleana* ("Transylvanian").[6]

Between 1906 and 1920 Kodály composed a small number of chamber works and songs for voice and piano, for the most part limited to Hungarian folk music characteristics as the source for tonal and rhythmic invention. In 1923 he, too, was awarded a commission to compose a work for the above-mentioned anniversary celebration. The result was his *Psalmus Hungaricus* (op. 13), for chorus, orchestra, and organ, set to the text of Psalm XLV. It is most interesting to note that, like Bartók's Dance Suite, the *Psalmus Hungaricus* also begins with a fusion of disparate styles. However, and quite unlike Bartók's, Kodály's musical language is specifically Hungarian: the melody is based on the ancient Magyar pentatonic scale, and rhythm schema, moreover, though derived from the galliard, a Renaissance court dance in triple meter, is ingeniously varied by use of Hungarian dotted rhythm.

The year 1923 also marks the appearance of *Transylvanian Hungarians: Folksongs* (*Erdélyi magyarság: Népdalok*), a collection of 150 melodies by Béla Bartók and Zoltán Kodály, which was published by the Budapest Popular Literary Society. Although Bartók transcribed most of the melodies, editorial control apparently was Kodály's responsibility, and the latter decided to classify the songs on a "lexicographic" basis, that is, according to the height of the end tones of each four-section melody.

The next year, however, Bartók's scholarly study, *The Hungarian Folk Song* (*A magyar népdal*), was published in Budapest, in which the basis of classification is his so-called grammatical method. The melodies are first grouped with regard to the three major types of Hungarian folk songs: old style, new style, and mixed style. Each of the three groups is then further classified according to the metrical, melodic, rhythmic, and formal structure of the melodies.

Bartók followed his "method of methods" with the preparation of his Slovak and Romanian materials for publication, according to similar grammatical principles of classification, including the determination of foreign as well as indigenous variant relationships of the melodies. He extended his investigation into choreographic details, and he developed a method for classifying the folk texts and their diverse variants. His extraordinary transcriptions, notated after patient, repeated listening to thousands of recorded vocal and instrumental melodies, brought to light the diverse rhythm schemata, altered scalar systems, and unique peculiarities of performance. In fact, many of these idiosyncrasies of peasant music eventually became an integral part of Bartók's new musical language.

Concomitant with his ethnomusicological studies, Bartók pondered the possibility of a new style of composition which would synthesize east European folk music with such west European art-music techniques of composition as the polyphonic texture of Bach, the progressive form of Beethoven, and the harmonic possibilities innovated by Debussy. The more or less strict contrapuntal practice of the German Baroque, however, was alien to Bartók's Hungarian temperament, and he looked elsewhere for creative inspiration.

In 1925, during his concert tour in Italy, Bartók discovered that Bach's Italian predecessors and contemporaries—Girolamo Frescobaldi (1583–1643) and Azzolino della Ciaia (1671–1755)—composed keyboard works in a more lyrical and less rigid contrapuntal style. The adaptation of this style in Bartók's "Synthesis of East and West" period began with his First Piano Concerto (1926) and continued with other masterpieces till his death in 1945, all of them now performed internationally as standard repertory works by "the composer par excellence of the twentieth century."

Turning again to Kodály's career during that time, he followed the *Psalmus Hungaricus* with such superlative works as *Háry János* (1929), Dances of Marosszék (1930), Dances from Galánta (1933), and a substantial number of important songs and choral works, all reflecting the spirit of Hungarian folk music to such a high degree that Bartók himself designated Kodály as "the best Hungarian musician . . . the greatest Hungarian teacher-composer."[7]

It should be obvious, of course, that Kodály's stylistic achievements resulted from his intensive study of the large corpus of Hungarian folk songs he had collected since 1905. In addition he minutely annotated Bartók's 1924 treatise and in 1937 brought out his book, *A magyar népzene* (The Folk Music of Hungary). The organization of his material into seven topical chapters shows how far his ideas digress from Bartók's concept of three style categories, particularly with regard to inclusion of German folk music, Gregorian chant, folk hymns, and popular art song (*magyar nóta*). And the sharp dichotomy in classification procedure is apparent in Kodály's emphasis on the lexicographical principle of grouping all melodies according to melodic design, thus enabling the reader to locate each tune quickly and easily, and, moreover, bringing together all variant melodies as far as possible.[8]

The very close friendship and mutual admiration that Bartók and Kodály had for each other—with regard to ethnomusicological aims and objectives—lessened in intensity to apparent estrangement beginning in 1934, when Bartók left his position as professor of piano at the Budapest Academy of Music and moved to the Academy of Sciences. Here he had the sole responsibility for preparing the complete corpus of Hungarian folk songs for publication, including his own material and the large number of melodies collected by Kodály.

Bartók decided to classify the entire material—about 14,000 melodies—according to the innovative "grammatical" method used in his *The Hungarian Folk Song* publication, with some minor modifications in terms of stylistic aspects and more detailed emphasis on rhythm schemata.[9] Kodály, who had long indicated a preference for his lexicographical system—"the many secret affinities come to sight only in a melodic system"—was not consulted.

When in October 1940 Bartók emigrated to the United States, leaving his completed work behind, and Kodály discovered what Bartók had done, he was deeply hurt by such "mysterious" behavior:

> If you had the intention to make the whole thing alone, why not tell it to me in 1934? I had plenty of other work. And the questions we couldn't decide, because during 6 years you found not a single afternoon to discuss them thoroughly. I wonder why you became deterred from "cooperation intellectuel" . . . . Well, we studied different things enough, to change ideas without loss for each other, and added experiences of two are of more value than any individual.[10]

At the end of the undated, unsigned letter (1941?) the content and poetic format of Emma Kodály's poignant postscript speaks for itself:

> I am not an angel, like Zoltán
> You don't like to write?
> Don't!
> You liked to forget us?
> Forget! (If you enable it!)

But Bartók, who had always followed strict principles of scientific research in his studies of east European folk music, in order to determine and separate foreign elements from indigenous material, had not forgotten "my only friend, Kodály," only differed diametrically from the latter's ethnomusicological objectives. In his last essay on Hungarian music, the year before his death in New York City, Bartók states:

> There are two of Hungary's contemporary composers who have gained an international reputation—Zoltán Kodály and myself. Although we have a common

outlook upon rural music and its part in the development of higher art music, there is a very marked difference in our works. Each of us has developed his own individual style, despite the common sources which were used . . . . Kodály studied, and uses as a source, Hungarian rural music almost exclusively, whereas I extended my interest and love also to the folk music of the neighboring Eastern European peoples and ventured even into Arabic and Turkish territories for research work. In my works, therefore, appear impressions derived from the most varied sources, melted—as I hope—into unity. . . . Apart from the great lessons we acquired from the classics, we learned most from those uneducated, illiterate peasants who faithfully kept their great musical inheritance and even created, in a so-to-speak mysterious way, new styles.[11]

Notes

1. The first version of the present essay appeared, with music examples, in the *New Hungarian Quarterly* 34 (Summer 1990), 134–38. The second version was commissioned by *Stagebill* magazine for the Winter 1990 season (book XIX) of the Chicago Symphony Orchestra, 78–84.

2. *BBL*, 29.

3. *BBE*, 409.

4. A symmetrical anhemitone construction, such as A-C-D-E-G.

5. Peasant inhabitants in the Biskra Oasis area of Algeria.

6. See Bartók's comments and related music examples in *BBSE*, 167, 187, 232–36.

7. *BBE*, 470.

8. *HFS*, xxxv.

9. Ibid., 4–11.

10. Ibid., xxxi.

11. *BBE*, 395.

20

Bartók in America[1]

It has been widely assumed that the conditions of American cultural and social life were the cause of the neglect and lack of appreciation experienced by Bartók between 1940 and 1945, the last years of his life in this country. Certainly the difficulties and frustrations experienced by artists prompted by events to take up residence in America were not then imaginary, nor are they today. But in Bartók's case there were extenuating circumstances.

The origin of the American guilt theory can be traced to the winter of 1942–1943. Bartók had emigrated here as a voluntary refugee in October 1940; earlier that year he had made inquiries about obtaining a position which would enable him to settle in the country. Though the Nazism then threatening Hungary would not affect directly his personal and professional status—he belonged to none of the political, racial, or religious groups denounced by it—his moral obligation to express protest against its political creed was strong enough to drive him from his homeland. Thus when the New York office of Boosey & Hawkes offered their managerial services for the 1940-1941 concert season, and Columbia University proposed a research position, Bartók unhesitatingly accepted and began preparations to take up permanent residence in America.

Bartók was under the impression that his Columbia University appointment involved permanence (as such a position would have done at a European university). In the Hungarian farewell notices, his post was described as a professorial one, and he surely understood it as such. He was not informed that it was to be a temporary research fellowship of a kind usually given to doctoral candidates, nor that it was financed by a special fund that did not permit even renewal, let alone permanence. He already had a worldwide reputation as a composer, and his assumptions were based on his awareness of his stature; the Columbia appointment, unknown to him but regarded at the university as a matter of common knowledge, was in conflict with those assumptions.

When the Columbia offer was made, bringing with it the chance to escape from life under an evil, dictatorial regime and instead teach or devote himself to folk music research, he was elated. The modest salary was not interpreted by him, as it might have been by an American scholar, as a symbol of the appointment's low rank. His true compensation would be the intellectual pleasure gained from his work on Milman Parry's collection of Serbo-Croatian folk-music material, awaiting its "discoverer" at Harvard University, which Bartók transcribed and annotated under Columbia's auspices.

One can well imagine, then, Bartók's disappointment when he learned that his Columbia position would not be renewed in 1943. He now faced financial insecurity in a foreign country engaged in an all-out war effort. Further, his work on the Serbo-Croatian project was unfinished; his year of creative work was now to be broken off and thus almost entirely wasted. He was discouraged, too, by the indifference toward the moral significance of the sacrifices he had made in abandoning home and country solely to join the outcry of other great men against Nazism. But in the United States no one considered it a sacrifice to emigrate to the country, whatever the purpose; ignorance of that attitude brought about another misunderstanding of American life.

No substitute income was within Bartók's reach. The royalties earned by his compositions, substantial before the war, could not be remitted from Europe; as for American royalties, performances of contemporary music in the United States were at their lowest ebb in the period just after Pearl Harbor. Bartók might have derived some income from recordings of his own works or the standard repertory, but the musicians union was then on strike against the recording companies, who had retaliated by suspending all recording. The indifference in academic circles toward the completion of his work on Serbo-Croatian folk music, which he held above all else, added moral insult to financial injury.

An appeal by Irving Kolodin, music editor of the *New York Sun*, to turn the esteem in which Bartók was held to practical benefit, fell on deaf ears. It was then that Victor Bator, later to become trustee of the New York Bartók estate, arranged with Columbia University for the renewal of Bartók's appointment, subject to a donation out of which his salary would be paid. József Szigeti, the Hungarian-born violinist, joined Bator in a campaign to raise the necessary funds. Despite the generous contributions from Eugene Ormandy, conductor of the Philadelphia Orchestra, and Benny Goodman, clarinetist and jazz-band leader, and lesser donations from members of orchestral societies, the results were poor; but the amount required by Columbia University was raised, Bartók's appointment was extended, and his study of Serbo-Croatian folk music completed.[2] The facts behind the renewal of his appointment remained hidden from Bartók, and he did not suspect that Bator's private resources were behind the donor's anonymity.

Others provided different kinds of help. Serge Koussevitzky, conductor of the Boston Orchestra, answered the plea with the response: "I trust to find another way to help Bartók morally as well as financially," and commissioned him to compose an orchestral work, sending him a fee of $1,000.[3] The commission resulted in the Concerto for Orchestra. On the initiative of Douglas Moore, chairman of Columbia University music department, the National Institute of Arts and Letters, which had a relief fund to assist recognized artists in overcoming temporary financial difficulties, offered Bartók a sizable loan. Aware that Bartók would refuse such a charitable gesture, Bator signed the note of indebtedness as the composer's attorney-in-fact, deposited the check in Bartók's name, and told him that the money was given as a prize, as one of the institute's annual awards.

After 1943, Bartók's financial circumstances, though modest, were no longer critical. Royalty income began to flow from England, an appointment came from Harvard University as a visiting lecturer, and Bartók's wife, Ditta Pásztory Bartók, acquired some private piano students. But at no time during his five American years did Bartók receive the honor, esteem, and glory he had enjoyed before his emigration. In the light of his now acknowledged stature, as composer and scholar, it is painful to look back on the two or three years when he was compelled to depend on the charity and magnanimity of lesser men.

Financial adversity was not the main disappointment of Bartók's life, not even during the crisis of 1942–1943. Nor was he desperate because of the indifference shown his music: he knew that he was a great composer, and the accolades from the most celebrated musicians of the day meant more to him than the petty snubs of provincial music critics and the general public.[4] The unrelenting and frustrating struggle of his life—and it was largely unsuccessful—was to preserve in authentic form musical folklore of eastern Europe, a cultural treasure threatened with engulfment in the flood of urban popular music that contaminates traditional folk art.

Since 1905, Bartók had collected, transcribed, compared, and described the peasant instrumental and vocal music of Hungary and its neighbors;[5] these activities grew out of his earlier need for folk music as a source material for composition. Where music making had been his only devotion, now, in the course of folk-music collecting, he became, as it were, a high priest of that other cult. It was not until 1945 that he completed the last of his five monumental volumes on the musical folklore of the Transylvanian-Romanians. He also wrote an important essay on Turkish folk music in 1943.

The preceding narrative underlines one sad fact: Bartók, in his lifetime, was unable to find a publisher, foundation, library, or private benefactor to provide the means that would make available to humankind the intellectual museum represented by his Romanian, Slovak, and Turkish folk music collections. Only minor parts of his folk-music works achieved publication, and even those were mostly subsidized from his own meager resources. When, early in 1940, Bartók arrived in New York for a concert tour, he paid for the printing of all the instrumental and half the vocal melodies in his vast Romanian material; his funds were exhausted before the remainder could be prepared for publication with prefatory studies. His passion for and devotion to folk music bound him to the extent that he felt compelled to preserve his transcriptions and their accompanying scholarly annotations in print, even if it meant the expenditure of income needed for living expenses or the rejection of full-time teaching positions.

In 1910, Bartók had written to Frederick Delius: "I am very much alone here apart from my one friend, Kodály; I have nobody to talk to." Bartók was virtually companionless throughout his life, and still more so in his last years on a strange continent.

NOTES

1. The previous version of this essay appears in the *Musical Times* 1596, no. 117 (February 1976): 123–24.

2. Originally published by Columbia University Press in 1951, six years after Bartók's death, and reprinted as *YFM*.i in 1978.

3. See the detailed remarks in *BBLW*, 153.

4. Bartók had been lauded as "fourth in the procession of the great B's of music: Bach, Beethoven, Brahms, and Bartók." See *BBLW*, 158.

5. BBSE, 174–240.

21

The New York Bartók Archive: History and Sources[1]

In 1948, three years after Bartók's death in New York, the idea of establishing a Bartók archive was conceived by Victor Bator, then cotrustee of the Bartók estate. Bator was motivated by the rapidly growing recognition of Bartók's genius and the resultant clamor for information about his life and works.

> The conscious recognition of my obligation to create a Bartók Archive was brought about not only by my obligation as fiduciary owner, trustee of the estate, to preserve and develop every facet and source of value entrusted to me, but also by the knowledge of the incessant care given by Bartók to the safeguarding of his manuscripts. The Bartók archive is the offspring of these two parents.[2]

During the fall of 1953, when royalties from performances and sheet-music sales of Bartók works enabled Bator to employ part-time assistants, selected manuscripts were prepared for photostatic reproduction.[3] At that time I was investigating bibliographic sources related to my proposed New York University dissertation on Bartók's *Mikrokosmos* for piano.[4] I wrote to Halsey Stevens, then professor of composition at the University of Southern California, for assistance in locating primary source materials. Stevens, whose outstanding Bartók biography appeared that year, advised me to contact Victor Bator, a Hungarian-born attorney who had been designated in Bartók's will as executor and trustee of the composer's estate. My letter to Bator, dated 29 December and addressed to his Manhattan office, enclosed a list of "the specific problems needed to be solved in the preparation of my dissertation." The letter continued: "Dr. Halsey Stevens has been interested in my study and has been offering valuable suggestions as to procedure. He states that his own research discloses no information, left by Bartók himself, that would be helpful in my dissertation. He suggested that you would be the only person to have the information I need, if it exists at all."

An immediate interview was granted, and, on 3 January 1954, I wrote another letter which summarized the results of our discussion, among them his offer "to lend me the photostats of the *Mikrokomos* MSS when they are ready. In return for this courtesy, I stated that I would supply you with a list of errors, if any, between the MSS and the Boosey & Hawkes publication." Following the interview, Bator opened the door to a large closet, the repository for an equally large chest of metal drawers, and permitted me to open them, one after the other. I was astonished to find the drawers crammed with well-worn, overstuffed envelopes, each one marked with one or several numbers and the Hungarian title in Bartók's holograph. During the summer, after photographic reproductions of the *Mikrokosmos* manuscripts as well as the contents of certain other envelopes had been readied for examination, my letter of 11 August—the first in a substantial number of them to the trustee—reports that:

> What I am doing now is to collect the tissue copies of the *Mikrokosmos*, the sketches, and the corrected tissue copies, and assemble them, with comments disclosed by my research. (I am working with the photostatic copies, of course!). A bound collection Mr. Wooldridge previously assembled was an excellent piece of work— unfortunately it contains music that belongs to the *Mikrokosmos* sketches (#59). The collection also includes certain manuscripts that belong to the First Piano Concerto (#58), and so forth. Additionally, I think we have located the missing tissue copies corrected by Bartók—they must be in London if they are not in your office. (According to the letter sent by Bartók to B. & H. in London.) I listed the missing pages and gave it to Mrs. Varga to copy and mail out.
>
> I have offered to help her assemble the various documents that relate to the composer. . . . I think it is a wonderful idea to collect every item of information concerning Bartók, if the estate is able to underwrite the expense. Periodicals must be secured or photostatic copies made of related articles. University libraries should be contacted to determine whether theses can be copied. A method of indexing and storing materials must be devised. A new system of numbering should be devised—such as Köchel did for Mozart. Publicity should be sought to promote Bartók's name, and suggested research topics sent to universities having graduate degree programs in music.

The actual building of the archive began in 1954, when royalty income permitted the allocation of modest funds to support the project and—as an outcome of my organization of Bartók's *Mikrokosmos* manuscripts as source material for my doctoral dissertation—when I was employed as assistant to the trustee and thereafter as curator. It was not until 1963 that we were able to announce the availability of *NYBA* holdings for study or reference by the public.[5] The matter of preservation of the manuscripts, for example, was a lengthy, painstaking procedure, for I had to find a way in which scholars could handle them without damage to the fragile papers. The solution was to encapsulate each leaf in chemically inert plastic envelopes and place them in ring binders. Equally important was the codification of the material, in chronological order of composition, and its subsequent stamping for identification and property ownership purposes. Finally, each manuscript was photographed in different processes (photostat, microfilm, photocopy), and sets of photostat copies were bound in book form as the basic reference collection. Then the precious originals were shelved in special cabinets in the lower vault of a New York bank. In 1966, after I attended the first seminar on computer-oriented music research at the State University of New York at Binghamton, an approach was devised for data processing of certain archive holdings.[6]

When the trustee died in 1967, the eventual probate of his estate required closure of the archive and placement of its contents in a warehouse. My appointment as successor-trustee was approved a year later, but legal problems delayed transfer of the trustee's papers, the Bartók estate, and its archival holdings to me as fiduciary owner. I was, however, able to provide the public with research and reference services to a certain extent. Finally, in 1975, I took possession of the warehoused materials and, following an agreement with the composer's widow, Ditta Pásztory Bartók, I reopened the archive in a suburban area close to New York, designated it as the New York Bartók Archive (*NYBA*), and organized its contents in sixteen categories.[7]

RESOURCES

1. *Compositions.* These consist of Bartók holographs, copyist autographs, and printed music with Bartók's handwritten addenda or corrigenda. Also treated as "holographs" are photocopies of Bartók compositions held by the Budapest Bartók Archive, the Library of Congress, and private collectors.

2. *Folk-Music Collections.* The physical makeup of these collections is similar to that of Bartók's compositions, but the folk-music collections are far more substantial. The largest are those devoted to Bulgarian, Romanian, Slovak, and Yugoslav musical folklore; smaller ones include Arab (Algerian), German, Gypsy, Ruthenian (Ukrainian), Turkish, and West Virginian specimens. There is also a small collection of Hungarian material, but the bulk of the more than 14,000 melodies Bartók had been classifying, transcribing, and correcting before his emigration to the United States in 1940 is held by the Musicological Institute of the Hungarian Academy of Sciences in Budapest.

3. *Letters.* The most extensive correspondences are between Bartók and his publishers: Universal Edition (in German) and Boosey & Hawkes (in English). Others are with Walter Schulthess (about Swiss concerts), Mrs. Oscar Müller-Widmann, Paul Sacher, Etelka Freund, and to a lesser extent with various university presses, ethnomusicologists, and other individuals. There are a number of letters to and from such musical personalities as Serge Koussevitzky, Yehudi Menuhin, Tossy Spivakovsky, Joseph Szigeti and William Primrose. Other letters published in various books, journals, and newspapers, particularly the volumes edited by János Demény (in Hungarian, German, Italian, and English), are on the *NYBA* bookshelves and have been catalogued chronologically, by name and to some extent by subject matter.

4. *Printed Music.* This category includes first editions and reprints of Bartók compositions and his annotated editions of keyboard works from the standard

repertory. Related materials include Hungarian folk-music and popular art-music collections; folk-music collections of ethnic areas where Bartók did research or that he was interested in; transcriptions of Bartók compositions by various arrangers; music composed or edited by Bartók's teachers, colleagues, and pupils; and so forth.

5. *Essays.* Holographs and published versions of Bartók's writings on musicological and ethnomusicological subjects are the core of this collection; other papers include typescript and autograph reminiscences by persons in contact with Bartók during his lifetime.

6. *Books, Monographs, and Offprints.* This extensive material comprises Bartók's own major folk music studies that were published during his career as ethnomusicologist; and the principal biographies by Halsey Stevens, József Ujfalussy, Serge Moreux, Benjamin Suchoff, and many other writers. There is a substantial collection of dissertations and other academic theses on Bartók works, reference books, related folk-music studies, and so forth. The books are cataloged by author and title.

7. *Journal Articles.* Bartók's published essays have been mentioned above. In addition is a very large accumulation of journals (or photocopied portions of them), all related to aspects of Bartók's life, times, and works. Of particular interest are several special Bartók numbers: *Musikblätter des Anbruch 3, no.* 5 (Vienna, 1921), *Zenei Szemle* 8 (Budapest, 1928), *Tempo,* nos. 13 and 14 (London, 1949 and 1950), *Uj Zenei Szemle,* 1, no. 4 (Budapest, 1950), *Musik der Zeit* 3 (Bonn, 1953), and *La revue musicale,* no. 244 (Paris, 1955). There are, too, copies of scholarly papers as yet unpublished, presented at various conferences in the United States and elsewhere.

8. *Cuttings.* The *NYBA* files contain many concert reviews and other items from newspapers and magazines, for the most part from Hungarian, English, French, German, Austrian, Swiss, and American sources. An important collection of such documentation, edited by János Demény, is contained in four volumes published by the Budapest Academy of Sciences, 1954–1962.

9. *Concert Programs.* The three classes in this category are Bartók's performances as soloist or with other artists; Bartók works played during his lifetime; and posthumous performances of his works that took place up until the late 1950s, because of the overwhelming, ever increasing number of concerts and recitals of Bartók compositions being given here and abroad.

10. *Iconography.* In this group are the many photographs of Bartók and his family and friends; of stage settings; Bartók caricatures; motion picture films and videotapes; and pictures of peasants taken by Bartók himself during his travels to collect musical folklore. There are also photographs of artists with whom Bartók performed, and the published collections of pictures, with anno-

tations, edited by Ferenc Bónis in various editions.

11. *Records and Tapes.* This category includes the commercial recordings of Bartók's own performances; pressings made by Peter Bartók for his company Bartók Records; the complete edition brought out by Hungaroton of Budapest; and many other recordings of Bartók works produced since the early 1950s. Tapes of Bartók's Hungarian and Romanian folk-music collections, originally recorded on Edison cylinders, enhance the collection.

12. *Personal Documents.* A number of family papers include immigration and tax forms; contracts with publishers; political items; travel documents; and Bartók's collection of cartoons appearing in various publications.

13. *Legal Papers.* A quite substantial number of documents make up this collection, which has attracted the interest of lawyers and law students in the United States. Perhaps the most significant case is that of the Concerto for Orchestra, which the courts ruled was not a posthumous work although it was published after Bartók's death in 1945. The various litigations, beginning in 1958 and ending shortly after my appointment as successor-trustee, may interest lawyers or scholars who specialize in estate and copyright law.

14. *Other Materials.* This small collection includes peasant costumes and embroideries, small and large plaques of Bartók's head in profile, and papers that do not fall under the preceding classifications.

15. *Scholarly Apparatus.* Accession lists, indexes of manuscripts and folk-music collections, catalog cards from the Library of Congress and the National Széchényi Library, Budapest, *NYBA* index-card catalogs (mentioned above), and various other lists and tabulations form the bulk of this category. Computer programs and permuted indexes of *NYBA* holdings, particularly in relation to folk-music collections, are an important resource for research and, moreover, represent the first instance anywhere of such archival electronic data processing as a scholarly tool.

16. *NYBA Papers.* The last category—a quite substantial one—is represented by correspondence with persons and institutions, and by other materials of historical value connected with the implementation and operation of the archive. *NYBA* contributions to the international world of music are an outcome of four functions, the first being the previously described collecting, preservation, and systematic classification of materials by and about Bartók. The second function is publication, represented by the *NYBA* Studies in Musicology series.

Publications[8]

Victor Bator, *The Béla Bartók Archives: History and Catalogue* (New York: Bartók Archives Publication, 1963). A concomitant aim of this short description of *NYBA* holdings was to attract the attention of the public to contribute materials and research services, and thus further the public service objective of the fledgling institution.

Béla Bartók, *Rumanian Folk Music*, ed. Benjamin Suchoff, trans. E. C. Teodorescu, et al, foreword by Victor Bator. (The Hague: Martinus Nijhoff, 1975). Five volumes: I. Instrumental Music (1967); II. Vocal Melodies (1967); III. Texts (1967); IV. Carols and Christmas Songs (*Colinde*) (1975); V. Maramureş County (1975). Bartók's seminal studies of Romanian musical folklore include morphological analysis of vocal and instrumental melodies, classification of the poetic texts, descriptions of folk instruments and choreography, and detailed tabulations of Romanian and foreign variants.

Béla Bartók, *Turkish Folk Music from Asia Minor*, ed.Benjamin Suchoff,(Princeton: Princeton University Press, 1976). Bartók's study of Turkish peasant music, vocal and instrumental, is the first of its kind in English and, like his other ethnomusicological treatises, has been described as a model for future scholarship in this area.

Béla Bartók, *Béla Bartók Essays*, ed. Benjamin Suchoff (London: Faber & Faber, and New York: St. Martin's Press, 1976; reprint, Lincoln and London: University of Nebraska Press, 1992). The first of two volumes of Bartók's writings; it also contains previously unpublished notes of his lectures given at Columbia and Harvard Universities, in which he summarizes his style and its relation to that of his contemporaries Schoenberg and Stravinsky.

Béla Bartók, *Yugoslav Folk Music*, ed. Benjamin Suchoff, (Albany: State University of New York Press, 1978). This four-volume work is the most substantial and thorough analysis of Yugoslav folk music in English; it is literally an ethnomusicological workshop in printed form and can serve as a basic reference text in this field.

Béla Bartók, *The Hungarian Folk Song,* ed. Benjamin Suchoff (Albany: State University of New York Press, 1981). Bartók prepared this work in Hungarian (Budapest: Rózsavölgyi, 1924), German (Berlin: Walter De Gruyter, 1925), and English (London: Oxford University Press, 1931). The enlarged, facsimile-reprint English edition contains Kodály's annotations, various tabulations in accordance with Bartók's later methods, historical and biographical narratives, and other editorial addenda which summarize related research in Hungarian ethnomusicology up to date.

The Piano Music of Béla Bartók, 2 vols, Bartók Archive Edition, ed. Benjamin Suchoff (New York: Dover Publications, Inc., 1981). Contains annotated facsimile reprints of Bartók's early Hungarian publications, with his final corrections, and editorial introductions which include program notes, music examples, and manuscript facsimiles.

Béla Bartók, *Studies in Ethnomusicology*, ed. Benjamin Suchoff (Lincoln and London: University of Nebraska Press, 1997. The second volume of Bartók essays, including his study of Arab folk music from the Biskra district of Algeria and his introduction to *Slovak Folk Songs.*

RESEARCH

The third archival function is research: to produce documentation—the so-called scholarly apparatus—that would facilitate support services to Bartók's publishers, performers of his works, educational and communications media, commercial and nonprofit organizations, scholars, and other qualified individuals. The unique feature of this function, as previously mentioned, is the use of computer-produced thematic indexes and other permutations of *NYBA* databases constructed at the Center for Contemporary Arts and Letters of the State University of New York at Stony Brook.[9]

SUPPORT SERVICES

The fourth function is represented by support services in the form of consultation; referencing; source validation, research recommendations; visits to the *NYBA* by recognized scholars, qualified graduate students, and performers of Bartók works; and so forth. The outcome of these services, in the form of publications, lectures, unpublished papers, and concert programs is too extensive to list here in their entirety. Another development was the exchange of card catalogues between *NYBA* and the National Széchényi Library Music Division, and data and documentation was provided by the Musicological Institute of the Hungarian Academy of Sciences in Budapest and its *BBA*).

AFTERWORD

Following the death of Mrs. Bartók in 1982, and in accordance with her husband's will, the New York Bartók estate and my trusteeship were terminated. Peter Bartók, the composer's younger son and designated remainderman, automatically became the sole inheritor of his father's estate. The probate of Victor Bator's estate and that of the widow followed in due course, and in 1984 I transferred Peter's inheritance to him, including *NYBA* holdings. He renamed them as the *PBA* and set to work preparing new performing editions and other publications of his father's works.

NOTES

1. This essay represents a compendium derived from the following sources: "Bartók," in *Proceedings of the Fifth Annual Conference, April, 1970*, ed. Barney Childs and

Paul Lansky (New York: American Society of University Composers, Inc.), 1972, 124–28; "The New York Bartók Archive," a paper read at the Bartók Seminar-Conference, University of Pittsburgh, 1975; and "The New York Bartók Archive," *Musical Times*, March 1981, 156–59.

2. Victor Bator, *The Béla Bartók Archives: History and Catalogue*. (New York: Bartók Archives Publication, 1963), 14–15.

3. By Mrs. Nike Varga, Hungarian-born librarian, and Clifford Wooldridge, Boosey & Hawkes rental-music librarian.

4. Published as *Béla Bartók and a Guide to the Mikrokosmos*. Ann Arbor, Michigan: UMI, 1957. A reprint is included in Benjamin Suchoff, *Bartók's Mikrokosmos: Genesis, Pedagogy, and Style* (Lanham, Md., and Oxford: Scarecrow Press, 2002.

5. An illustrated brochure was prepared, a board of trustees selected, and the archive was designated as an official New York City cultural institution, open for research purposes by qualified scholars and musicians.

6. Benjamin Suchoff, "Computer Applications to Bartók's Serbo-Croatian Material," *Tempo* 80 (1967): 15–19.

7. See also the descriptions in the Bator *Catalogue* (note 2, above), 22–39.

8. The *NYBA* alphanumeric designations of Bartók's manuscripts are listed in *BBLW*, 219–54.

9. Similar database construction is illustrated in Benjamin Suchoff, *A Musician's Guide to Desktop Computing with the Macintosh* (Englewood Cliffs, N.J.: Prentice-Hall, Inc., 1994), 94–124.

Index

About the Author

Benjamin Suchoff is an adjunct professor in the Department of Ethnomusicology at the University of California, Los Angeles, and a member of the American Society of Composers, Authors, and Publishers (ASCAP, 1960–). Dr. Suchoff was curator of the New York Bartók Archive (1953–1967), successor-trustee of the New York Bartók estate (1968–1984), and editor of the thirteen volumes comprising the Bartók Archive Studies in Musicology series and the two volumes of piano works in the Bartók Archive Edition. His most recent books are *Bartók: Concerto for Orchestra: Understanding Bartók's World* (1995), *Béla Bartók Studies in Ethnomusicology* (1997), *Bartók Perspectives* (coeditor, 2000), *Béla Bartók: Life and Work* (Scarecrow Press 2001), and *Bartók's Mikrokosmos: Genesis, Pedagogy, and Style* (Scarecrow Press 2002). He was awarded the Béla Bartók Diploma and Memorial Plaque from the Hungarian Republic in 1981 for his "great contribution to the understanding of Bartók's oeuvre" and is generally recognized as the dean of Bartók scholars.